Warren Zevon and Philosophy

Pop Culture and Philosophy®

General Editor: George A. Reisch

For full details of all Pop Culture and Philosophy® books, and all Open Universe® books, visit www.carusbooks.com

Pop Culture and Philosophy®

Warren Zevon and Philosophy

Beyond Reptile Wisdom

Edited by
JOHN E. MACKINNON

OPEN UNIVERSE
Chicago

Volume 10 in the series, Pop Culture and Philosophy®, edited by George A. Reisch

To find out more about Open Universe and Carus Books, visit our website at www.carusbooks.com.

Warren Zevon and Philosophy: Beyond Reptile Wisdom

ISBN: 978-1-63770-028-0

This book is also available as an e-book (978-1-63770-029-7).

Library of Congress Control Number: 2021941770

*Dedicated, with love,
to my brothers and sisters,
Bernie, Carol Ann, Paula, Ellen, and Ron,
and in loving memory of our dear sister,
Mary Rose MacKinnon
(1960–2020)*

*Remember when our songs were just like prayers
Like gospel hymns that you called in the air?
Come down, come down sweet reverence,
Unto my simple house and ring,
And ring . . .*

—GREGORY ALAN ISAKOV, "The Stable Song,"
from *That Sea, The Gambler* (2007)

Contents

Preludes

I would like to express my gratitude to George A. Reisch and David Ramsay Steele at Carus Books for their interest in and support of this project.

Thanks also to all the contributing authors for their enthusiasm and commitment, and for responding promptly to my queries over the past year.

My thanks to Fatema Ali of the Department of Philosophy at Saint Mary's University for her administrative help and constant good cheer, and to Matthew Salah, formerly of the Software and Applications Support (SAS) Lab at Saint Mary's, for his invaluable assistance in preparing the manuscript for submission.

My brother Bernie was a source of sage advice, as my wife and sons were of encouragement and something more than glancing interest. I share their relief that there'll be no more questions about how "the Zevon thing" is going.

JOHN E. MACKINNON
Window Seat
LF Bakery
Halifax, Nova Scotia

Writing is like shooting: complete stillness, the subject caught in the sights, the trigger squeezed.

—AIDAN HIGGINS, *Ronda Gorge and Other Precipices*

Talkin' about the Man

JOHN E. MACKINNON

If Only, When I Made My Debut

In the 1970s, the respected music critic Paul Nelson declared himself "the world's number one Jackson Browne fan." From the basement bedroom I shared with my older brother and our record player, I would have begged to differ. Of Browne's brilliant albums *For Everyman* and *Late for the Sky*, I knew every note, every lyric, every modulation of voice, every scrape and wail on the electric fiddle and slide guitar of that greatest of sidemen, David Lindley. I was eager for any news I could get of Browne. So, when I read in *Rolling Stone* that he was producing a friend's album, I had to know more. That friend, it turned out, was a guy named Warren Zevon.

Before meeting Browne, Zevon had already begun to make modest inroads into the Los Angeles music scene. Born in Chicago in 1947, and raised in Fresno and Los Angeles, he was the only child of an ill-starred union between a Scottish Mormon, hypochondriac, alcoholic mother and Ukrainian-born Jewish gangster father, who had worked with Mickey Cohen, for Sam Giancana, and fondly remembered Al Capone as "a nice guy" (*I'll Sleep When I'm Dead*, pp. 10, 241; *Accidentally Like a Martyr*, p. 91).

At the age of thirteen, in the company of the conductor and writer Robert Craft, Zevon visited Igor Stravinsky on several occasions at his Hollywood home, where they would read scores, and discuss conductors and conducting. Classical music was, indeed, what James Campion calls Zevon's "initial seducer," and for the rest of his life he would labor to compose a symphony that he was never able to finish (p. 77). In 1966, as a member of the duo lyme and cybelle, Zevon had a minor hit with "Follow Me," an infectious pop number that producer Bones Howe describes as "the first psychedelic rock record" (*I'll Sleep When I'm Dead*, p. 22). Zevon's song "Like the Seasons" appeared as the B-side on The Turtles' "Happy Together," which bumped the Beatles' "Penny Lane" from the Number One spot on the Billboard Top 100 in April 1967. In 1970, Imperial Records released his debut album, *Wanted Dead or Alive*, to the sound, Zevon mordantly recalled, "of one hand clapping" (*I'll Sleep When I'm Dead*, p. 32). Though the album was largely forgettable, one song, "She Quit Me," was included on the soundtrack of the Academy Award-winning movie *Midnight Cowboy*. A second Zevon album, which Howe describes as "very adventurous and experimental," was never released (p. 40). After serving as piano player and band leader for The Everly Brothers, Zevon and his wife, Crystal, having concluded that their prospects in Los Angeles weren't improving, bought two one-way tickets to Spain "to start a new life." While there, Zevon received a postcard from Browne, urging him to come home, insisting that it was too soon to give up and that, somehow, Browne would get him a recording contract. Shortly after returning to Los Angeles, Zevon was signed by David Geffen at Asylum Records.

Just as Henry James disowned his first novel, *Watch and Ward*, preferring to count *Roderick Hudson* as his proper debut, Zevon, along with others in the industry, treated *Wanted Dead or Alive* as a piece of largely regrettable juvenilia, regarding *Warren Zevon* (1976) as his true debut album. Produced by Browne, it was warmly received by critics, including respected producer Jon Landau, who described it as, "in reality, one of the truly great first albums." The songwriting, which included "Frank and Jesse James," "Poor, Poor Pitiful Me," "Mohammed's Radio," "The French Inhaler," and "Desperadoes under the Eaves," was simply "state of the art" (pp. 112, 114).

Zevon's follow-up album, *Excitable Boy* (1978), boasted his lone international hit, "Werewolves of London," as well as a number of other memorable songs, including the title track, "Johnny Strikes up the Band," "Roland the Headless Thompson Gunner," "Accidentally Like a Martyr," "Veracruz," "Lawyers, Guns, and Money," and "Tenderness on the Block." Zevon's third album, however, *Bad Luck Streak in Dancing School*, clearly represented a step back. The title track, along with "Play It All Night Long," "Bed of Coals," a rousing cover of The Yardbirds' "A Certain Girl," and "Jeannie Needs a Shooter," co-written with Bruce Springsteen, are all fine songs, but more like solid second-order material on a much stronger album.

Shortly after *Bad Luck Streak*, Zevon released a live album, *Stand in the Fire*, that, along with Neil Young's *Live Rust*, Nelson describes as "the best live rock'n'roll LP I've ever heard" (*I'll Sleep When I'm Dead*, p. 174). By then, though, it had become apparent that, due to a life of addiction and debauchery that Crystal Zevon so ably, and disturbingly, documents in her book, Zevon's career had begun to fall apart. David Landau, Jon's brother and long-time guitarist in Zevon's touring band, marveled, "the only thing I ever saw that came close to how Warren drank was Nicholas Cage in *Leaving Las Vegas*," adding bluntly that Zevon's career "was on a downswing." As Crystal Zevon confirmed, his star "was dimming" (pp. 154, 173, 185).

When *The Envoy* was released in 1982, it was warmly reviewed by Robert Palmer in the *New York Times* and later described by his *Times* colleague Jon Pareles as Zevon's "best album," just as it is occasionally praised, still, on-line. I remain unmoved from my own verdict, however, that, as an album, it is a middling work. And yet, it contains fine individual songs, including the raw, searing "Ain't That Pretty at All," the lilting cuckold's lament, "Hula Hula Boys," the raucous "The Overdraft," and the sweetly solemn "Jesus Mentioned." Regardless, the album didn't sell well, Zevon's erratic behavior continued, and his career tailspin accelerated.

Roaming the Philadelphia neighbourhood to which he had relocated during a particularly chaotic and destructive period in his life, Zevon happened to read in *Rolling Stone* that his label, now known as Elektra/Asylum, had "dropped" him. "I was freaked and enraged," he scribbled in his journal. Andy Slater, who managed Zevon when no one else could bother, and heroically struggled to revive his career, laments, "with his guns and his knives and his prescriptions and his guitars . . . none of it was working, and it was getting worse and worse," while George Gruel, photographer and aide-de-camp to Zevon through many difficult years, recalls with brutal frankness, "the abuse . . . had caught up with him" (p. 194). His resources exhausted, his possibilities pinched and narrowed, Zevon seemed destined to learn the meaning of limbo.

Feints and Jabs

It would be another five years before Zevon's next studio album appeared. "I tried to stay away long enough," he quipped, "to make a comeback when I came back" (*I'll Sleep When I'm Dead*, p. 202). *Sentimental Hygiene*, recorded by a resolutely sober Zevon and released on the Virgin label, featured the stately title song, the beautiful ballad "Reconsider Me," the propulsive "Boom Boom Mancini," and the witty and arch "Even a Dog Can Shake Hands." With contributions from Bob Dylan, Neil Young, Jennifer Warnes, Brian Setzer of The Stray Cats, and the members of R.E.M., *Sentimental Hygiene* was more polished in its production than *The Envoy*, and generally a much better album, but nonetheless failed to hit the heights of Zevon's first two Asylum records.

It was followed in 1989 by *Transverse City*, often described as a concept album, or song-cycle, about a culture in collapse. Steeped in the language of the cyberpunk fiction Zevon had lately been devouring, it ultimately fails to convince, in part because it trains its dystopian dread on some obsessions, like traffic jams, computers, and crowded shopping malls, that seem dated, even trite. Once again, though, there are fine individual songs, including the dark lament "Run Straight Down," featuring Roger Gilmour of Pink Floyd on guitar, the limpid "Splendid Isolation," the unusual and haunting "They Moved the Moon," and the rueful "Nobody's in Love This Year," complete with Mark Isham's flugelhorn solo.

In light of poor sales, Virgin decided to drop Zevon, who eventually signed with Irving Azoff's new label, Giant Records. The first album that Giant ever released was *hindu love gods* (1990), a roughly recorded, day-long jam session, mostly of blues standards, with Zevon and three members of R.E.M., Bill Berry, Peter Buck, and Mike Mills. Though never intended for release, and though reportedly used as a bargaining chip by Andy Slater to coax a deal for Zevon out of Azoff, it's a terrific album. Zevon also released with Giant a live solo album called *Learning to Flinch* (1993), mainly comprising acoustic versions of already recorded material, except for a handful of new songs, including an inspired performance on slide guitar of a song called "Worrier King," which sounds a bit like Leo Kottke on a muggy day.

The first studio album Zevon recorded with Giant, *Mr. Bad Example* (1991), sold so poorly that, not only did it fail to chart, but it became the first of Zevon's records taken out of circulation (p. 280). And yet, it remains unjustly neglected, a solid effort throughout, from the clangorous "Quite Ugly One Morning" and the rollicking "Things to Do in Denver When You're Dead" to the lithe "Suzie Lightning" and "Searching for a Heart," as well as the stirring Confederate pledge of faith, "Renegade," and "Heartache Spoken Here," which sounds like it ought to be an old and honored country standard.

The quality of song-writing on *Mutineer*, Zevon's second studio album for Giant, remains reasonably high, including the title song, "The Indifference of Heaven," "Something Bad Happened to a Clown," and "Similar to Rain," described lovingly by Zevon as a "Streisand-type tune" (p.305). But the production is so muddy and plodding that the whole effort is sadly compromised. Zevon recorded the album at home, and it sounds like it. When he was dropped by his label after the disappointment of *Transverse City*, he scrawled in his journal, "I'm taillights at Virgin" (p. 253). Almost seven years before, of course, he had been taillights at Elektra/Asylum, and now he was taillights at Giant.

The sequence of albums released over the course of these years confirms Zevon in reduced circumstances. In an article on the abstract expressionist painter Willem de Kooning, the art critic Peter Schjeldahl offers some reflections that are strikingly relevant to Zevon. De Kooning, he says, was "an intellectual giant among painters, with an analytical grasp that registers in every move with pencil or brush." Noting the "violent intelligence" of certain of de Kooning's work, he describes other paintings as "savagely comic," as if an angel choir were chanting "a dirty limerick." For a while, he adds, "the very ruin of the world seemed to drive his brush," while de Kooning himself seemed at ease "only on the lip of chaos." It took years of what Schjeldahl calls "woodshedding"—a term that C.M. Kushins, in his biography, uses twice in connection with Zevon (pp. 76, 118)—for de Kooning "to recover his own wavelength." Any retrospective view of such a career would do well, Schjeldahl concludes, to avoid "the Greatest Hits approach," since, for de Kooning, the "feints and jabs set up his knockouts." As de Kooning's career progressed, it may have seemed as if he had been "left behind," but it was in fact he, Schjeldahl assures us, who would eventually be shown to have been, like Zevon, "waiting ahead" (pp. 12–14).

To Rally What Remains

In *Rock Me on the Water*, Ronald Brownstein refers to those acclaimed movie directors whose later work can often feel "like the epilogue of earlier triumphs," while Morris Dickstein notes

Talkin' about the Man

the tendency of musicians in the later stages of their careers to settle for anthologizing, "cannibalizing," or otherwise rehashing, their earlier work. Late-Zevon, however, amounts to something far greater than mere epilogue or rehash. As Jon Landau notes, one of "the interesting and unusual things" about Warren Zevon was "how productive he stayed. In many ways, he got better creatively; he continued to grow" (*I'll Sleep When I'm Dead*, p. 112).

In December 1998, Jackson Browne, who remained a staunch advocate, once more intervened on Zevon's behalf, urging veteran record executive Danny Goldberg, who had recently left Mercury to found his own label, Artemis Records, to listen to a tape of new Zevon material. "I thought Jackson was right," Goldberg recalls. "These songs were great." Eventually, Goldberg offered Zevon a deal (pp. 358–359, 361). In his journal, Zevon had earlier confided that he was enjoying "a surprising burst of creativity" and, as he completed "Fistful of Rain" and continued to work on "Porcelain Monkey," declared to his friend and collaborator Jorge Calderón, "Jorge, you don't know what we're doing. This is high art. We've been together for years, but we're at the top of our game. We write so well together" (pp. 322, 364). The resulting album, *Life'll Kill Ya* (2000), is a triumph, a virtually flawless collection. The next album with Artemis, *My Ride's Here* (2002), features some fine individual songs, including the suitably smart, funny, and brilliantly orchestrated "Genius," but remains, as Goldberg concedes, "less focused" as a record (p. 258).

Just as *Life'll Kill Ya* is preoccupied with aging, death and dying, so *My Ride's Here*, Zevon's self-described "spiritual" album, amounts to a personal "meditation on death" (pp. 381, 413). As such, both proved prescient. In 2002, while touring Western Canada, Zevon, who had been suffering from shortness of breath, was eventually diagnosed with pleural mesothelioma, a rare and untreatable form of cancer, and given roughly three months to live. Zevon contemplated a retreat to an ashram, perhaps even a visit to India, or a last-gasp fishing trip to Florida with his friend Carl Hiaasen, but, charged with fresh purpose, resolved to devote the time that remained to him to recording one last album. Goldberg invested generously in the project, which attracted contributions from a pantheon of stars, from Browne and Springsteen to Don Henley and Tom Petty, Ry Cooder and Emmylou Harris to Dwight Yoakam and Billy Bob Thornton.

One particularly important source of comradeship, for

Zevon, over the last few years of his life had been The Rock Bottom Remainders, a rock band of published authors that included, among others, Mitch Albom, Dave Barry, Roy Blount, Jr., Carl Hiaasen, Stephen King, and Amy Tan. Although King recalls finding Zevon a "reclusive" fellow, he marvels at the strength Zevon had to have mustered to abstain from at least some of his most destructive vices, remarking, "I have no idea to this day how Warren dealt with not drinking. All I know is that he didn't drink. That, to me, is really the story of Warren Zevon" (*I'll Sleep When I'm Dead*, p. 349). But, with his strength diminishing and death looming, his seventeen-year run of sobriety dramatically buckled. Ryan Rayston, his friend and neighbor, describes how he began by taking the medication the doctors had given him, what he called "the Elvis drugs," but then started to mix the medication with alcohol, before "getting completely loaded and wasted and losing himself" (pp. 400, 402).

Another important source of solace and encouragement during this period was David Letterman, whom Zevon described as "the best friend my music ever had" (p. 441). On October 30th 2002, Letterman devoted the entire episode of his *Late Show* to Zevon, who, though desperately weak, managed to perform "Roland the Headless Thompson Gunner," "Genius," and "Mutineer." Back in L.A., as his condition, and behavior, deteriorated, progress on the album ground to a halt. "After the first songs were recorded," Calderón recalls, "it got really hard. He never came back to the studio. He got very depressed, started drinking" (pp. 402–03). According to Jordan Zevon, his father's medical need for painkillers overwhelmed his long-standing commitment to sobriety, so that, by Christmastime, he was "drinking and taking every pill you could get as well as liquid morphine. He was totally isolated, living off of groceries delivered to his doorstep" (*Bumping into Geniuses*, p. 270).

Through the patience and persistence of those who loved him, Zevon was eventually coaxed to finish the vocals for the remaining tracks. In August 2003, *The Wind* was released, debuting on the charts at number fourteen, the highest position any Zevon album had attained since *Excitable Boy* hit number eight twenty-five years before. Zevon lived to see not just the completion of his final album, but the birth of his and Crystal's twin grandsons, Max and Gus, born to their daughter, Ariel. On September 4th, Goldberg phoned to tell him the album would soon be gold. Three days later, on September 7th 2003, Zevon died. He was fifty-six. The following February, *The Wind* won the Grammy for Best Contemporary Folk Album, while the song "Disorder in the House," performed by Zevon and Springsteen, won for Best Rock Duet.

In his memorable book, *The Anxiety of Influence*, the great scholar and critic Harold Bloom argues that poetry begins "with our awareness, not of a Fall, but that *we are falling.*" What remains for the poet is neither "to sanctify nor propound," but "to rally everything that remains" (pp. 20–22, 33). Since what's true for the poet applies no less to the songwriter, this fittingly describes not only Zevon's efforts to complete *The Wind*, but also the motivation required to persevere in the face of the very adversity that, so often, he created for himself.

Madeleines, Music, and Memory

When, in *A Remembrance of Things Past*, Proust's narrator, Marcel, eats a madeleine dipped in lime-blossom tea, it triggers a process of recollection that brings his past to life. For most of us, though, it's music, far more than cookies and tea, that triggers the memories. "Nothing else," writes the novelist E.L. Doctorow, "can as suddenly evoke the look, the feel, the smell of our times past," releasing us "into a flow of imagery that whirls us through our decades, our eras, our changing landscape." Though "short and linear things," songs name us, he says, establishing for us "our timely place," managing "in their lyrics and lines of melody" to represent "wars and other disasters, moral process, the fruits of experience, and, like prayers, the consolations beyond loss" (pp. 61, 64, 65).

I recall an overcast late-Saturday morning, hinting at a humid day ahead, early summer, 1976. I'm playing my new album, *Warren Zevon*, on the stereo in the living room. When "The French Inhaler" concludes, my father busily folds the newspaper at the kitchen table and, clearly intrigued, calls in, "Who was *that?*"

A couple of years later, with younger brothers and sisters in the living room, flooded with summer light. "Johnny Strikes up the Band" is playing, when our mother pokes her head in from the kitchen and, smiling, asks, as perhaps only she could, "Is that James Taylor?"

Later. A crisp December afternoon, the sky ultramarine above a crooked line of gold, where the sun is setting behind the bare, blackened trees at the top of Portland Street. There's no snow yet, but the high grass and milkweed in the neighboring field have been flattened to a brown stubble. At its edge, my sister Carol Ann, fifteen or so, strolls home from school in her yellow, waist-length ski jacket. A blade of light from the setting sun catches her auburn hair. Standing by the wood stove, my parents watch from the sunporch window. Without turning, Mom says to Dad, "Isn't she pretty, dear?" Whenever I hear "Tenderness on the Block," I never fail to recall this scene.

Later still. Home for the holidays. I wander in from the living room, where "Accidentally Like a Martyr" is playing, to find Mom in her housecoat at the kitchen table, her head bowed over a cup of coffee. It takes me a while to realize that she's crying. Please, she asks, could I change the song?

The years intervene: study, work, travel, more study, more work. I'm teaching philosophy part-time at a small university in Canada, where my habit is to return to campus in the evening to prepare classes for the following day. On the radio in my temporary office, the dial is set to CBC. A program called *After Hours*, from Winnipeg, is on, hosted by Ross Porter, whose voice sounds like it's been cured in whiskey and smoke. He introduces a Zevon recording I've never heard before, a spare but stirring song called "Jesus Mentioned." I listen, rapt, recalled at once to Zevon. Where had he got to? How had I managed to lose track of him?

In the short-lived police series "Boomtown," the riveting actor Neil McDonough plays an assistant DA with a drinking problem. In "Blackout," the penultimate episode of Season One, having made a spectacle of himself at an awards dinner, he climbs into his car, riffles through the glove compartment and under the seats, looking for a swig, even just a drop, of liquor, then, coming up empty, cranks the radio. "Lawyers, Guns and Money" is playing. As he starts the car, he smiles and purrs, "Zevon!"

Exactly.

I

Laughing at
Shadows

1
The Incongruous Humor of the Excitable Boy

ERIC V.D. LUFT

On a cloudy weekend in late November 2005, my wife and I unexpectedly spent an extra day in London because British Airways had screwed up our return flight from Berlin to New York. Making ad hoc plans for this additional time, we decided to find out whether Lee Ho Fook, the Chinese restaurant which Warren Zevon mentioned in "Werewolves of London," was real.

It was! Just over on Gerrard Street, it was not far from our hotel in Piccadilly. We walked there and found it cheerful, spacious, and not highly decorated, except for posters of Zevon plastered all over. We had an overpriced but fairly decent dinner. It seemed to us that they traded more on Zevon's name than on the quality of their food.

We were struck above all by incongruity. The brightness of Lee Ho Fook contrasted with the usual darkness of Zevon's songs. That he should sing of an ordinary Chinese restaurant in lyrics about murderous monsters of European folklore presents a bizarre juxtaposition of the benign and the deadly.

Dirty Life and Times

This sort of weirdness is normal for Zevon. Just as Kurt Vonnegut found humor in the firebombing of Dresden, so Zevon finds it in bizarre and often nasty situations. He makes us smile at what should disgust us. We might laugh at the rapist and murderer who builds a cage out of his victim's bones, or at little old ladies getting mutilated, but this is uncomfortable laughter. Yet his apparently sympathetic view of predators is mitigated by his ironic and often implicit condemnation of their behavior. The laughter he sparks is sarcastic and wickedly human, but not cynical or contemptuous.

Zevon's humor is based on normalizing the abnormal, or contrasting the ordinary with the extraordinary. There is significant precedent in Western culture for such contrast, especially in the nineteenth century. Charles Baudelaire did it in poetry; Francisco Goya and Théodore Gericault in painting; Mary Shelley, Emily Brontë, and Bram Stoker in literature; Baron Cuvier in comparative anatomy; and Arthur Schopenhauer and Friedrich Nietzsche in philosophy. Like them, Zevon shows an almost Victorian fascination with juxtaposition between the common and the uncommon. This juxtaposition can either blur or sharpen the line between the two.

Not only Zevon's lyrics, but also his visual presentation gives us a jolt. One side of the record sleeve of the *Excitable Boy* vinyl LP has the lyrics to all the songs on the album. The other side has no words, but just a life-size photo of a plateful of delicious vegetables, perfectly cooked, and presented in a very appetizing way—with a Smith and Wesson revolver laid across them. Talk about incongruity!

Does Zevon's incongruity express pessimism? Resignation? Cynicism? Self-pity? None of the above? All of the above? Something else? Nothing? We can at least say that it expresses itself, that it is what it is, and that we can just take it at face value, laugh at it, and let it go. But we could also push it toward a greater depth of meaning. His lyrics seem to encourage this, and such scrutiny could reveal hidden facts about ourselves that we might prefer not to know. He seems to relish this result, not just because he wants us to feel something nasty, but because he seems to want us to become more aware of ourselves and our dirty little secrets.

Reconsider Me

Mark Roche puts it succinctly: "In comedy we laugh at contradictory positions; we don't take them as the final truth" (p. 427). Sometimes these contradictions are resolved, sometimes not. Sometimes the resolution is funnier than the contradiction, but usually not. That's because a contradiction typically shakes our sense of comfort and its resolution seldom restores that sense completely. Despite any resolution, we remember the contradiction and how it shook us. Yet in general, contradictions scream to be resolved. Zevon often deliberately disappoints us in this regard, refusing to resolve his contradictions, which makes his incongruous comedy not less funny, but more poignant. Zevon's incongruity seems more powerful when there is no resolution. It is certainly more savage.

Philosophers of humor discuss "incongruity and resolution." A clear case in point is Gilbert and Sullivan's *The Pirates of Penzance*, where incongruity is apparent between Frederic's duty to his loving friends and his duty to fight piracy—and this incongruity is funny. Later, this conflict is resolved, as his true birthday is revealed and one of these duties evaporates—and this resolution is funny too. But in Zevon's lyrics there is much incongruity and little resolution. Even though they remain funny in the absence of resolution, they also remain eerie, dark, absurd, even surreal, precisely because their content is not resolved. Of course, Roland "didn't say a word"; he was headless. Zevon gives no explanation.

There are dozens of types of philosophical theories of humor. One of these types is focused on incongruities, disconnects, contradictions, and paradoxes. Oddly enough, it's called incongruity theory. Most of it fits Zevon's output pretty well. Some of it even tries to reduce all humor to incongruity, but that position is difficult to maintain.

Critics of the incongruity theory of humor point out that not all incongruous juxtapositions are funny. But, we may note with amusement, some of these authors seem to have no sense of humor of their own. Just because the philosophy of humor is usually not funny does not mean that it can't be fun. Analysis often kills the spirit of whatever is being analyzed, but only if we take analysis too seriously. We can take it semi-seriously and remain true to ourselves as intelligent humans. If we readers have a sense of humor, we can sometimes find laughable, or even hilarious, passages that authors didn't intend to be so. This doesn't mean that these authors are ridiculous or don't know what they're talking about. It doesn't even mean that we're laughing at them. It only means that we see something in their writings that they didn't. This is perfectly normal. Readers are always finding things that authors didn't intend. Some authors are too serious. Most readers aren't.

Looking for the Next Best Thing

Robert Latta discounts incongruity as source of comedy. He says instead that humor proceeds in three stages, describing the transitions from stage to stage as "cognitive shifts." First, we are "unrelaxed," then we are even more "unrelaxed," then, finally, we laugh and "relax." Comic situations disturb us. Our heightened "unrelaxation" triggers laughter, which brings, or returns, us to a state of relative "relaxation," a more comfortable feeling. Nevertheless, "unrelaxation" may be our natural or default state. Latta hints that, perhaps, no one is "ever totally relaxed" (p. 37). There is no full catharsis.

Latta's theory of cognitive shifts, which he calls "Theory L," offers a physiological or behavioral explanation of why we laugh. He claims that incongruities are not funny in themselves, but only in how we physically react to them. Thus, Theory L is a response-side theory, as opposed to a stimulus-side theory, which traces the source of humor to the situation itself. The general difference between response-side and stimulus-side theories is expressed by asking whether our feelings come from our brains acting on things or from things acting on our brains. If the former, then, as Hamlet says, "There is nothing either good or bad, but thinking makes it so" (II.ii.259). But if the latter, then we are just knocked about at the mercy of a probably hostile world of external forces beyond our control.

All philosophical theories of humor can be classified as either response-side or stimulus-side. Incongruity theory is a species of stimulus-side theory. That is, if we have a sense of humor, incongruous things make us laugh. We can't help it. We may stifle a chuckle, but the reaction itself is just a reflex. We do not decide, even subconsciously, whether or not some state of affairs is funny. It just hits us. We can only decide what to do with our reaction: let it all hang out, hide it, be embarrassed by it, worry about it, or whatever.

Steven Gimbel traces two thousand years of debate between response-side and stimulus-side theorists. Unlike arguments about behaviorism, the difference between the two does not come down to a role for free will in response-side theory versus no role for free will in stimulus-side theory. Rather, both response-side and stimulus-side theories acknowledge that laughter is involuntary, a reaction beyond our control, unless we're faking it.

Although this reaction is automatic, we are not robots. We react to the stimulus with our emotions, bringing all of our previous experience to the reaction. At this point, the line between stimulus-side and response-side theories becomes gray and blurry. The stimulus may be funny in itself, but it is not actually funny until we respond to it, recognize it as funny, and either laugh at it or deliberately stifle our laughter. As with many of Zevon's lyrics, this debate itself is an incongruity without resolution. Neither side is hard and fast. Neither is likely to win the battle against the other. The truth probably lies somewhere in the middle.

Something Bad Happened to a Clown

Even though John Morreall may well be the main proponent of modern incongruity theory, he doesn't fully accept it, although he is more friendly to it than most theorists. He traces it back to Aristotle, who wrote in the *Poetics* that misfortune, ugliness, or distortion can all incite laughter if they are not too painful, malicious, or harmful. The incongruity apparent in such situations lies between what is expected or hoped for and what is actually seen or experienced. The transition from one pole of this incongruity to the other must be funny if the whole incongruity is going to make us laugh. Aristotle's translator and commentator, Samuel Henry Butcher (1850–1910), emphasizes "the blending of contrasted feelings. The pleasure of the ludicrous . . . arises from the shock of surprise at a painless incongruity" (p. 376).

Morreall admits two problems with incongruity theory. First, we sometimes laugh at things which are not incongruous. Ticklish people laugh when tickled, but there is no incongruity in that. Second, incongruity theory does not cover all cases. Finding a cougar in your bathtub is incongruous, but it won't make you laugh (p. 130). On the other hand, if the "cougar" is a middle-aged, sexually predatory woman instead of a mountain lion, the incongruity could be highly amusing.

If not all humorous situations are incongruous, and if incongruity theory does not, therefore, cover all cases, then what are some possible alternatives? On the theoretical side, Charles Gruner agrees with Latta's claim that incongruity alone is not sufficient to cause laughter, cannot be relied upon to cause laughter, and may indeed cause any of the whole range of emotions, including disgust, indifference, or hatred. But, on the more practical side, we recognize a general hierarchy of humor, with puns and slapstick at the bottom and paradox, satire, and sarcasm at the top. High-end humor tends to be more incongruous than low-end humor. Puns and slapstick are low forms of humor because of their lack of subtlety. Paradox, satire, and sarcasm are high forms of humor because they require a certain level of sophistication to get the joke—not just to tell it, but also to frame it.

Zevon's lyrics have been favorably compared with those of Randy Newman, Frank Zappa, Elvis Costello, Lou Reed, and others, but his sense of humor is more macabre, and hence more incongruous, than that of any of these other songwriters. His paradoxes are poignant, satirical, and sarcastic. He seldom uses puns. Even though many of his scenarios contain slapsticky elements, that is not their main point. His slapstick points beyond itself, usually toward something nasty, and almost always toward something incongruous.

I'll Sleep When I'm Dead

We all have a lot to do, and little time to do it, alive or dead. There's no time to sleep. We can worry about sleeping after we're dead. In the meantime, life is full of peaks and valleys of pleasure and pain. Zevon wants to experience it all, sometimes simultaneously. We learn in "Ain't That Pretty at All" that he would rather suffer than feel nothing. He makes a similar point in "Hostage-O," where he prefers being bound, gagged, dragged, chained, maimed, and treated like a dog to being lonely. So, he maximizes his experiences, often in contradictory ways. He wants to visit the Louvre, not to see the artworks, which may leave him unimpressed, but to bang his head against the wall. He implies that banging his head against an exotic wall in Paris would be more thrilling than banging it against a mundane wall in Los Angeles.

What does he mean by musing over what to do in Denver once he's dead? Probably not the idea that Herodotus attributed to Solon: "Call no man happy until he's dead." Solon's quip was about fortune, or good luck, and its transience—or "transigence"—but Zevon's lyrics are about misfortune, or bad luck, and its apparent permanence or intransigence. All sorts of things can kill you, but that shouldn't stop you from doing what you do, even after you're dead. We're back to Roland again. The impossibility. The lack of explanation. Van Owen felt it—the hard way. Is this realistic? Supernatural? Well, it's probably at least psychologically real. As a metaphor, Roland's revenge on Van Owen—and, by extension, on the CIA, for which Van Owen worked as an agent—reflects the persistence of rebellion against oppression, no matter how many rebels are killed in the process.

Heartache Spoken Here

If Zevon's humor isn't absurd, it's certainly the first cousin of the absurd. His juxtapositions make us wince. Even worse, they make us re-examine ourselves, often to our own detriment. Are we the schlemiels and schlemazels that he portrays in songs like "Poor, Poor Pitiful Me"? How would we behave if we found ourselves in the tempting situations he describes? Would we be ashamed or proud of ourselves later? His refusal to talk about the sadomasochistic encounter that may or may not have happened at the Hyatt House suggests that he has not yet escaped from the Waring blender. The effect that his failed sexual relationships have had on him is permanent. Isn't that true for all of us? That's why "Poor, Poor Pitiful Me" hits home, even if we are not self-pitying fools.

Zevon presents the stereotype of the sad clown as a juxtaposition between bright fantasy and ugly reality. Even in his self-pitying songs, he does not whine, but deprecates himself. His expectations are low. He wants a woman with low self-esteem. In "Dirty Life and Times," we see that only such a woman can give him any kind of solace. Perhaps that's because of his own low self-esteem. Like a real schlemazel, he can't get a break. The waitress he thinks he seduces in "Lawyers, Guns, and Money" turns out to be a Russian agent seducing him. He loses more than he risks in Havana. He can't even commit suicide properly in "Poor, Poor Pitiful Me," laying his head on railroad tracks that are no longer in service.

Worrier King

"Uneasy lies the head that wears a crown," the king laments in Shakespeare's *Henry IV, Part II* (III.i.31). But a king's worries should be because of and on behalf of his subjects and his kingdom, not because of his own neuroses. He should be the king who worries, not the king of worries. Zevon hints that subjects ought not to obey such a maladjusted, self-absorbed king.

"Monkey Wash Donkey Rinse" is reminiscent of Tom Lehrer's "We Will All Go Together When We Go" or Blue Öyster Cult's "Don't Fear the Reaper." Here, Zevon mentions the inevitability and universality of death, suggesting that there is still plenty of room in Hell for everyone. But he juxtaposes these morbid thoughts with the idea of having a good time in Hell, partying at the Earth's core. Death is a festival. Zevon invites us to welcome the event and join in the fun, as if it were the debut of a fancy rich girl into high society. There will be excitement all night, and the night will be infinitely long. We will not only witness, but also participate, in the twilight of the gods of Valhalla. Also in attendance will be Shiva the Destroyer, the third member of the Hindu trinity, who oversees the necessary function of death and destruction so that there can be further life and creation.

The stark contrast between two lifestyles presented in "Detox Mansion" provides insight into Zevon's apparent obsession with death. Both lead to death, but different kinds of death. As we approach death, we may feel either rapid burnout or slow plodding. Everything leads to our last breath, whether in the wide world or at the secluded farm, whether we shoot up dangerous substances or just rake leaves.

Gorilla, You're a Desperado

Zevon's frequent primate metaphor shows the implicit incongruity between simians and humans. Often the simian comes out on top, but even when it doesn't, the human has some significant foibles exposed. At first, "Leave My Monkey Alone" seems like a simple plea for humans to quit messing around with nature, but further reflection reveals it as a condemnation of colonial wars and imperialistic attitudes.

"Gorilla, You're a Desperado" and "Excitable Boy" both satirize the same social phenomenon: self-indulgent parents and apathetic society letting miscreants run wild. Living with no accountability, like the gorilla or the wanton boy, is ultimately shallow, pointless, and unfulfilling. The escaped gorilla luxuriating in the high life is just as much a prisoner as the man he left behind in his old cage at the zoo. The spoiled boy does not go to prison for rape and murder, but only to a hospital for the criminally insane. When, after ten years, he is "cured" and released, his family, friends, and other enablers are still only amused by his bizarre, sociopathic antics.

What would resolution mean in these cases? Would the gorilla meekly return to his cage? Would he be happier there? Would the man in the cage drive away to better times in his BMW? Would the criminal be locked up for good? Would society then respond to him "with howls of execration," as Albert Camus's antihero Meursault desires at the end of *The Stranger* in order to counter "the benign indifference of the universe"? Probably none of these resolutions, or any others, would work. Zevon achieves greater pathos by leaving his incongruities unresolved.

My Shit's Fucked Up

Alexander Kozintsev counsels us to avoid being inoffensive. By this, he is not suggesting that we should go out of our way to be offensive. Rather, he's only saying that offending people is often funnier than not offending them. Offensive people can be funny if they're not mean. Offended people can be funny if they're not permanently harmed. This dynamic of offensive banter has been a mainstay of comedy since ancient times, from Aristophanes to Shakespeare to the Three Stooges to Jack Benny to Don Rickles to Zevon and beyond.

Pie in the face might offend the recipient, but no one else. It's naturally funny, an example not only of slapstick, but of incongruity. Gruner writes, "Custard pie in the face of an elaborately tuxedoed stuffed shirt might be a hilarious incongruity. But would a lovely, smiling child sitting unscathed in the ruins of her demolished hut in Vietnam? Such an incongruity would hardly elicit laughter" (p. 7). Nevertheless, Zevon could probably pull it off. He had a knack for illuminating the darkness, for mollifying the horrific.

In a chapter aptly titled "Incongruity, Degradation, and Self-Parody," Kozintsev cites the same passage in Aristotle's *Poetics* that Butcher does, but uses Aristotle's example of laughable ugliness to segue into the superiority theory of Thomas Hobbes (1588–1679). Hobbes claims that laughter is essentially egotistical. We feel good when we put other people down. Tragedy is when something bad happens to me; comedy is when something bad happens to you. When superior, or wannabe superior, people imitate or ridicule inferior people, or those whom they consider inferior, they chortle vaingloriously because they believe themselves "nobler, smarter, and more beautiful" than the butts of their jokes (p. 2). Zevon is not so mean. Rather, in some of his more introspective songs, he identifies with "inferior" people. Cruelty has no part in Zevon's worldview.

Well, maybe that's not quite true. Sometimes it seems that Zevon is either cruel to himself, expecting someone to be cruel to him, or perhaps even asking someone to be cruel to him, as in "Hostage-O"—and we still don't know what happened at the Hyatt House. But all of these instances are presented without malevolence. In "I'll Sleep When I'm Dead," he coyly suggests that he might shoot himself for acting stupid. In "Accidentally Like a Martyr," he doesn't seem to mind the hurt getting worse or the heart getting harder. Then there's his constant smirking threat in "Ain't That Pretty at All" to run headlong into a wall. Would he ever really do such a thing? Of course not! But the comic threat perfectly expresses his state of mind.

Ain't That Pretty at All

Zevon was a true rock'n'roller. He did not write or record mere novelty songs, such as Dr. Demento might play on his radio show. Nor was he a witty parodist like Weird Al Yankovic. Rather, his dark lyrics, set to original tunes, were more akin to the poetry of Dorothy Parker or the satire of Tom Lehrer. He sought to wake us up, not to entertain us with silliness. He expressed his jaded cynicism in provocative oxymorons.

Zevon saw it all, heard it all, and what he saw and heard wasn't pretty. He took a little vacation, and on vacations we're supposed to relax, be happy, be frivolous, rejuvenate ourselves, ready ourselves for our eventual return to the real world. But he spent his vacation getting a root canal. The pain didn't bother him—or if it did, it didn't discourage him. He would rather be alert than anesthetized. He knew that many people enjoying silly pastimes deceive themselves into thinking that they feel happy, when in fact they feel nothing, or at least nothing worthwhile.

Right now, as I write this, I'm sitting at a picnic table on the south shore of Oneida Lake in upstate New York. It's a gorgeous day. All around me are people having a good time: fishing, kayaking, wading, skipping stones, chatting, staring at their phones, listening to music, playing music—and not a single unhappy face in the bunch.

But what dark secrets might any of them hold? Would Zevon's lyrics make them cringe, see more of themselves than they want to see, or reveal what they prefer to hide? If so, then Zevon was a success.

2

Red Noses and Squirting Roses

SHALON VAN TINE

In 2002, Warren Zevon revealed on *The Late Show* that he had been diagnosed with lung cancer, which had spread throughout his body. When David Letterman asked how he took the bad news, Zevon responded dryly, "Well, it means you better get your dry cleaning done on special."

Taken aback by Zevon's response, Letterman commented that he doubted he would be able to make jokes had he received such disheartening news, to which Zevon retorted, "I know you could." When Letterman asked Zevon if his cancer diagnosis gave him any insight into life and death, he simply advised everyone to "enjoy every sandwich" (Letterman, Episode #1895). Zevon died less than a year later.

Throughout his career, Zevon was known for his quirky, dark sense of humor. Beginning as a session musician and jingle writer, Zevon struggled to make it as a solo artist, despite his undeniable musical talent. Always a bit out of place among the mellow sounds of his fellow singer-songwriters, he is mainly remembered for his kitschy one-hit number that gets trotted out every Halloween, "Werewolves of London," sometimes referred to as "the thinking man's 'Monster Mash'."

His music often dealt with themes not suited to radio: rape, murder, drugs, alcoholism, crime. As his friend and frequent collaborator Jackson Browne put it, Zevon wrote "song noir" (*Nothing's Bad Luck*, p. 257). But Zevon's uniqueness stemmed from his preference for dealing with the macabre through humor. He grappled with questions that philosophers have tried to solve since ancient times: Why do we laugh? What's the function of humor? What role does comedy play in our lives?

Philosophers have proposed various theories to answer these questions. One of the oldest gags in vaudeville acts (and later in cartoons) involves a man slipping on a banana peel and falling down while the audience erupts in laughter. This classic joke illustrates what's called superiority theory, which emphasizes how humor involves laughing at others' misfortunes (the German concept of *Schadenfreude* captures this same idea). Relief theory, on the other hand, proposes that we laugh to release nervous tension. Whereas the former suggests that humor is a kind of social phenomenon, the latter maintains that it's psychological. Prominent among more recent views on the comic is incongruity theory, according to which humor stems from a reaction to the absurd. When our perceptions are challenged by something unexpected, we find the situation funny. For instance, when a stand-up comedian gets to the joke's punchline and it doesn't fall within the range of our expectations for a normal telling of events, we laugh. Essentially, incongruity theory argues that humor is a natural response to the irrational.

Zevon's music exemplifies these three models of humor, but it also demonstrates the way humor is highly dependent on historical context. In other words, what we find funny is directly connected to the historical period in which we live. Zevon's most famous songs were written predominantly during the 1970s and 1980s, the last couple of decades of the Cold War era. During this time, many popular comedy forms shifted to a darker tone that reflected broader societal problems.

Comedy has always provided artists with a way to address social and political issues, but in the crisis-ridden 1970s, artists reacted to trying times with a darker, more jaded sense of humor. In this decade, American culture shifted sharply, as multiple economic crises occurred, the entertainment industry became increasingly corporatized, and the public lost faith in trusted institutions. It's perhaps no surprise, then, that artists responded with sardonic detachment. The magazine *National Lampoon* and the television show *Saturday Night Live*, for instance, got their start in this era, when it seemed as if the only reasonable defense against the compounding problems was to laugh at them. In this way, Zevon's ironic tunes were in sync with troubled times.

The One about Grandpa Pissing His Pants

Plato was one of the first philosophers to explore the nature of humor. In his *Philebus*, Socrates tells Protarchus that comedy always involves "a mixture of pleasure and pain" (47d). When people deviate from how they should act in public, usually due to ignorance about proper behavior in certain social settings, the ridiculousness of the situation prompts us to laugh. Jokes about immigrants that were commonplace in the United States during the nineteenth century, for instance, made fun of their accents or customs that seemed unusual to native-born Americans. Such jokes rested on the notion that immigrants were ignorant about appropriate ways of acting and talking, so how they acted and talked seemed silly and thus ripe for parody. This joke structure depends on a power dynamic where those who are the butt of the joke are deemed inferior in some way, while those laughing are deemed superior.

In his *Republic*, Plato suggests that the ideal society is one based on reason and political order. Since comedy often elicits frivolous emotions that can hinder your ability to think clearly about serious matters of state, Plato views comedy as intrinsically dangerous. "There's a part of you which wants to make people laugh," he argues, "but your reason restrains it, because you're afraid of being thought a vulgar clown" (606c). For Plato, when we exploit the misfortunes of others for a cheap laugh, we are debasing ourselves. In his song, "Play It All Night Long," which describes Grandpa pissing his pants and Brother Billie wandering about with both guns drawn, Zevon depicts Southerners as dirty, trigger-happy, incestuous alcoholics.

The image of the ignorant redneck has become a stereotype, frequently exploited as an easy comedic punchline. But these lyrics demonstrate why Plato is uneasy about this form of humor. Those who listen to and laugh at these caricatures clearly feel superior to the people they are intended to depict, but the depictions themselves do not offer any actual intellectual commentary on the plight of the Southern poor, for if they did, the result would expose the tragedy of their situation and would not actually be very funny.

For the most part, Aristotle echoes Plato's sentiments about comedy, but instead of writing off comedy altogether, insists that it must take the right form and be used in moderation. Aristotle differentiates between laughter and wit, associating the former with mockery, while regarding the latter as more sophisticated. His views on humor are related to his system of ethics. For Aristotle, we develop our character by embodying virtues, character traits that are balanced between deficiency and excess. In his *Nicomachean Ethics*, Aristotle argues that those "who go to excess in raising laughs seem to be vulgar buffoons. . . . Those who would never say anything themselves to raise a laugh, and even object when other people do it, seem to be boorish and stiff. Those who joke in appropriate ways are called witty, or, in other words, agile-witted" (1128a). For Aristotle, having a good sense of humor is ideal—not too much, not too little.

Thomas Hobbes, the philosopher known for describing human existence as "solitary, poor, nasty, brutish, and short," also addresses the nature of humor. For Hobbes, humans are in a relentless struggle for power, so when we see our opponents fail, we are compelled to laugh at them. In his *Leviathan*, Hobbes explores the underlying reasons for our natural human emotions and passions, including why we laugh. He says that laughter occurs "by observing the imperfections of other men" (p. 125). Pointing out others' flaws seems to be a natural human tendency, but superiority theory also works the other way around by pointing out our own flaws to get others to laugh. This approach suggests that it is better for people to laugh *with* you than *at* you. Take, for example, Zevon's song "Lawyers, Guns, and Money," which makes us chuckle at the narrator's errors in judgment, as well as his embarrassing reliance on his father's money and connections to get him out of trouble. Or consider the track "Poor, Poor Pitiful Me," in which the comic desperation of laying his head on a track to be crushed by a train that doesn't run anymore is bound to elicit a laugh. On the assumption that these songs are even in part confessional, Zevon makes himself the object of ridicule, thereby making us feel superior to him and thus allowing us to laugh at his expense.

The One about the Headless Gunner

Self-deprecating humor also works by relieving tense situations. If someone with a black eye walks into a room, most people would react with concern. But if that person immediately jokes, "You should see the other guy!" then the room is put at ease and everyone can laugh at his unfortunate appearance. This approach to humor is an example of relief theory, the notion that we laugh to release a kind of nervous or psychological tension.

Francis Hutcheson, one of the representative figures of the Scottish Enlightenment, thinks that the prevalence of self-deprecating or situational humor posed an alternative to the idea that we laugh only to show our superiority to others. In his *Reflections Upon Laughter*, Hutcheson challenges Hobbes's harsh interpretation of human nature, saying, "If Mr. Hobbes's notion be just, then, first, there can be no laughter on any occasion where we make no comparison of ourselves to others, or of our present state to a worse state," suggesting that a good deal of humor stems from circumstances that do not rely on making fun of others (p. 7).

As more people learned about the theory of evolution in the nineteenth century, philosophers began inclining more toward relief theory because it provides a physiological, rather than a moral, basis for humor. In his *Sense of Beauty*, George Santayana says that humor is "a much more directly physical thing," and that laughter is the result of a kind of "nervous excitement" (p. 151). This perspective echoes the views of the two major proponents of relief theory, sociologist Herbert Spencer and psychoanalyst Sigmund Freud. In his essay "The Physiology of Laughter," Spencer cites the example of being tickled in order to show how laughter can be described as the result of a physiological response to a stimulus, arguing that "nervous excitation always tends to beget muscular motion, and when it rises to a certain intensity, always does beget it" (p. 195).

Like Spencer, Freud regards jokes as a way to relieve nervous tension. In *The Joke and Its Relation to the Unconscious*, he synthesizes previous theories of humor with his own theories about the inner workings of the psyche. For Freud, most human behavior is the outward manifestation of fears, anxieties, or desires lodged deep within the unconscious. Like a "Freudian slip," where someone accidentally utters a wrong word or phrase that reveals their true desires, a joke is humorous because it makes fun of those things that often go unsaid. Freud argues that "the presence of several inhibited drives, whose suppression has remained to some degree unstable, will provide the most favorable disposition for producing tendentious jokes" (p. 138).

A joke is a way for us to release pent-up energies in the psyche, and the more the urge is suppressed, the more controversial a joke is likely to be (and the funnier we're likely to find it). Just as sports allow us to channel our violent tendencies into a socially acceptable activity, humor allows us to approach difficult topics in a socially safe way. With the ground quaking underfoot and water levels rising, California's prospects depend upon Zevon paying his bar tab. Werewolves pause from their cruel marauding to thumb Chinese menus. Vengeful Roland, still headless, doesn't say a word. In a world of murder, mayhem, and looming natural disasters, the comic twist offers relief.

The One about the Pot Roast

In his *Critique of Judgement*, Immanuel Kant develops another theory about humor. "Something absurd (something in which, therefore, the understanding can of itself find no delight) must be present," he writes, "in whatever is to raise a hearty convulsive laugh" (p. 161). This idea forms the basis of incongruity theory, which claims that laughter arises from perceiving something which, since it's out of place, defies our expectations. In his essay, "On Wit and Humor," William Hazlitt notes that "man is the only animal that laughs and weeps, for he is the only animal that is struck with the difference between what things are and what they ought to be" (p. 1). While scientists have observed some animal behaviors that may resemble laughter, the ability to understand the absurd is a purely human trait that forms the basis of much of what we find funny. To put it another way, the human mind is not simply the sum of our primal instincts, but aims instead to organize experience into a rational whole. So, when presented with something absurd, the natural response is often to laugh.

Similarly, Søren Kierkegaard argues that humor arises at the point where there is a disparity between what we expect and what actually occurs. He relates this to the concepts of irony and tragedy, suggesting that incongruity can lead either to laughter or melancholy. In his *Concluding Unscientific Postscript to Philosophical Fragments*, he says that "the tragic and the comic are the same, in so far as both are based on contradiction; but the tragic is the suffering contradiction, the comical, the painless contradiction" (p. 514). For Kierkegaard, a good sense of humor is directly tied to a higher level of ethics and aesthetics, amounting to "the last stage of existence— inwardness before faith" (p. 291).

Having a good sense of humor about the absurd permeates Zevon's worldview. His song "Mr. Bad Example" illustrates how incongruity is crucial to humor. The lyrics of this song begin by telling a little coming-of-age story, but the listener quickly learns that the main character does not study religious practices or help move furniture for altruistic motives. The "punchline" in each stanza produces a humorous response because we expect a different outcome entirely.

However, probably the best example of how Zevon deals with the macabre and the absurd through humor is found in his song "Excitable Boy," where he takes a grisly scenario and makes it funny by adding a bit of social commentary. Listeners are almost as disturbed by the indifferent responses of the psychopathic killer's family and friends as they are by the grue-some deeds themselves. The unexpected reaction to the song ends up being laughter.

The One about the Village Idiot

In an interview with Steve Roeser, Zevon talked about the valu-able role that humor played in those of his songs that deal with dark or absurd themes. He explained, "If you can say something serious and important and moving, and something about your feelings and/or humankind, that's great. But as soon as it gets stupid, you better get 'em laughing because, otherwise, it'll be horrible" (p. 80). Being able to respond with humor to tough top-ics helps us face difficult realities when we are armed with nothing else. In this way, Zevon's approach aligned with the larger changes happening in American comedy in the 1970s and 1980s.

The Seventies marked a time when many Americans felt the effects of stagflation, the combination of high unemploy-ment rates, high inflation, and slow economic growth. A good deal of manufacturing moved abroad, adding to rising unem-ployment levels. As we have seen, many lost so much faith in formerly trusted institutions that political polarization inten-sified. Leftwing liberation movements clashed with growing rightwing coalitions, while, through the Eighties, the gap be-tween the wealthy and the poor continued to grow (Schulman 2001 and Rossinow 2015). This era was pretty bleak, a histor-ical reality that was reflected in the shift in the style of American comedy.

Starting in the 1970s, comedy took on a surlier, more cynical tone. Television shows like *Saturday Night Live* and *All in the Family*, which used humor to tackle contentious political issues, debuted during these years, as did satirical magazines like *National Lampoon*. Another key development was the opening of The Comedy Store, a stand-up comedy club where many well-known comedians got their start. Comedy in popu-lar music, however, was still somewhat of a novelty. The Dr. Demento radio show, for example, helped to popularize comedy musicians like Weird Al Yankovic, but these acts were still far removed from the mainstream. Popular radio in this era often featured saccharine singer-songwriters who rarely broached the grim topics that Zevon was inclined to. It's probably no sur-prise, then, that many of Zevon's best tunes did not get much radio play. Still, that did not stop him from using humor to address the many historic changes that American society was contending with at the time. Zevon frequently poked fun at the economic troubles and political malaise of the era. For instance in "Mohammed's Radio," he notes everyone's desperation, but in the context of observing the village idiot wandering around with his face all aglow, pressed up against the radio, and the General whispering cautionary advice to his aide-de-camp. Zevon resorted to humor in his art as a way of commenting on the social and political problems of the age, placing him among the most sharply observant songwriters of his time.

Punch Line

In his posthumous work *The Will to Power*, Friedrich Nietzsche says, "Perhaps I know best why man alone laughs: he alone suffers so deeply that he had to invent laughter" (sec. 91). As someone who was plagued by illness his entire life, Nietzsche understood at a gut level how humor can relieve the worst of situations. Just a couple of years before his cancer diagnosis, Zevon released the song "My Shit's Fucked Up," which anticipated his failing health.

Throughout his career, Zevon's music reflected elements of humor that reflect the assumptions of the superiority theory, relief theory, and incongruity theory of humor as a way to deal with the bleakness of life. When nothing in life is actually funny, sometimes the best medicine is simply to laugh at it.

II

Intrusions in the Dirt

3
What Can "Boom Boom Mancini" Teach Us about Boxing and Ethics?

HEINRIK HELLWIG

Ray Mancini killed a man. It happened in a boxing ring in Las Vegas on November 13th 1982. Mancini punched Duk-Koo Kim in the head. Kim went down, but got back up. Moments later, he collapsed, fell into a coma and never woke up again. Kim had suffered a massive brain injury from the punch. He died five days later. He was twenty-seven years old. Mancini was twenty-one.

Mancini didn't intend to kill Kim. It was an accident. Mancini and Kim were professional boxers. Their fateful encounter is the focus of Warren Zevon's song, "Boom Boom Mancini," the second track on his album *Sentimental Hygiene* (1987). After Kim's tragic death, there were loud calls for boxing to be abolished: "Boxing is about hurting people. Why should any civilized society tolerate that? In all other sports, if you hurt someone on purpose, you'd be disqualified, because it's immoral. It doesn't matter if the fighters are willing to put their health at risk. This sport is too brutal and too dangerous." Such criticisms of boxing weren't new, but they took on a new life after Mancini vs. Kim. As Mark Kriegel puts it in *The Good Son*, Ray Mancini became "Exhibit A" for the abolition of boxing.

In "Boom Boom Mancini," Zevon accuses Mancini's critics of making "hypocrite judgments," and yet doesn't explain *how* their judgments are hypocritical. How is someone a hypocrite by criticizing Mancini's actions or boxing in general? What might Zevon have had in mind? These aren't easy questions, because, as we'll soon see, there's some evidence that Zevon wasn't trying to say *anything* meaningful about boxing. By looking closely at Zevon's lyrics and connecting them to philosophical ideas, I'll show that "Boom Boom Mancini" teaches us three valuable lessons about boxing and ethics:

- A well-known moral principle called The Doctrine of Double Effect would say that boxing is not allowed for moral reasons and should be banned.

- Moral hypocrisy happens when people don't follow the moral principles they advocate and apply to others. Anyone who invokes the Doctrine of Double Effect to criticize boxing while at the same time supporting it is a moral hypocrite. Similarly, a person who supports boxing and applies the Doctrine of Double Effect to defend it when tragedy strikes is a moral hypocrite.

- Moral hypocrisy is very bad.

A Boxing Tragedy

Ray "Boom Boom" Mancini was one of the most popular American fighters of the 1980s. He had an "all action" fighting style—the kind of fighter who wasn't afraid to take a punch to land one and who kept coming at his opponent with wild flurries like a whirlwind. Crowds flocked to watch Mancini fight because they knew they'd probably see a knockout. Usually, it was Mancini knocking out his opponents and winning the fight. He retired with a record of twenty-nine wins and five losses, with twenty-three of his victories coming by way of knockout.

Mancini, whose fights were broadcast on CBS, competed in the lightweight division (130–135 pounds). Network television was capitalizing on new interest in smaller weight divisions after the US boxing team's dominant performance at the 1976 Summer Olympics. Though he wasn't an Olympian, "Boom Boom" was a must-see fighter. Between his exciting style and Italian heritage, many boxing fans and journalists saw Ray Mancini as a mini-Rocky Balboa.

Mancini also had a great story. Hailing from Youngstown, Ohio, a steel town that had flourished for generations but fell into permanent decline after the steel mills closed in the 1970s, Ray was a local hero. He knew the quality of life that many steel workers had enjoyed and lost. Ray was proud of his Youngstown roots, proud to represent his town's struggles and fighting spirit on a national stage. His father, Lenny Mancini (also nicknamed "Boom Boom"), had boxed professionally from the late 1930s through the 1940s. Lenny was a lightweight contender whose career was interrupted by World War II. After the War, he tried to resume his boxing career, but he was wounded in combat in 1944 and his injuries limited what he could do in the ring. Lenny Mancini never won a world title. Ray made it his sole purpose in life to become a world champion for his father.

After challenging and losing to lightweight titleholder and eventual Hall of Famer Alexis Argüello in 1981, Ray's first pro loss, he finally fulfilled Lenny's dream on May 8, 1982. In his twenty-fourth professional fight, Ray Mancini knocked out Arturo Frias in the first round to win the World Boxing Association Lightweight Championship.

Unfortunately for Ray, his entire world would be turned upside down only seven months later. In his second lightweight title defense, Ray fought Duk-Koo Kim, a tough South Korean fighter not widely known at the time. After thirteen unrelenting rounds, in which neither fighter went down and both fighters dished out and absorbed hundreds of heavy blows, Mancini connected with a right hand to Kim's head. Kim's entire body flew backward onto the canvas in a motion that resembled the "blown-away" guy from the old Maxell cassette commercials. Kim used the ropes to pull himself up, but referee Richard Green had seen enough. Green stopped the fight and Mancini was the winner by technical knockout in Round 14. Kim was stretchered out of Caesars Palace, having suffered a massive subdural hematoma, a blood clot in the brain. Emergency surgery was performed by Dr. Lonnie Hammargren, who hypothesized that Kim's brain injury was caused by one punch, possibly the last right hand (*The Good Son*, p. 146). The doctors could not save Kim's life. He was pronounced dead on November 18th 1982.

The Aftermath of Mancini vs. Kim

The Duk-Koo Kim tragedy changed Ray Mancini's life and career permanently. Personally, Ray was devastated. That Kim's passing was an accident offered little consolation. To Ray and to many of the public, it was *Ray's* fault, and subsequently he wrestled with depression and a guilty conscience. He also lost some of his trademark aggression in the ring. Ray Mancini would defend his lightweight title two more times, but according to his longtime promoter Bob Arum, "Ray's heart wasn't in it anymore. When you kill a man in the ring, it must always be in the back of your mind that it could happen again" (p. 204).

Professionally, Ray Mancini was no longer the beloved "Boom Boom" or the fighting pride of Youngstown, Ohio. Now he was "the guy who killed Duk-Koo Kim." Boxing deaths had happened before—Jimmy Doyle in 1947, Benny "The Kid" Paret in Madison Square Garden in 1962, among numerous others. A few had even been televised. But this one was different. Millions of people saw Duk-Koo Kim suffer a fatal injury on network TV at the hands of a fighter whose wholesome, all-American, working-class image touched mainstream audiences. Although Mancini still had supporters, sportscasters, advertisers and large contingents of the American public wanted nothing to do with boxing after his fight with Kim. They wanted answers, as well as changes to the sport; the fight game was too violent and unsafe in its current state. The press disseminated those opinions, sparking a national debate. The American Medical Association's position was that boxing should be banned outright.

Additional tragic consequences related to the Kim fight fueled the outcry and the mass media coverage. Soon after Kim was pronounced dead, it emerged that Kim's fiancée was pregnant with their son, Jiwan, who would never meet his father. In January 1983, Kim's mother, Sun-Nyo Yang, heartbroken and overwhelmed over the settling of Duk-Koo's estate, committed suicide. Then, on July 1st 1983, referee Richard Green was found dead of a gunshot wound, a revolver by his side. Las Vegas police ruled Green's death a suicide. No note was found. There's no evidence that grief over Kim's death caused Green's demise, but it was widely assumed that Green, too, was a casualty of the fallout from the Mancini-Kim bout.

The Kim tragedy ended up changing professional boxing permanently. The main change concerned the maximum number of rounds in championship fights. Fifteen-round fights were no longer permitted. In December 1982, the World Boxing Council (WBC) announced that their title fights would henceforth be twelve rounds. The other three sanctioning bodies, including the World Boxing Association (WBA), eventually followed suit. State athletic commissions also changed their rules to afford fighters more protection. A standing eight-count was adopted, although most commissions no longer use it.

Mancini did his best to move forward, but it wasn't easy. Over the next three years, he could not escape endless questions from the press about Kim. Quickly, Kim's death became the main thing people knew about Ray Mancini, not his accomplishments as a championship-level fighter. Mancini fought and won three more times in 1983 against decent, but not high-quality, opposition. He wouldn't compete in another big-time fight until January 1984, when he fought Bobby Chacon—the same fight Zevon refers to in the chorus of "Boom Boom Mancini." (Chacon died in 2016; in his later years, Chacon would tell people that Zevon wrote a song about him.) Impressively, Mancini stopped Chacon in three rounds. It would be his last victory. Mancini retired in 1985 at the age of twenty-four. After two unsuccessful comebacks in 1989 and 1992, he retired from the ring for good. Outside of boxing, Mancini found mild success in acting. He was inducted into the International Boxing Hall of Fame in 2015.

Is Zevon's "Boom Boom Mancini" a Commentary on Boxing?

Say His Name, Say His Name

In interviews, Zevon could be coy about his songs. In an article published in *Uncut* magazine in September 2002, Nick Hasted relates a 1989 exchange he had with Zevon about the meaning of "Boom Boom Mancini":

> Every song I write I try to make sound like the songs I like. The main purpose of "Boom Boom Mancini" was to sound like "Start Me Up." Lyrics can be something morally adequate to sing for three minutes when I feel like it. "Boom Boom Mancini" is about saying the guy's name. None of it is very conscious, and there are no resolutions. This is the material world, Nick, and there are no resolutions anywhere.

According to Zevon, the song doesn't aim to resolve any moral or social controversies about boxing. It's actually an *amoral* song, from Zevon's perspective. He wants to sound like The Rolling Stones, it occurs to him that the phrase "Boom Boom Mancini" is valuable for achieving that sound, and it's "morally adequate" to that extent. It's less clear what Zevon means about the material world. (Was Madonna playing on his Walkman?) One possibility is that he's suggesting that we shouldn't romanticize musicians' intentions. Musicians are people trying to make a living. They do that by writing good songs, and that's mostly it. We shouldn't assume that musicians are intending to contribute to society, much less trying to resolve social issues.

C.M. Kushins provides an additional reason to believe that Zevon didn't intend "Boom Boom Mancini" to be a socially conscious song. In Kushins's excellent biography, *Nothing's Bad Luck: The Lives of Warren Zevon*, we learn that Zevon wrote "Boom Boom Mancini" while living in Philadelphia with his girlfriend Anita Gevinson in 1984. Zevon was at a low point in his life: his alcoholism was destroying his relationships and stifling his creativity, and he had just learned, while perusing an issue of *Rolling Stone* magazine, that he'd been dropped by his label (p. 198). Kushins explains how the song came into existence:

Warren had written the song while watching the Mancini-Chacon fight on HBO in real time. Anita Gevinson remembered, "I was working a telethon that night and I called home to remind Warren to tape the fight for us to watch together, since we both were excited to see the outcome. He kept saying to me, 'Well, hurry on home, hurry on home.' I told him I'd be as fast as I could . . . When I got home hours later, he was sitting on the couch with his guitar. The song was already completely done by the time I walked in." (p. 230)

So that earworm of a chorus—*Hurry home early, hurry on home, Boom Boom Mancini's fighting Bobby Chacon*—is not a *planned* tribute to Mancini or Chacon. Zevon simply took his comment to Gevinson and put it to some chords. The original HBO *World Championship Boxing* broadcast of Mancini-Chacon contained twenty minutes of pre-fight hype, including two video packages on both fighters' lives and careers. It's possible the song's verses about Mancini's life were simply drawn from what Zevon saw and heard on HBO while he was riffing. That would explain why the song was completed by the time Gevinson got home.

Zevon's Boxing Commentary (No, It's Not Blow-by-Blow)

Even if Zevon didn't intend to convey a particular message or reach some resolution in "Boom Boom Mancini," it would be disingenuous to suggest that the song contains *no* commentary on boxing, or that the subject of boxing is incidental to the melody. Both suggestions seem plainly false. A close inspection of the lyrics reveals that Zevon is expressing how he feels about boxing generally, and the Mancini-Kim fight specifically.

The song opens with Zevon announcing that he is excited to watch the big fight. ("Hurry on home...") Obviously, he likes boxing. His father, William "Stumpy" Zevon, was a boxer in his youth. As a fellow son of a boxer, Zevon can relate to that part of Mancini's story. ("From Youngstown, Ohio, Ray 'Boom Boom' Mancini, a lightweight contender, like father like son . . .")

In the second verse, Zevon expresses an appreciation for Mancini's toughness—not only for bouncing back quickly from defeat ("When Alexis Argüello gave Boom Boom a beating, seven weeks later he was back in the ring."), but also for Mancini's swarming style. Argüello was an elite boxer, a precision puncher with incredible technique and power, more skilled than "Boom Boom." ("Some have the speed and the right combinations . . .") Yet there's an air of understanding, almost an argument, from Zevon about what boxing demands.

Boxing aficionados might criticize Mancini's style for lacking elegance, just as casual viewers might think him unwise for always coming forward. Zevon would probably challenge both opinions. The ability to take a punch is a virtue—an excellence—of being a good fighter, apparently the foremost virtue in Zevon's opinion. ("If you can't take the punches, it don't mean a thing.")

Why would anyone believe that? Suppose we saw Mancini go down after every good punch that Argüello landed. What would we say? We'd likely remark that Mancini is missing something and shouldn't be fighting. Or suppose we saw Mancini run from Argüello for fear of getting hit. We'd likely make the same remark and add that this fight stinks! A "throw-caution-to-the-wind" fighter like Mancini (or Kim) commands respect, by Zevon's lights.

The song's bridge contains the closest thing to a moral commentary on boxing:

> When they asked him who was responsible
>   for the death of Duk-Koo Kim,
> He said, "Someone should have stopped the fight,
>   and told me it was him."
> They made hypocrite judgments after the fact,
>   but the name of the game is be hit and hit back.

An ESPN article written for the twenty-fifth anniversary of Mancini vs. Kim confirms that the first two couplets aren't true (Ron Borges). Perhaps Zevon was misinformed about the Kim incident. Or, perhaps he was taking poetic licence. It doesn't matter, because the last couplet is what's important. ("They made hypocrite judgments after the fact, but the name of the game is be hit and hit back.")

Zevon seems to be simultaneously defending Mancini and admonishing those who blame him for what happened to Kim. Boxing is called "the fight game"—a professional boxer's job is *to fight*. The whole point of boxing is for people to buy a ticket to watch two people hit each other with their fists in a controlled environment. No one will be interested in "Boom Boom" if he doesn't hit his opponent, which means no future paydays for him. (This is why fighters who punch and engage less, like Floyd Mayweather Jr., rely heavily on marketing and trash-talk to generate interest in their fights.) In any case, Mancini has to hit his opponent to protect himself. How, then, could anyone justify blaming him?

Some reporters later complained that the fight was a mismatch. Zevon might reply that any such complaint is hypocritical.

Sure, we sometimes confront situations that cause us to reflect on our values, and we're always free to change our minds, but Mancini fought Kim the same way he fought his previous opponents—like a warrior. The only difference was the outcome. Thus, Mancini's detractors—the fans, the network, the sports reporters who won't let up about Kim—are opposing the *exact* same behavior they were cheering on very recently. Furthermore, even if the fight were a mismatch, that's not Mancini's fault. There are other powerbrokers—the athletic commission, the promoters—whose job it is to prevent mismatches and minimize risk to fighters.

I think we can say Zevon is a strong supporter of both boxing and Ray Mancini. Can we say more than that? Yes! Zevon doesn't specify what "hypocrite judgments" he has in mind, or who "they" are. Ironically, though, the vagueness affords us an opportunity to pursue, and perhaps resolve, an important question: What hypocrite judgments might be involved in boxing? An important idea from moral philosophy, called The Doctrine of Double Effect, may provide us with a possible answer.

Boxing and the Doctrine of Double Effect

What's Moral Philosophy Got to Do with Boxing?

Unlike other sports, the object of boxing is to inflict physical damage on your opponent, enough to incapacitate him for ten seconds (knock him out), or to prevent him from being able to win the fight on points (Sokol, p. 513). In most every other competitive sport, purposely inflicting physical damage on your opponent will get you disqualified. It may also earn you a fine or a suspension, depending on the sport and the offense. In extreme cases, a civil lawsuit or criminal charge is conceivable. Can you imagine a cricketer charging and walloping another player with his bat?

Even in contact sports like hockey and tackle football, there are rules. Fighting is illegal in hockey despite its frequency, and the NHL penalizes both instigators and aggressors. In tackle football, physical contact is essential to blocking and tackling, but inflicting damage on the opponent is not the point of the contact. Nor is it essential for winning the contest. That's why certain blocks (crackbacks), tackles (horse-collar), and targeting are illegal and will get a player thrown out of a game. They are seen as "dirty" plays because they pose a high risk of injury, and the players know it.

In boxing, certain maneuvers are illegal. Intentional headbutts, hitting behind the head ("rabbit punching"), and hitting below the belt can all result in disqualification, because they can seriously injure a fighter. Otherwise, in a boxing contest you're allowed to inflict physical damage on your opponent. More than that, you can't win a boxing contest *unless* you inflict damage on your opponent; that's how the contest is structured. Thus, you must make it your goal (at least intermediately) to inflict damage on your opponent if you want to win. Note, therefore, that *the behavior that boxing allows and requires for success—purposely inflicting physical damage—is the same behavior that almost every other sport forbids.*

Why do we forbid it? There are several reasons, but there is an especially obvious moral one, namely, the belief that intentional physical harm is generally wrong. Intentional physical harm can cause pain and suffering, long-term or permanent injury, even death. Rarely if ever can anyone claim to have a right to harm another intentionally. Intentional physical harm also requires people to act on bad, typically very bad, reasons. When someone chooses to cause others pain or destruction, whether they took the time to plan it (that's evil) or they're just being reckless, such choices expose humanity's dark side. This disturbs our sense of safety and interpersonal trust, to say nothing of sportsmanship. Consequently, we create rules forbidding intentionally harmful, as well as seriously risky, behaviors, and we use sanctions to make sure that people follow the rules. (Criminal law relies on similar logic: crimes that require strong intention, such as murder or rape, receive the harshest punishments.)

Because boxing doesn't protect against intentional harm nearly to the degree of other sports, it is considered inherently dangerous. And it is. The risk of acute brain injury is high, as are bodily injuries, like detached retinas and damaged organs. We know Kim's story. There have been boxing deaths in the hundreds. In fact, in 2019, there were four in a span of four months. Muhammad Ali battered Joe Frazier's face in Round 14 of the "Thrilla in Manila," their third fight. And who can forget seeing Ali himself, inspiring though he was, shaking while lighting the Olympic cauldron at Atlanta 1996? All provide evidence of serious harms that might be diminished if boxing were safer (after the Mancini-Kim bout, authorities considered implementing a headgear rule). But why not go one step further? We could prevent the harms altogether and save lives if we banned boxing, and since boxing by its nature runs afoul of a basic moral belief that other sports and many people share, why not abolish boxing? Such questions were entertained both after Kim's death and long before. With every reported boxing death or traumatic brain injury, we revisit them. They still linger, unresolved.

I can imagine a boxer objecting. "You're being too negative about the sport and too restrictive about purposefully inflicting damage," he might say. "I never try to *hurt* my opponent on purpose. I respect the hell out of my opponents in the ring. We know we're going to cause each other some pain, but we accept it. We know what we're getting ourselves into, and the risks are always there. But I'm trying to do good things when I fight. I'm trying to win and make a better life for my family. So are other fighters—don't forget that many of us come from dirt-poor backgrounds. "Boom Boom" wanted to win a world title for his dad. Some fighters fight to stay off the streets. Others fight to lift the spirit of their country. Those are all good outcomes, right? Right. And they're all because of boxing. What do you say to that?" Here's where the Doctrine of Double Effect comes in.

The Doctrine Explained—and a Checklist

The Doctrine of Double Effect, or Double Effect for short, is a principle that tells us what actions are allowed (philosophers say "permissible"), morally speaking. It was introduced by St. Thomas Aquinas, a thirteenth-century philosopher and Catholic theologian. Zevon had an enduring interest in Catholicism, so perhaps he'd appreciate the discussion!

Double Effect applies to a certain kind of situation. Sometimes our actions produce good and bad effects at the same time. The basic idea of Double Effect is that you may perform a good action even if you can foresee (reasonably predict) that it will have a bad effect, but you are not allowed to perform a bad action in order to achieve a good effect.

To find out if an action is permissible according to Double Effect, we can see if the action meets four conditions. Philosopher Lewis Vaughn summarizes them:

1. The action is inherently (without reference to consequences) either morally good or morally neutral. That is, the action itself must be morally permissible. Things like lying or purposely killing an innocent person are morally bad.

2. The bad effect is not used to produce the good effect (though the bad may be a side-effect of the good).

3. The intention must always be to bring about the good effect. For any given action, the bad effect may occur, and it may even be foreseen, but it must not be intended.

4. The good effect must be at least as important as the bad effect. The good of an action must be proportional to the bad. If the bad heavily outweighs the good, the action is not permissible. The good of saving your own life in an act of self-defense, for example, must be at least as great as the bad of taking the life of your attacker. (p. 139)

An action must meet all four conditions to be allowed, according to Double Effect. If the action fails to meet any one of the conditions, that is, then it is not allowed. When I teach Double Effect to students, I present it like a checklist. I go through each condition one at a time. If the action passes Condition 1, I can say, "Check-mark!" If it doesn't pass, I'll say "X!" The same goes for Conditions 2, 3 and 4. If I end up with four check-marks, then the action is allowed. If I end up with even one X, then the action is not allowed—in other words, it's forbidden. The main point of Double Effect is that we want the world to contain as few bad acts as possible. Intentional bad acts are the worst kind, so we should do all we can to prevent them.

Why Double Effect Forbids Boxing

I said that we believe intentional physical harm to be generally wrong. Yet there are some physical harms we think are morally acceptable. Surgery involves a doctor intending physical harm (cutting), but we would not forbid this (in most cases of surgery, anyway) because there's a good intention behind it. "Intentional physical harm" is not a good category for running through the Double Effect checklist test because it's too broad. We need a more specific category, such as stabbing, shooting, punching. Hey, let's try punching!

Is punching morally allowed by Double Effect? First, I check Condition 1: Is punching in and of itself a morally good or morally neutral act? I say it's morally neutral. When I make chicken parmesan at home, I punch the chicken breasts on my countertop to flatten them. I haven't done anything bad there. What makes an act of punching good or bad is the intention behind it. So, since punching itself is morally neutral, it would pass Condition 1—check! Onward to Condition 2. What are the potential good and bad effects of this act of punching? Moreover, what's the intention behind it? What's at stake? We need to know more about the situation because not all acts of punching are the same. Some punching may be allowed by Double Effect pending more info about both the intention and the effects. So, we need to be more specific than just "punching."

How about "punching in a boxing contest"? The act itself seems morally neutral. Not every punch thrown in the ring is necessarily aimed at another person. When boxers shadowbox to warm up, they're punching the air. Watching them do it may be intimidating, but they're not doing anything wrong. So, "punching in a boxing contest" would pass Condition 1.

The outlook isn't good for Condition 2, however. In an obscure but fascinating article, philosopher Colin Radford explains how "punching in a boxing contest" fails to meet Condition 2. According to Radford:

> What each boxer is trying to do is not merely to score points or to win rounds by punching his opponent, and to avoid being hit himself, he is also trying to stop his opponent from scoring points, and the best way to do that is to *stop him* . . . If he is wise, he therefore tries to hurt the other man and hurt him so much that he will be unable to fight back for a minimum of ten seconds. And since the activity is either entertainment for paying spectators or a preparation for that and perhaps for a professional career, the more spectacularly a boxer can do this the better his prospects, reputation and self-esteem. So let us be clear: the boxer's intention is to win, and he can only do this by knocking his opponent out, or by out-pointing him, and he can only do that by punching his opponent more frequently, clearly and effectively than he is punched himself. And he tries to do that, in part—unless he lacks a heavy punch—by hitting his opponent so hard that the opponent's capacity to make effective punches in reply is impaired. A boxer, therefore is hoping and trying to hurt his opponent. (pp. 69–70)

Radford's point is this. Punching in a boxing contest mainly has the bad effect of hurting the opponent enough to inhibit what he can do with his body. Fighters must exploit this bad effect to produce the good effect of winning; it's the only way to win a boxing match. But Condition 2 of Double Effect says a bad effect *must not* be used to produce the good effect. Which means that if Radford has described the boxer's actions correctly, we must say "X!" Boxing is not allowed by Double Effect because it fails to meet Condition 2.

Worse, if Radford is right, then boxing also fails Condition 3. To intend to hurt is to intend a bad effect, which Condition 3 forbids. Failing one condition is bad enough, but the fact that boxing fails more than one means that boxing is very wrong, according to Double Effect.

How Can Boxing Fight Back?

What does all this Double Effect stuff mean for those who want to defend boxing? At the very least, it means they are confronted by a big challenge. My imaginary boxer from earlier would likely be frustrated. None of his arguments work if Double Effect is true, since they all fail Condition 2. All the good effects he mentioned—more money, a better life, personal satisfaction, national pride—can't be achieved without the bad effect of hurting.

Some boxers might insist they're not trying to hurt their opponent. Despite the announcers routinely exclaiming "He's hurt!" when a fighter is wobbly from getting rocked, there's hurting, and then there's *hurting*. "What Radford describes as hurting," our imagined boxers might say, "is allowed by the rules of boxing. It's only bad if you're looking at it from outside the ring. But inside the ropes the blows aren't bad because they're allowed, so it's not true that a boxer intends a bad effect to produce a good effect. The only bad effects are *injuries*. We fighters can foresee injury, and death is the worst-case scenario, but understand that we do not try to injure each other. Boxing even has rules to minimize the risk of injury." Such a plea would amount to arguing that boxing doesn't violate Conditions 2 or 3 of Double Effect.

The claim that "it's not bad if it's allowed by the rules of boxing" is a shaky premise, but let's grant it for the sake of argument. Boxing would then meet Condition 2, because the boxers aren't doing something bad in order to produce something good. Thus, the boxers could say they're intending good effects the entire time while merely foreseeing that brain damage or death may happen to their opponent. Boxing would thereby pass Condition 3 as well. And let's say that, as mentioned earlier, "punching in a boxing contest" also passes Condition 1. That's three check marks—one more to go. What about Condition 4 (the requirement that the good effect must be at least as important as the bad effect)? Now we have a problem. No amount of money or contentment or number of lives improved, not even a victory that lifts a nation, as when Joe Louis KO'd Max Schmeling in their rematch, could outweigh the importance of one unnecessary, preventable death or traumatic brain injury. At least that's what I suspect believers of Double Effect would say. If they're right, this defense of boxing we've been considering won't work, because it fails to meet Condition 4 of Double Effect.

We see, then, that boxing and Double Effect are incompatible. To persist in your defense of boxing, you could argue that Double Effect should not be accepted in the first place. In other words, you could find good reasons not to commit to Double Effect, picking different moral principles that don't conflict with what boxing requires, then do your best to act in accordance with those reasons and principles. Some philosophers—called *consequentialists*—argue that Double Effect is wrong because we ought to judge the rightness or wrongness of an action by its consequences, not the intentions behind it: boxing is morally wrong to the extent that it has bad consequences and right to the extent that it has good consequences. Although I can't go into detail about those arguments here, I will point out that arguing convincingly against Double Effect is not easy.

The Difficulty of Penetrating Double Effect's Guard

Arguing against Double Effect is hard because the basic idea of Double Effect seems to be reflected in various generally accepted practices, particularly in law and medicine (palliative care). Bioethicist Greg Pence notes that Double Effect permits physicians to give terminally ill patients increasing dosages of morphine, as long as the intention is to relieve suffering and not to kill the patient (p. 14).

Let's talk about US self-defense law. Suppose I'm jumped from behind and my attacker is armed with a knife. May I use deadly force to save my own life? The legal answer is, "it depends." Several state jurisdictions (though not the majority of the US) allow that I have a legal duty to retreat, that, in certain circumstances, I must try and get away safely before I can kill in self-defense.

There's a clear parallel with Double Effect here: killing is a bad act, and while the attacker is certainly doing something bad, killing is worse, so I should avoid it as much as possible. Suppose I can't get away. If I'm punching to fend off my attacker and I accidentally land a fatal blow to the head, the law likely wouldn't prosecute me for homicide. Double Effect would say that's the right result. Why? Well, punching for my health and life isn't an obviously bad act (passes Condition 1); I didn't kill the attacker on purpose, so I didn't use the bad effect of their death to produce the good effect of saving my life (passes Condition 2); there's a good intention behind my punch (saving my own life), and at most the attacker's death is a foreseeable side-effect of the punch (passes Condition 3); and, finally, the good of saving my life is as great as the bad of ending the attacker's life (the most important effect balances the worst effect—passes Condition 4). Many people would likely agree that not prosecuting me in such a case is the right move. Double Effect provides a moral rationale as to why.

Now, imagine a variation on this case. Suppose I've fended off my attacker and kicked the knife away. The attacker backs off. He's assaulted me, but he's no longer a threat. Enraged about being attacked, I run up and purposely beat him to death. Understandable though my anger might be, the law would prosecute me (perhaps for manslaughter, because I lost my cool, but probably for murder) because I was retaliating. Instead of defending myself, I killed somebody intentionally and unnecessarily for my own gratification, an act which fails *all four* conditions of Double Effect.

Consider one more variation. Suppose I'm on my back, with my attacker on top of me. He holds the knife above his head. He makes like he's about to stab, but a gun is within my reach, which I manage to grab. I fire and kill the attacker. I tell the police that my intention was to kill the attacker in order to save my life. Would I be charged with homicide? Again, it depends. The law would need to investigate a few things. Was my life in imminent danger? Did I have an objectively reasonable belief that using deadly force was necessary? Double Effect is relevant to the law's investigating these things. If I kill an attacker *in order to* save my life, I am using a bad effect to produce a good effect, which flatly violates Condition 2 of Double Effect. Yet it's hard to believe I've acted wrongly in this case. If I'm pinned and practically certain I'll be killed, must I let the attacker take my life because it'd be morally wrong for me to kill him? I doubt anyone except Saint Augustine would say yes.

By stipulating that I must be in imminent danger and that my belief in using deadly force must meet an objective standard, *perhaps* the law is acknowledging that justifiable homicide requires us to contravene an important moral principle, namely, the Doctrine of Double Effect. The world *is* better when there are fewer intentionally bad acts, so if we're going to allow one, we ought to have extremely good reasons.

To be clear, I'm not saying that Double Effect is *the* moral-theoretical rationale for traditional self-defense law, since there are other possible explanations. I'm not even arguing that Double Effect is correct. My point is simply that, in real life, a person's intentions matter when it comes to judging whether actions are acceptable or unacceptable. Intentions matter for holding people responsible and for deciding how much blame or punishment a person should receive. Both the legal system and professional medicine take that point seriously, as do ordinary folks in their personal and work lives. Double Effect is an old, familiar idea from moral philosophy that guides our thinking about what the role of intentions should be in judging actions right or wrong. Even if we don't consciously commit to it, Double Effect has a non-trivial presence in our moral lives, both in our practices and as a rule of thumb. For that reason alone, critics will have a hard time convincing people that Double Effect doesn't work.

Where's the Hypocrisy?

We've gone many rounds with Double Effect in order to find more meaning in Zevon's lyric about hypocrite judgments in boxing.

Moral Hypocrisy

Boxing and boxing fandom may involve a kind of *moral hypocrisy*. Moral hypocrites are people who themselves don't follow the moral principles they advocate and apply to others (Isserow). If we allow boxing *and* we sincerely want to be moral, then we can't accept Double Effect and boxing simultaneously. Anyone who did would be a moral hypocrite in the plainest sense. How could anyone who accepts Double Effect justify watching the fights for enjoyment? By going along with Double Effect, someone who supports the idea that a person may not use a bad effect to produce a good effect. But by watching the fights, that same person is supporting the idea that people (specifically, the fighters) *may* use bad effects to produce a good effect! That's pretty clear hypocrisy. The hypocrisy is crystal clear if people who enjoy boxing have consciously committed to Double Effect or declared their support for it.

Some hypocrisy can be brushed off as inconsequential and annoying, but moral hypocrisy isn't like that. Quite the contrary, it's worrying. In boxing, people often buy tickets in hopes of seeing a fighter beat up and humiliate another fighter they vehemently dislike. (Indeed, Ali and Floyd Mayweather, Jr. were both major attractions in large part because people hoped to see them lose.) If a fan who supports Double Effect does this, that would be like saying, "I'd be *most* satisfied with a result that contradicts what I believe."

That's worrying for a few reasons. First, maintaining consistency between your actions and value principles is part of what it is to have integrity, an important ingredient for being good to others and living well. A bloodthirsty fan may honestly believe that morality is important, but if the fan is willing to downgrade or violate his principles for a passing spectacle, then such a fan is, at the very least, fickle. He's not acting with integrity. Mere enjoyment isn't a good reason for compromising a moral principle. If a Double Effect-believing fan were to have no reaction to my claims, or responded flippantly, "Oh well, I like boxing. Guess I'm a hypocrite, then," we might laugh at his irreverence, but would you call on him for moral guidance or entrust him with anything morally significant? You'd surely better call someone else.

Also, moral hypocrisy can cause real anguish. In *The Good Son: The Life of Ray "Boom Boom" Mancini*, a 2013 documentary film directed by Jesse James Miller, Mancini tells a painful story about the day after the Kim fight:

> When I got into the Cleveland airport, we got met off the plane by reporters and cameramen . . . They kept asking, y'know, "How do you feel about Kim? How do you feel that he's on life support?" How do I feel? How am I supposed to feel? How am I supposed to . . . ? I'm dyin' inside.

The moral hypocrisy in the story is that the reporters hold Ray accountable for the physical damage to Kim but never once hold him accountable for the damage he inflicted on previous opponents. Actor and longtime friend Ed O'Neill elaborates:

> What hurt Ray so badly after the Kim tragedy was the fact that he was seen as this all-American boy, wanted him in our living rooms, you know . . . And then it was a certain betrayal. "Oh, he's a killer. He killed a guy." Other fighters have killed fighters in the ring and went on, y'know, without that stigma.

Prior to Kim, the press was happy to ignore moral issues about damage in Mancini's fights. Imagine if, after winning the lightweight title, a reporter asked Mancini how he felt about pummeling Art Frias, and he'd said, "Gee, I feel terrible about hitting him. I'm dying inside." They would've labeled Mancini a soft champion and his marketability would have plummeted. Yet if Mancini had said after Kim, "I'm a warrior till the end—death doesn't faze me," he would have been reviled as a cruel monster. It's as if the press wanted Mancini to be an amoral fighter with a moral image and an immoral figure all at the same time, an impossible burden to shoulder, on top of overwhelming grief he felt. Remember the old saying, "It's all fun and games until someone loses an eye?" The reporters are treating it like a principle, not a saying.

Depending on the situation, if moral hypocrisy is not called out, it can lead to nightmarish situations. Ray Mancini affirms as much in the movie, telling us that his young daughter has had to deal with classmates calling her dad a murderer.

Boom Boom's Moral Hypocrisy

No one likes hypocrites. At the same time, a lot of hypocrisy is unintentional. Sometimes we don't notice that we're behaving in ways that undermine principles we had earlier advocated, either explicitly or implicitly. It's hard enough to get through a normal day, and we might've plum forgot what we had said or done before.

Although Zevon defended boxing in general and Mancini in particular against others' "hypocrite judgments," "Boom Boom" and his camp are guilty of a little moral hypocrisy themselves. During the HBO broadcast of Mancini-Chacon, in a pre-fight interview, Mancini said this about Kim: "In effect, yes, the man died at my hands, but I didn't have the intention to kill him. I didn't *kill* him in effect." We can see that Mancini is basically invoking Double Effect (emphasizing Condition 3) to defend his actions: he never intended to kill Kim to win the fight, and the bad effect of Kim's death was an unintended side-effect.

Thus, Mancini explicitly advocates Double Effect, or something like it. Problem is, *Double Effect can't be invoked to defend boxing when tragedy strikes, because boxing is and always was forbidden by Double Effect.* As we have seen, as long as Mancini fights, he fails to meet at least Condition 2 of Double Effect. In other words, he isn't actually following the moral principle he's applying to himself and presumably others—a case of moral hypocrisy by definition. If Mancini were to concede that he's being hypocritical and reply that he believes in Double Effect except when the fight is on, he'd be no different than the fickle fan who believes in Double Effect at all times except for fight night. Absolute moral principles don't come with a pause button, alas.

The terror of witnessing death is the main reason people had a hard time getting past the Kim fight. I suspect that Mancini didn't realize his defense was hypocritical. But I do wonder if the hypocrisy played a part in others finding his defense inadequate, without their realizing that Double Effect was the reason.

Are There No Resolutions?

Barry McGuigan, another Hall-of-Fame fighter, once said, "The trouble with boxing is that too often it ends in sadness" (Hubbard). Death, moral hypocrisy, pain and suffering abound, and still the fight game rolls on. Zevon's quip that there are no resolutions anywhere in the material world suddenly seems apt.

All hope is not lost, though. I'd like to think my words here can resolve some confusion about the moral issues at play in ethical debates about boxing. More personally, I think I've pin-pointed why boxing was a guilty pleasure of mine for fifteen years. (Seriously, I felt *guilty* about watching it, usually after the excitement wore off, but sometimes during the fight.)

Boxing can't be reconciled with some of my working moral commitments. I still enjoy books and movies about boxing, but I'm not watching fights for fun these days. I'm glad to have resolved that. For those who have been directly affected by boxing's sadness, like "Boom Boom" Mancini, resolution can be found. In 2011, Duk-Koo Kim's son, Jiwan, then aged twenty-nine, traveled to America to meet Ray Mancini in person. Jiwan told Ray, "It's not your fault. It's not just on you . . . You don't need to live guilty (Miller).

Jiwan's visit and words gave both men the answers they needed.

4
Mr. Bad Exemplar

Fernando Zapata

Warren Zevon's songs feature outlaws, rogues, ne'er-do-wells, and morally vicious characters of all types.

"Excitable Boy," for instance, recounts a youngster's progressively bad behavior, from the aesthetically disgusting to the morally evil, from rubbing a pot roast all over his chest to raping and murdering his prom date.

"Lawyers, Guns, and Money" narrates the plight of a womanizing, degenerate gambler (after all, he goes home with the waitress, like he *always* does). Without taking a great interpretive leap, the lead character of perhaps Zevon's most famous number, "Roland the Headless Thompson Gunner," appears to fight on behalf of colonial economic interests in Nigeria and the Congo. The protagonists of some of Zevon's most memorable songs are bad guys, given to morally contemptible behavior.

In some cases, we admire bad fictional characters, just as we can admire immoral people. However, should we admire the immoral? Take, as an example, Zevon himself. We admire Zevon, his excellent songs and literary lyrics (no other songwriter can claim to have mentioned in his songs brucellosis, fluorocarbons, Naugahyde divans, regal sobriquets, and Lhasa Apsos), but not his abusive alcoholic behavior, his philandering, or, more generally, his dirty life and times. Zevon's songs commonly concern characters whom it may be fitting to admire in some way, but whom we should not admire from the moral point of view, because they have vicious characters.

Mr. Bad Example is just such a person. And, as an example, we may consider him an *exemplar*, that is, a model of a person living a life that promotes or realizes ideals that we deeply value. Obviously, he is not a *moral* exemplar, since so many vicious character traits are manifested in his exploits, ensuring that he falls well short of the ideal of virtuous character. Typically, we admire exemplars for living up to ideals that we have reason to value, or for living or being in a way that we strive to live or be. So, if we admire Mr. Bad Example as a person, without qualification, this suggests, as Zevon sings on the album *Sentimental Hygiene*, that there's trouble waiting to happen.

Admiration as a Moral Emotion

When we admire a person, say, David Letterman, we experience what moral philosophers consider a *moral emotion*. Moral emotions, such as guilt, shame, anger, and envy, are products of our capacity for moral reasoning and moral behavior. The emotions of admiration and contempt, for instance, are responses that capture our moral judgments of character and action, our own and others', and so evince our moral beliefs and ideals, even if we do not have a clear idea of what they are. Admiration for Letterman, in this technical sense, involves a positive evaluation of him as a person exercising lasting traits and talents, and not just for his regularly featuring Zevon as a musical guest on his talk show over the course of many years. If we admire Letterman, we see him in a positive light, judge him as excellent, and single him out as an exemplar who should be admired, if not emulated, because he personifies an ideal that we value and may want to realize in our own lives.

Admiration is a morally significant emotion because it indicates the projects and pursuits that matter to us and that we may be inspired to strive to achieve. When we admire Letterman, we compare him to other talk-show hosts and regard him as better than them at this activity. He informs our ideal of what a talk-show host should be, perhaps even to the point that we're motivated to be in show business like he is. Admiration is a fitting emotional response when the people we admire actually have the traits, commitments, and values that explain the things that we admire them for. There is something excellent about Letterman for which he, as an agent, is responsible, qualities that are manifest in his appearances, that are no accident or fluke. Fitting emotions accurately correspond to what the world and the people in it are like, and admiration is no different.

Admiration and Immorality

No matter how much we admire a television host, a musician, a painter, a thinker, a politician, or a friend for promoting or realizing a worthy ideal, it's appropriate to abandon admiration for someone when he does morally reprehensible things. This does not refer to just *any* action judged to be immoral from a particular perspective, such as binge-drinking, but significant or severe moral wrongs. We might, for instance, admire a gifted songwriter who intends to drink up all the salty margaritas in Los Angeles, not for his addiction, but for his lyrical prowess. In admiring him, we don't run the risk of causing moral injury or harm to others who may have been wronged incidentally by his drinking. And yet, we may imperil ourselves if, in emulating him, we come to glorify irresponsible behavior.

We can think of conduct as significantly morally wrong if it carries great risks of harm for those who are wronged and for whoever happens to admire it. However, there are many cases where we admire people who have acted wrongly, people whom it is fitting to admire for some reason, but who have engaged in morally bad, though not morally terrible, behavior. What should our response be to people who are admirable *and* immoral, even though they have not committed grave moral wrongs?

Mr. Bad Example is this type of person. His case confirms that we should not admire people who just *seem* to be admirable. Perhaps we are devout churchgoers, to whom Mr. Bad Example appears admirable because of his service as an altar boy, because no one carries the liturgical books, nor the bread and wine for consecration, with the zeal that he does. In such a case, however, our admiration is not fitting, because Mr. Bad Example does not actually lead a life that meets the ideal of piety or religious obligation that we consider important and take him to endorse.

Mr. Bad Example, the altar boy, is not a fitting object of admiration, it turns out, because he studies religious rites for the sole purpose of learning how to take advantage of the devout and trusting, of honing those oratory and social skills that prove useful in confidence games, and of deftly stealing from the offertory box, labeled "Children's Fund." If we were to admire Mr. Bad Example, we would do so mistakenly, since he acts, not out of respect for the ideal of religious devotion, but for selfish material interests, including a determination to serve those interests by becoming an agile swindler. In sharp contrast to an exemplar of a religious devotee, Mr. Bad Example lacks the enduring purposes and character traits, such as benevolence, required for us to count his altar service as meeting the religious ideal that we value.

To admire Mr. Bad Example for choosing to have sex with married women, then stealing their furniture to auction in

Spokane, can only be a marginal view, the result of poor moral education and the formation of regrettable emotional habits. Admiration is an emotion that may encourage us to imitate the exemplar of ideals we support, and if the clever but morally confused admire Mr. Bad Example's reckless behavior, then perhaps they'll try to emulate him. We have moral concerns about the people we admire, whom we single out as exemplars of some type, because of the tendencies of that emotion to motivate action, as it may inspire us to emulate our heroes in an effort to live up to the ideal that they realize in their lives. There is no necessary one-to-one correlation between admiration and emulation, however. We may be inspired to dress in a gold lamé suit like Elvis, even if we admire him for filial piety, as reflected in his care of and devotion to his mother, Gladys, or we may admire Philip Habib's tact in helping to hammer out a peace deal without ourselves wanting to pursue a career as a diplomat.

Even if we are mistaken to admire Mr. Bad Example for his immoral or superficially admirable acts, are there other ways in which we might fittingly admire him?

The Boom Boom Mancini Example

Say, for example, we admire the boxer Ray "Boom Boom" Mancini. If so, our emotion would be focused on Mancini as a kind of person, as an exemplar of courage or perseverance, and not just for a single fight, even though that match belongs to a larger sequence of performances that, taken together, exemplify the excellences that we admire Mancini for. Mancini's excellence can be explained by stable attitudes and character traits, among them his ability, whether native or trained, to take punches. We can admire Mancini for a particular act or choice—say, his continued dedication to the sport of boxing even after his partial responsibility for the death of Duk-Koo Kim—but, if so, it is because we take it to indicate something valuable about the kind of person Mancini is, to reflect his deeper aims and commitments, particularly in upholding the ideal of athletic excellence that we value. Granted, we can morally evaluate a single act or trait by itself as praiseworthy or blameworthy without it reflecting some fundamental fact about who a person is, but we tend to admire people, their conduct and dispositions, as fully integrated wholes. When we admire Mancini, this is the nature of our emotional response.

Although it is fitting to admire Mancini for his greatness as an athlete, his achievements in the boxing ring can't possibly realize the ideals of a theoretical physicist, like Einstein, or maybe even an actor, like Charlie Sheen. But none of this takes away from the ideals of a fighter that he aims to realize over the course of his career. If Mancini fought well past his prime, staying in the game too long, or had as many, or more, failures than successes in the ring, our admiration for him as a boxer would diminish. However, if he were guilty of morally bad behavior, it would decrease the admiration we have for him as a person, no matter how exemplary a fighter he may have been. And if he committed morally heinous crimes, it would be inappropriate to admire him at all.

We do not admire Mancini less, as a person, for failing to propose a groundbreaking theory of everything that elegantly reconciles general relativity and quantum mechanics, or because his cameo performances in the 1980s sitcom *Who's the Boss?* are forgettable, but we would find him contemptible if he enthusiastically participated in, say, a program of ethnic cleansing. We would have a compelling moral reason not to want to admire Mancini, period.

Admiring Mr. Bad Example

Mr. Bad Example's activities say something about his persisting traits and aims, in other words, his character. If we were charitable, we'd concede that it would be possible to admire him from other points of view. For instance, we could admire his multi-tasking, his competence at balancing and completing different endeavors, provided they were not manifestations of vice, such as exhibiting excessive pride, gluttony, or sloth.

We could admire his earning a law degree, if only he didn't use his legal knowledge to help clients evade justice by encouraging them to plead insanity. We could admire his success in the field of hair transplantation, since dermatology is a respectable profession, if only he hadn't defrauded his patients, then squandered those ill-gotten gain in games of *chemin de fer* and purchased sexual services from a prostitute in Monte Carlo. We could admire his business acumen and initiative in founding a mining company, if only he hadn't exploited aboriginal workers, garnishing their wages, denying them workers' compensation insurance in order to pay his private debts, and leaving them destitute and immiserated. In other words, it may well be fitting to admire Mr. Bad Example from many points of view, but not so that we could consider him morally admirable, since he fails to meet any ideal of moral character that we can reasonably endorse.

We can say that Mr. Bad Example lives up to the inverted ideal of a *morally vicious person*, an exemplar of immorality. He is excellent, that is, at being morally bad. His characteristic behavior, for which an impartial and sympathetic spectator would feel nothing but contempt, reflects lasting but vicious traits, attitudes, and motives, as he regularly lies, cheats, and takes advantage of others. We should be reasonably skeptical about the possibility of his quitting his immoral ways once he's relocated to Sri Lanka, because, judging from his conduct, he has a settled disposition to think, feel, and act in vicious ways.

This is not to say that Mr. Bad Example could not become morally admirable, over time, if he were drastically to change his behavior, to the extent that it comes to form a regular pattern of morally praiseworthy acts in different situations. For instance, he might earn a fortune from stem-cell research aimed at stimulating hair growth, then use it to aid the world's needy, or he might become a formidable advocate for the working poor. In some sense, his earlier immorality would be canceled by his subsequent admirable actions, just as a person who is admirable at an earlier point in time can cease to be so, if he subsequently commits severe moral wrongs.

Moral Admiration

Many of us regard morality as carrying a special weight in human affairs. Although Mr. Bad Example's record of bad behavior is so noteworthy that he cannot be considered admirable from a moral point of view, the nature of his deeds does not make it inappropriate to admire him in other ways. When a public or historical figure whom we fittingly admire from an artistic, intellectual, or political point of view does something morally wrong, it counts as a reason against admiring him as a person. This problem is compounded if that person has a history in his private life of morally terrible behavior.

We might find Lord Byron artistically admirable for the originality and biting satire of his poetry, and politically admirable for his bravery, but we couldn't help but admire him less if we discovered that he had a penchant for torturing animals. In such a case, moral considerations override all others. Let's say, for instance, that we have a date at the Rainbow Bar, but chance upon a person who has lain his head on the railroad tracks. What we morally *ought* to do, in this case, is to ignore our self-interested urge to get to the bar as quickly as possible and try to help the person in mortal danger. Judgments about what is morally right or wrong influence how we feel and act, although the strength of our motivation to act morally may be weak, since we are not fully rational. However, we should desire a world where we would be moved on moral grounds to help others in need, no matter how much that duty conflicts with our own desires or interests.

We find it hard to admire people who are deeply contemptible from the moral point of view, even if we find them admirable in a way that bears on their occupation, whether as a bellboy, a hockey enforcer, a gambler in Havana, a bank robber fleeing across state lines, or a drug-dealer. This is because moral ideals, since they reflect our hopes for the world and the people in it, command an authority in human life that other ideals do not. Moral ideals differ importantly from aesthetic, legal, economic, and athletic values, because they concern what we ought to do in any circumstance, not just what it is best or most valuable to do in a game, in political society, or in a market economy. Perhaps we can fittingly admire Mr. Bad Example as an ideal adventurer or traveler, for his devil-may-care attitude and *joie de vivre*, which may qualify as deep facts about who he is. We can identify character traits that, provided they are not facets of a morally vicious character, strike us as admirable. But we can hardly admire someone for these traits if he doesn't care who gets hurt in the process of his having a good time.

This is not to say that anyone is admirable without qualification, from all points of view. We can admire someone as a novelist, for instance, and yet not think highly of her as a parent. However, failing to be morally admirable in significant ways disqualifies her from being admirable as a person, as a moral agent.

A Qualified Admiration

People can be admirable even though they have done morally bad things, provided those bad things don't constitute severe moral wrongs, such as planning or participating in war crimes, supporting racist regimes, or wantonly committing murder. Admiring such a person may not only intensify the harm done to those who have suffered wrongs, but also morally injure the admirer.

As for Mr. Bad Example, he could be *worse*, morally, and yet hardly count as an exemplar of any valuable ideal, since he has no qualities, and can claim no achievements, that contribute to the rational interests and hopes of humanity. If he is admirable at all, it is, as we've seen, for non-moral reasons. As a moral emotion, however, admiration's focus tends to extend from a single trait or action to the whole person, favorably coloring our perception of who they are and what they do. There are moral risks involved in admiring any of Mr. Bad Example's qualities or escapades, as we may come to admire, and perhaps even justify or excuse, his wrongdoing. In some cases, we idealize the people whom we have good reasons to admire, even to the extent that we ignore or minimize the moral wrongs that they commit. If we admire Mr. Bad Example's roguishness, we may come to believe that it is acceptable for him to harm all the people he screws over, for the sake of, not just adventure, but ultimately having a thrilling story to tell.

Our admiration for accomplished but flawed people must resist idealizing them, but at the same time challenge that smug moralism which obscures the complexity of life by demanding that we withhold honor from anyone who occasionally offends our moral sensibilities. We have the capacity to educate our emotional responses, and to judge when it is, and is not, appropriate to admire someone in spite of their moral failings. We can admire Mr. Bad Example, who after all is more like Mr. Not-So-Bad Example when compared to many historical and fictional figures, while openly acknowledging his ethical failings. Our disposition to praise or honor a person must always be tempered by an acknowledgement of their conduct, suspect or otherwise.

When All Is Said and Done

Mr. Bad Example is an agent, albeit a fictional one, and so may be admired from various points of view. For a person to be fittingly admired in a particular way, he must act intentionally, for the right reasons, and make manifest in his life some ideal, like that of, say, being an accomplished artist or athlete. Mr. Bad Example, however, is by nature a swindler, an exploiter, and while it may be fitting to admire him for living up to some non-moral ideal, perhaps that of being an intrepid world traveler, his behavior is far from praiseworthy, given his depraved way of life and his social role as an "intruder in the dirt." He is the inverse of a model of moral excellence or perfection, since his actions betray a character that we have good reason not to want to emulate.

So, while it may be fitting to admire Mr. Bad Example from some points of view, we ought not, morally, to want to. We can find him captivating, a fascinating character, value him as someone we can relate to, since we too lead morally imperfect lives, but while we may decide that there is much to admire him for, moral admiration is harder to warrant. This is perhaps how we should morally evaluate our admiration of any cultural or historical hero, and, as his admiring fans, Warren Zevon himself.

5

The Mystery of "The French Inhaler"

CONALL CASH

Warren Zevon's "The French Inhaler" is a hard song to keep track of. As with Zevon's "Roland The Headless Thompson Gunner," the song's final lines offer a stunning and bewildering shift that turns an already complex narrative into a seemingly inscrutable tale, leaving us with many unanswered questions.

What's the relationship between the narrator and the woman he addresses throughout the song? What's the time-span of the song's events—that of the course of an extended relationship, or merely the few minutes of a brief and aborted encounter between two strangers at a bar? Who is the "French Inhaler" of the song's title, appearing without warning in the penultimate line? And who the hell is "Norman," the object of the woman's address in the song's final words: "And she said, 'So long, Norman'"?

We listeners may find ourselves as disconcerted as the song's narrator when he sings, "You said you were an actress, yes I believe you are." We are without guardrails in determining what is real and what is mere appearance.

Reality, Appearance, and Lyric Address

This undecidability between reality and appearance will turn out to be an essential theme of "The French Inhaler," a theme that we will explore through the song's complex use of lyric address. Who is addressing whom, and from what perspective are they speaking? Even as the accumulation of detail over the course of the song conjures a narrative that listeners will try to make sense of, the enigmatic immediacy of lyrical address continually interrupts every narrative explanation of what is happening.

What's most interesting and complex (and frustrating) about this song is how it raises this tension between lyric and narrative, between the immediacy of direct address and the sequential order of a plot. In this, Zevon's song can be understood in relation to the account of *apostrophe* developed by the literary theorist Jonathan Culler.

"Apostrophe," here, refers to the poetic act of address, or the invocation of an absent object as the poet's addressee. Etymologically, "apostrophe" means to turn away: rhetorically, speakers apostrophize when they turn away from the world in front of them to address a person or substance that is not present. For Culler, the power of apostrophe to invoke what is absent brings it into tension with the narrative functions of poetry. He explains:

> If one brings together in a poem a boy, some birds, a few blessed creatures, and some mountains, meadows, hills and groves, one tends to place them in a narrative where one thing leads to another; the events which form ask to be temporally located. . . . But if one puts into a poem *thou shepherd boy, ye blessed creatures, ye birds*, they are immediately associated with what might be called a timeless present but is better seen as a temporality of writing. . . . So located by apostrophes, birds, creatures, boys, etc., resist being organized into events that can be narrated. (p. 165)

In "The French Inhaler," Zevon draws on this power of apostrophe to suspend or resist narrative, making the addressed woman present by conjuring up her image, even as our sense of who she is and her relationship to the speaker remains unclear. In one respect, the song addresses her in a quite conventional and sexist way by making her into the abstract image of "woman": as a woman, she *is* nothing but her image, on the speaker's account. Since she's not "cut out for working," she must sell her appearance, her attractiveness, in a way that clearly alludes to sex work ("How you gonna get around in this sleazy bedroom town / If you don't put yourself up for sale?").

She is appealing as the abstract image of a woman whom everyone would like to "possess," as a way to overcome their loneliness ("All these people with no home to go home to / They'd all like to spend the night with you / Maybe I would too"). The woman as she's evoked here is not really a person, but a kind of fantasy object, and the fantasy is poised between adoration and contempt. The speaker is drawn to her by her beauty, but he also hates her for it and for what he thinks of as her profiteering from this beauty; he wants her, and wants her to want him, but he knows that in wanting her he is just like everyone else, that there is nothing special about this desire (and he kind of hates her, and himself, for this too).

Identifying "Norman"

A dramatic shift occurs in the final lines of the song. This shift can first of all be understood, in Culler's terms, as the return of narrative: and the first thing that this return will do is to dispel the fantasy of the woman as an abstract, timeless presence.

The spark of this return to reality is a distinctly temporal, narrative event: namely, the lights coming on at the bar to announce that it's closing time. "When the lights came up at two / I caught a glimpse of you / And your face looked like something death brought with him in his suitcase / Your pretty face looked so wasted." She is no longer "woman" in the abstract, the perfect object of desire; she is *this* woman, sitting at this bar at this time (2:00 a.m.), drunk and "devastated."

In and of itself, this shift is not so remarkable: it participates in a familiar, and equally sexist, tradition of depicting women as desirable for their immaculate perfection and contemptible for their living imperfections. But this return to narrative and to the reality of the bar scene leads into the astonishing conclusion, which will upend the speaker's own sense of things and the misogynistic logic he has been working within.

This conclusion is introduced by an instrumental flourish, with the solo piano leading the transition into the enigmatic finale with a descending movement, before Zevon sings the final lines: "The French Inhaler, he stamped and mailed her / So long, Norman / She said, 'So long, Norman.'" Clearly, the meaning of the song is tied up with whatever allusions are entailed in these two names ("the French Inhaler," and "Norman"), and interpretations of this point have abounded among fans. "French inhaling" refers to the act of blowing smoke out through your mouth and inhaling it through your nostrils: the French Inhaler is therefore someone who *blows smoke*, with all the allusions that phrase conjures.

One possible association of these final lines, which previous listeners have picked up on, is to the infamously macho writer, Norman Mailer (note the proximity of "Mailer" to both "inhaler" and "mailed her"). With this allusion, it would seem that Zevon reveals the song to be a kind of satire of Mailer's machismo and his corresponding presentation of women as ideal objects of male desire who exist to spur male ambition, as in Mailer's 1973 biography of Marilyn Monroe. Mailer, like the French Inhaler with whom he is identified in the song, blows smoke, creating a kind of allure about himself without any real content. "Stamped and mailed" would then refer first of all to Mailer's packaging of Monroe for his own fantasies about women and male power (as well as his own financial benefit from sales of his book about this dead actress), and, secondly, to a man at the bar who seduces the woman whom the song's speaker has been hitting on, a man whose performance of masculinity is as grotesque as Mailer's. With this allusion, then, the song harshly detaches us from the male fantasy of "woman" by reminding us of the misogyny and the delusion this fantasy entails.

But what of the final words, spoken by the woman herself? If she's leaving the bar with the French Inhaler, who is she saying "so long" to? The name "Norman" appears strangely attached to both men, the two rivals for her affection. Another reference, to another author, is needed to make sense of this: the author of the song himself, Warren Zevon. The woman appears to have misheard Zevon's name, substituting "Norman" for "Warren." Thus, the speaker (and the author, with whom he is indirectly identified in this moment) faces the ultimate indignity: left for another man, by a woman who gets his name wrong as she leaves the bar with this rival.

Both the Mailer reference and the self-reference to "Warren" seem plausible. But this leads to a difficulty: how exactly are the two to be reconciled? Is the song about Norman Mailer, or about Warren Zevon? Does it conclude with a savage critique of machismo, or an ironic (and perhaps bitter) allusion to the author's own impotence, his failure to "get" the woman? After all, if we are to understand that the woman leaves the bar with this French Inhaler, leaving poor, pitiful Warren misrecognized and alone, the song might be read as the lament of what we would today call an "incel," an unsuccessful man who hates women for spurning him. In so doing, does the song really criticize Mailer-esque machismo, or does it merely envy such men their supposed success with women?

The full, devastating power of this ending emerges if we realize that there is no incompatibility between the readings of the song as an allegory alternately for "Norman Mailer" and "Warren Zevon." Rather, what is most disturbing, and what makes the critique of machismo so powerful, is that the song ends up *associating* Zevon with Mailer, through the woman's mishearing of "Warren" as "Norman." Zevon enacts a self-criticism of his own self-pity in this final line, establishing his own

link to Mailer's toxic masculinity through the woman's mis-
naming of him. The very position of the cynical, all-knowing
speaker is undermined, since the speaker of the song is now
revealed to be another self-aggrandizing, deluded man. All of
the earlier expressions of bitterness and contempt towards the
woman are now replayed differently in light of the ending, as
we learn to see the speaker himself as someone who "stamps
and mails" women, packages them according to his own fantasies of self-importance.

What this ending reveals, then, is that *everyone in this scene*
is performing, not only (or primarily) the woman berated for
being an "actress," and not only the obviously offensive man
who blows smoke (the French Inhaler), but equally the knowing, satirical speaker himself. Men who obsess over women as
images also turn themselves into performers, acting out fantasies of their own masculine power. Much the same would
later be said of Mailer by Monroe's former husband Arthur
Miller, who remarked that Mailer "was himself in drag" in writing the biography, "acting out his own Hollywood fantasies of
fame and sex and unlimited power" (p. 532).

Zevon wryly acknowledges his own tendency toward such
fantasizing through the association of the names "Norman"
and "Warren" at the end of the song. More significant still is
the fact that "The French Inhaler" has been widely understood
to mark Zevon's break-up with his long-term partner, Marilyn
"Tule" Livingston, with the name "Marilyn" linking Zevon's ex
to Monroe, the object of male obsession whose own humanity
is misrecognized in the process. Zevon thus seems, by the end
of the song, to be offering a reflection on his own misrecogni-
tion of the woman he has just split up with, through this association between Marilyn Monroe/Norman Mailer and Marilyn
Livingston/Warren Zevon.

You Must Try It Again 'Til You Get It Right

"The French Inhaler" thus arrives at the radical idea that all
gender is a kind of performance, that individuals are defined
according to gender only through performing, rather than
through any innate characteristics. In a weird way, Norman
Mailer himself knows this when he obsesses over women as
objects/images, and conceives of male power through the possession of women, for he is effectively saying that it is only
through the woman that a man *is* a man. To be himself, he
needs to perform himself in such a way as to be selected by the
right woman as her "possessor."

This idea of the *performative* character of gender is famously associated with the theorist Judith Butler, and her book *Gender Trouble*. Butler argues that gender "has no ontological status apart from the various acts which constitute its reality" (p. 173). In other words, a person only attains the status of "man" or "woman" by "acting like" a man or like a woman, acting according to social conceptions of what gender-appropriate behaviour is. Notably, Butler refers to *drag* in the development of her account of performativity, in a way that dovetails with the remark from Arthur Miller cited above. According to Butler, "In imitating gender, drag implicitly reveals the imitative structure of gender itself—as well as its contingency" (p. 175). The act of performing in drag, Butler suggests, only makes explicit what is going on implicitly in all gendered behaviour, what she calls its "imitative structure" and its "contingency." Gender only exists through imitation (a man becomes a man by imitating actions that he is told or shown are manly), and what it is to *be* a man or a woman is therefore contingent upon the social practices that produce gender in any particular time and place (if it's only through imitating others that someone becomes a man or a woman, then when the actions to be imitated change, so do the definitions of "man" and "woman"). Butler goes on to propose that "part of the pleasure, the giddiness" of performing drag "is in the recognition of a radical contingency in the relation between sex and gender" (p. 175). By showing how femininity and masculinity are constituted through performance—through "acting like a woman" or "like a man"—in a way that makes obvious the discontinuity between this performance and any basis in biological sex, drag reveals what we are always doing when we act in gendered ways.

The central theme of gender and performance in "The French Inhaler" thus has an unexpectedly Butlerian quality, especially in light of the interpretation of the song's ending laid out in this chapter. The idea of the woman's femininity as a performance is indicated from early on: "Drugs and wine and flattering light / You must try it again 'til you get it right." She is trying to position herself, to make herself into a certain ideal image of femininity, and she can only achieve this through practice, through the repetition (or imitation) of a series of conventional actions and setups (like the "flattering light" she surrounds herself with, and which she will lose later, at 2:00 a.m., when the lights come up). Zevon's speaker here suggests that, while the woman may not be "cut out for working" in the familiar sense of what "work" means, making herself a (certain image of) "woman" is itself a kind of work, which must be carried out repeatedly if it is to get results.

This line of thought is continued by the more or less explicit association to sex work that we have already heard ("If you won't put yourself up for sale"), and that is now reiterated: "Maybe you'll end up with someone different every night." Sex work *works*, the song seems to tell us, because the men who desire this woman are seeking to define themselves *as* men through sexual congress with her: they need her in order to be themselves, and just as she needs to "try it again" until she gets it right, so the men must constantly repeat this search for the woman who will make them feel like men, must constantly repeat "masculine" actions so as to define themselves as such. This is why she has something to sell.

The song is deliberately ambiguous about whether the woman is engaged in literal sex work, or if this may be some fantasy (alternately desirous and hateful) of the male speaker; but the point of this ambiguity is to show that no clear line exists between the kind of male/female relationship at stake in sex work and that which is at stake in more conventional heterosexual relationships. In both cases, the norm is that the woman "performs" and "sells" her femininity as a product that men desire, because in possessing this product the man gets to perform his own "maleness." In this sense, both the man and the woman are "working" in their enactment of gendered roles. And Norman Mailer is arguably performing a kind of sex work himself when depicting his lurid fantasies about Marilyn Monroe, selling to readers his masculine identity as the man who can penetrate the feminine mystique.

If the woman in the song allusively stands, via the Mailer/Monroe reference, for Tule Livingston, then on one level the suggestion of sex work may appear as Zevon's insult of his ex-partner. Perhaps she wasn't sincere in the relationship, was just an "actress," faking it for personal gain, a no-good untrustworthy tramp, the feminine ideal in makeup and the right lighting, but a garish, embarrassing mess when the lights come up and her true colours are revealed. But as we know from what we've unpacked here, the song is smarter and more self-aware than this.

"The French Inhaler" both plays out this male fantasy about women's untrustworthiness, rooted in the recognition that femininity is a performance, *and* reveals this male fascination/revulsion as a performance of its own, constituting masculinity through the performance of a desire to possess this mysterious and elusive femininity. If the macho, Mailer-esque French Inhaler represents one version of this performance of maleness, the cynical but secretly romantic speaker (Warren/ Norman) represents another. Through the confusion between the two names in the song's final line, the culpability of the songwriter himself in constructing a certain self-interested performance of masculinity—like Mailer in his Monroe biography—hits with a deliciously ironic force.

Zevon's Deconstruction of the Lyric

"The French Inhaler" carries out this self-reflexive critique by drawing upon particular powers of the lyric form. The lyric is a poetic form that calls up things and beings that are absent, making them present within what Culler calls the "temporality of writing"—present to us in our encounter with the poem or the song. Zevon makes use of this power of the lyric to carry out a kind of deconstruction of the form itself. In "The French Inhaler," the absent woman is conjured up by the male speaker through his poetic power, but this conjuring is revealed to be the confused act of someone trying to establish his own masculinity through the act of address, or apostrophe.

The shift of voice in the song's final line, from the man to the woman, with her three devastating words—"So long, Norman"—completes this self-destruction of the very setup of the lyric form as an expression of the male speaker's power to make absent things present. What happens when the object of address—an object of alternate adoration, resentment, and degradation—talks back? Here, her words dislodge the picture that the speaker has been constructing of her and of himself, revealing a fragility to the lyrical act itself which the speaker has sought to hide behind his own lyrical prowess (just as the macho, Mailer-esque French Inhaler hides his fragility behind the seductive tricks he plays).

"The French Inhaler" stands as a work of brutal self-examination and self-criticism, drawing on Zevon's personal self-reflection to mount an auto-critique of the very form of the lyric, and the performances of gender that this form enables.

III

Reptile Wisdom

6

Warren Zevon's Poetry about Animals

BRUNO ĆURKO AND MARINA MILIVOJEVIĆ PINTO

Nikola Visković, a Croatian lawyer, professor, and bioethicist, asks:

> How much of a culture would it be and how would we perceive ourselves and our environment were there no birds, butterflies, ants, fish, bears and wolves, horses and donkeys and cows on the plains, camels that breathe life into the desert, countless creatures that inhabit our memory, imagination, religion, art in a familiar and mysterious way, responding to our emotional and rational needs to receive and to display our wealth, mysteries and beauty? (Visković, p. 18)

What would the human world be like without animals?

Among the world's creatures, animals are biologically and psychologically the most similar to humans. Perhaps because of this, they are present in all forms and expressions of human culture, including music. Animals serve as the themes and motifs of many compositions, from those that mimic animal sounds (such as Rimsky-Korsakov's "Flight of the Bumblebee") to tales of particular animals (Poulenc's "The Story of Babar the Little Elephant"), and from classical music to contemporary rock and heavy metal.

Warren Zevon's poetics are no exception. We can't help but notice that he often mentions animals in his lyrics. We cannot say with certainty why, of all animals, he most often mentions primates. Or dogs. In some cases, though, he gives them human characteristics, while in others he attributes animal traits to humans.

Around the mid-1990s, Visković introduced a new scientific discipline, which he called Cultural Zoology, defining it as the representation of the multifaceted relationships between animals and humans over the course of the history of life on Earth. While animals have been primarily a source of food and labor throughout history, they have also assumed over the course of time significant cultural roles. In many ways, culture is interwoven with animals and our representations of them.

The Great White Hunter and a Gorilla

Zevon never sought to conform to trends. His songs often tackled bizarre, morbid, even grotesque themes, the dark aspects of life that he would spice up with humor, irony, and cynicism. Primates serve as the main motif in no less than five of his songs, with a monkey's hand playing an eerie role in a sixth.

Zevon's first album, *Wanted Dead or Alive* (1969), features the song "Gorilla," in which he humorously describes a hunter arriving in the jungle. Here, Zevon appears to be mocking those who hunt gorillas. A hunter enters the jungle believing he is superior, physically and intellectually. He rustles, makes noise, and talks on the phone, enabling the gorilla easily to slip away. Yet Zevon refers to him, ironically, as "the great white hunter," one among those who continue to mock and kill innocent apes.

Since the ape is the animal closest to humans in behavior, emotion and intelligence, it not only fascinates, but repels us, the most. We tend to recognize our worst qualities in it—our primitivism, ugliness, ignorance, greed, malice, self-indulgence and destructiveness. These are the very qualities that we find most difficult to admit about ourselves. So, when the hunters laugh at the gorilla's faults, they are at once laughing at their own.

The Gorilla Desperado

Zevon's fourth studio album, *Bad Luck Streak in Dancing School* (1980), features the song "Gorilla, You're A Desperado," which tells the story of a big gorilla from the L.A. Zoo that snatches the glasses off his face and takes the keys to his BMW, leaving him to take its place at the zoo, while taking over his life. Zevon neither complains nor resists. In fact, all he wants is for the gorilla to succeed, even apologizing to the gorilla for his apartment being in such a mess. He also predicts that the gorilla won't end up behaving all that differently than Zevon himself does. This suspicion is confirmed when, in spite of the swap, both Zevon and the gorilla feel equally imprisoned. One is caged in a zoo, while the other is weighed down by an expensive platinum chain, which symbolizes the perils of musical fame. Obviously, Zevon and the gorilla are one and the same, for just as Zevon attributes animal characteristics to himself, so he attributes human characteristics to the gorilla. Zevon thereby overcomes the conceit of anthropocentrism, the view that humans are superior to animals, by equating one with the other. This may sound extreme, but in the song's very title, the gorilla is described as a desperado, an antisocial person who lives on the margins of society, often in conflict with established social values. With all this in mind, we can call both a man who prefers to trade places with a gorilla and a gorilla who prefers to trade places with man desperados.

The Endangered Apes and Humans

There are also a few positive characteristics of primates that make us just like them. They are curious and playful, learn from observing, and make tools that they can use, for example, to fetch food. Females will adopt motherless young, carry their wounded, clean each other's fur of parasites, and display signs of altruistic behavior. It is precisely due to these positive qualities that it makes sense to regard monkeys as representing innocence and needing protection from human cruelty.

In the song "Leave My Monkey Alone," featured on the album *Sentimental Hygiene* (1987), Zevon addresses the Mau Mau rebellion in Kenya (1952–1960) by repeating the line, "Leave my monkey alone." So persistent is this refrain that it constitutes most of the lyrical content of the song. The white man has taken over most of the land in Kenya, leaving the Indigenous people with little room and fewer resources. By lyrically foregrounding the monkey, which is unable to defend itself against man's greedy incursions into its natural habitat, Zevon draws attention to the need to preserve the wilderness and its creatures. In other words, if the great white hunter leaves the monkey alone, nature and those who are native to the land should also be left alone.

A Monkey and a Donkey

In the West, monkeys tend to be regarded as ugly and stupid, as objects of mockery. Regarded as the most foreign of animals, they have tended to be viewed in a negative light. Where do these prejudices come from? In Greek mythology, for instance, Zeus punishes the Cercopes for their lies, transforming them into ugly, inarticulate monkeys. By contrast, the ancient Egyptians worshiped Thoth, the god of wisdom, who was depicted with the head of a monkey or an ibis, both sacred to him. While the ancient Greeks associated Thoth with their Hermes, the early Christians, possibly owing to his monkey head, regarded him as a malevolent figure, often synonymous with the devil.

During the Middle Ages, monkeys were kept at court and in the homes of the wealthy, where they were trained to entertain people. Often dressed in human clothes, the monkeys' clumsy attempts to imitate humans made the crowds laugh. In some countries, like Morocco, monkeys are still commonly found entertaining tourists in town squares. Zevon's album *Mutineer* (1995) features the song "Monkey Wash, Donkey Rinse," which declares that, since "hell is only half full," there's "room for you and me," and invites the listener to "a party in the center of the earth."

In his book, *Warren Zevon: Desperado of Los Angeles*, George Plasketes claims that the monkey referred to in this song serves as a metaphor for the devil, but also cites David Lindley's recollection of how Zevon, during a visit to Marrakesh, found himself in a courtyard where street performers were playing. "They brought in a donkey and his 'very, very good friend,' a monkey, who was happily riding the donkey's back," says Lindley. "The satisfied monkey climbed down and gave the donkey a fast and vigorous massage, which in turn made the donkey very happy. And because he was very happy, the donkey reacted in a certain way." As Lindley recalls, "the monkey washes, and the donkey rinses, to which Warren said, 'I realized humanity is dead'" (p. 145).

By portraying this primitive way of exploiting an animal for human entertainment, the song illustrates how, when we abandon decent human values, we begin to approach the gates of hell, at the center of the earth.

The Porcelain Monkey

The song "Porcelain Monkey," released on the album *Life'll Kill Ya* (2000), was inspired by a figurine that Elvis Presley displayed on the coffee table in his TV room at Graceland. Zevon uses this porcelain monkey as a metaphor for the decadence of Elvis, who succumbed to the burdens of fame and fortune, including all those nights in Las Vegas and "his face on velveteen."

Why, of all things, did Zevon choose to focus on a porcelain monkey? He was known to have his reservations about Elvis, describing his life as "a very sad story, and not an interesting sad story, just a sad story" (*Nothing's Bad Luck*, p. 316). He was convinced that there were other quality artists who deserved attention and respect from the public and the media. By associating Elvis with a fragile porcelain figurine of a monkey, Zevon managed to emphasize the absurdity and vanity of Elvis's turbulent life.

The Monkey's Paw

Owing to their rather unattractive and grotesque appearance, when compared to humans, and their unrestrained nature, apes and monkeys are often portrayed as unappealing, somewhat intimidating animals. This, of course, reflects the human perspective. Consider, for example, Franklin Schaffner's movie *Planet of the Apes* (1968) or the Edgar Wallace and Merian Cooper film *King Kong* (1993). At the heart of W.W. Jacobs's short horror story, "The Monkey's Paw" (1903), a mummified monkey's paw is able to grant three wishes to whomever possesses it. Each of the wishes, however, comes with its own tragic consequences. Zevon draws on this image of the monkey's paw in his song "Genius," which is featured on the album *My Ride's Here* (2002).

Ever since ancient times, humans have tended to ascribe magical and protective properties to certain objects. Often, such amulets or talismans were made from animal parts, particularly those animals considered to have desirable qualities. In this case, though, the monkey's paw, which is very similar to a human hand, possesses such great power that it can grant any wish, albeit with a fatal outcome. As such, it represents the evil that can ensue when you tempt fate. Therefore, in this example, too, the monkey, or at least its paw, symbolizes regrettable human qualities. In "Genius," Zevon appears to depict the way man, the only rational animal, will often use his intellect to blame others for his mistakes, even to the extent of blaming this poor animal's paw for his misfortune.

What Is a Dog's Life?

Four of Zevon's songs feature the motif of man's best friend, the dog. The first animal domesticated by man was the wolf, which, after thousands of years of selective breeding, became, in the form of the dog, a servant of man, as well as our protector and friend. According to Visković, dogs' sense of hearing, smell and eyesight have, over the course of time, been significantly weakened, since they no longer have to protect themselves and search for their own food. Their brains are roughly twenty percent lighter than those of their relatives that survive in the wild. So, Jean de la Fontaine's fable, "The Wolf and the Dog," is scarcely fictional. Would you be willing to trade thirty per cent of your brain capacity for being protected and provided with food?

On Zevon's sixth studio album, *Sentimental Hygiene* (1987), there are two songs comparing a dog's life to that of a human. The first is called "Bad Karma," which describes a man who works hard to succeed, but fails. Who's to blame for this bad karma? The narrator doesn't understand why his life is full of such difficulty, convinced that there is nothing he can do to change things for the better, as if he were entirely helpless. "It's a dog's life," he says, "a low-down dirty shame," and yet not his fault.

The expression, "a dog's life," dates back to the sixteenth century, when dogs were relied on exclusively for hunting or protection. They slept elsewhere than in human dwellings, fed on waste and had a short lifespan. So, the expression also refers to the lives of those who are confronted by difficulties over which they have no control. The big difference between a dog and a human, however, lies in the fact that the dog is largely dependent on the human. A dog doesn't care about the qualities of its owner, whom the dog will adore and defend, if necessary at the cost of its own life, even if his owner is a vicious fool. Since dogs have no choice but to obey man's will, the phrase, "a dog's life," can also be associated with a distinct lack of freedom.

When Dogs Shake Hands

The other song about dogs featured on *Sentimental Hygiene* (1987) is called "Even a Dog Can Shake Hands," which conveys the idea that, when you're successful, everyone wants, not just to be your friend, but to bask in and benefit from your fame. Zevon compares those who are suddenly desperate to hang around, "trying to be a friend of mine," to a dog that knows crowd-pleasing tricks, including how to shake hands. Handshaking is one of the most common ways that people have of greeting one another.

This custom is believed to have roots dating back to ancient times, when shaking hands proved that people had no hidden weapons in their possession. The movement of the hand during hand-shaking ensured that any weapon that happened to be concealed would fall out of its cover. But when a dog is taught to shake hands, it has no idea why it gives us humans so much joy. It is simply happy to earn its master's approval.

Zevon uses the line, "Even a dog can shake hands," to compare fake friendships, friendships of mere convenience, to a dog's groveling devotion. A dog will do anything, after all, to gain the favor of its master, who, in turn, will ensure that the dog's needs are met. But if a dog's behavior is driven in large part by the desire to gain some advantage and avoid unpleasant consequences, can't humans be said to behave in a similar way? In psychology, the term "projection" refers to our habit of attributing to other people those of our own characteristics and emotions that we don't like. That way, we feel justified in criticizing them, while shielding ourselves from the same criticism. Possibly, the dog, while fascinating for its extraordinary qualities, many of which we share, reminds us at the same time of how shamelessly we can ingratiate ourselves, of how slavish, cowardly and pathetic we can be.

Gangster Rottweiler

Zevon's ninth studio album, *Mutineer* (1995), features the song "Rottweiler Blues," about gangsters and their guns. The narrator tells us he has a Glock in his bedside table, as well as a machine gun and a Kevlar vest that he keeps in the same room. The gangster attitude is particularly well suited to the dog, and not just any dog, but the Rottweiler.

The example of the Rottweiler illustrates how humans have constantly changed animals to fit their needs, so that they can use them both for noble and malevolent purposes. In Roman times, the Rottweiler is thought to have been used for herding livestock. They would travel across the Alps with the Roman legions, guarding both the armies and their livestock. Until the nineteenth century, Rottweilers were commonly relied on in Germany for guarding cattle, but also for pulling carts loaded with butchered meat. In modern culture, though, we tend to view the Rottweiler as an especially dangerous dog, one that shouldn't be messed with. It's not uncommon for gangsters and those committed to a life of crime to own Rottweilers, so it's no surprise to learn that the guy with the Glock and Kevlar vest in Zevon's song also owns one. If you don't know his Rottweiler's name, he warns, don't even bother knocking on his door.

A Dog's Life

Zevon's tenth studio album, called *Life'll Kill Ya* (2000), features a song with the intriguing title, "Hostage-O." The lyrics could be described as suicidally romantic in a rocker kind of way. The narrator expresses his willingness to be humiliated, promising to stand in line in order to make whatever sacrifice is necessary for "shame-faced love." He will be his lover's unswervingly loyal slave. Such a man accepts these terms because of love. Completely at her mercy, he invites his lover to treat him as the most submissive and miserable of creatures, bound, gagged, and "dragged behind the clown mobile."

This confirms the cruelty of man to animals, especially those closest to him. Thus, the expression, "You treat me like a dog," indicates that the object of mistreatment is completely subordinated to the one who dishes out the punishment. This is why, over the course of the entire song, the narrator offers himself without reservation, going so far as to express his willingness to be treated in the worst ways possible, namely, the way individuals treat their dogs.

A Lamb, of the Sacrificial Kind

The opening song on the album *My Ride's Here* (2002) is called "Sacrificial Lambs." In this "spiritual song," Zevon sings ironically about spirituality. What would all the Coptic monks, as well as the Rosicrucian and Zoroastrian spiritual leaders, be willing to do if they ran out of sacrificial lambs? The term "sacrificial lamb" refers to someone who is regarded as an innocent victim. And innocent lambs and sheep have been sacrificial animals since roughly 4400 B.C. Most of our ancient ancestors also made animal sacrifices. Once a sacrificial animal (usually a sheep) was killed, its blood would be splattered all over the altar and its inedible parts burned in the sacred fire. The rest would be eaten by the priests and worshippers.

Most Greeks believed that the offered animals were happy to be sacrificed. According to the Bible, animal sacrifices represent gifts to God. They were mandatory sacrifices, offered on altars, of immaculate rams, lambs, bulls, oxen, and pigeons. Both the title of Zevon's song and the phrase itself refer to the usual innocent victim. But why precisely a lamb? What makes a lamb more innocent than other animals? One possibility is that lambs and sheep are the very epitome of meekness, although their meekness and innocence may be due to the simple fact that they were the most simple and cost-effective to sacrifice. Regardless, the image suits Zevon's purposes well. In his turbulent life, when the public failed to appreciate his talent, he never bowed down to the demands that others made upon him. He never agreed to sacrifice his integrity and become a sacrificial lamb.

Anxious Little Bird

On the live album *Learning to Flinch* (1993), Zevon recorded three new songs, one of which is "Worrier King." In this song, the narrator sings about a bird that, quite naturally, he is worried about. This song challenges our habit of perpetually worrying about things, which results in our being beset by fears about the future and everything around us, even if there is little reason to feel that way. Zevon himself battled personal demons, suffering in particular from obsessive-compulsive disorder (OCD). Chances are that when he wrote "Worrier King," he was actually referring to himself and his troubles. Then again, there are always those who are eager to exploit people's anxiety, including for political ends. Who knows what November may bring, the narrator sings, whether an attack on our country by, say, Vladimir Putin or some other dictator who manages to convince his people to follow him blindly.

It's interesting to note, here, how Zevon starts the song, the narrator declaring that he's got a bird that whistles, a bird that sings, before adding, hesitantly, "I've got a bird that . . . I've got a bird," then assuring us how much he worries about that bird, because he worries about everything. Even though it's sheltered in a cage, that tiny, helpless bird is perhaps the most protected thing of all, but he worries about it. And yet, Zevon never wonders if the little bird itself is worried. So, how might this protected bird feel? Would it choose freedom or the safety of the cage? Would it risk being free, struggling to cope with the many dangers that threaten free beings, or would it prefer to be caged and carefree?

This again recalls Fontaine's fable, "The Wolf and the Dog." A well-fed dog guards his master's home, while chained in his backyard. A hungry wolf, meanwhile, must fight for every morsel of food. So, when he is offered food on the condition that he agree to be chained, we might expect him to accept such terms with gratitude. But instead, he refuses, preferring his freedom. Who would you rather be, a hungry but free wolf or a well-fed but dependent dog? Or, to return to Zevon's song, would you choose to be a safe, carefree bird in a cage or an alert and anxious bird roaming free?

How Did Warren Zevon Represent Animals in His Poetry?

Having considered the animal imagery in Warren Zevon's lyrics, it's clear that he mainly wrote songs about primates, from different points of view, comparing them to humans in a variety of ways. On the one hand, he mocks the "great white hunters" for their vanity, and because they are so easily outwitted by their prey, the gorilla. He proceeds to suggest that humans and apes could easily swap positions with each other, as they are virtually on the same level. He implies that the "great white hunter" endangers both primates and humans, due to both his arrogance and his consuming need to exploit nature. Zevon anticipates the exploitation of animals, in particular of monkeys and donkeys, even in an uncrowded hell. Does this mean that we are creating a hell on Earth for non-human animals? Or perhaps for ourselves?

The second most common animal that Zevon sings about is "man's best friend," the dog. In his songs, he highlights the view that humans bred dogs out of wild wolves, as well as the popular opinion that humans can make a dog's life very difficult. Besides dogs and wolves, Zevon sings about birds and lambs to address perennial concerns, like cosmic anxiety and religious belief. We can conclude that Zevon's anthropocentrism is not typical. Standard anthropocentrism suggests that human beings are superior to all other creatures and that, consequently, those other creatures must be assessed in human terms. Although Zevon occasionally relies on certain prejudices about some animals, he does not consider them inferior.

We have admittedly missed the opportunity to analyze Zevon's most popular song, in which he sings, "I saw a werewolf with a Chinese menu in his hand." However, that will be worth considering when we are certain that the werewolf is a non-human animal, rather than a bizarre form of human being.

7
On Being a Werewolf

CHRISTOPHE POROT AND LUCIE TARDY

Warren Zevon describes "Werewolves of London" as a dumb song for smart people, but his interpretation is just one among many. Here are some curious thoughts on what we consider to be a smart song.

Have you ever laughed at a moment when you felt you should scream? According to Friedrich Nietzsche, you might be onto something. Sometimes, when you are powerless in life to change your circumstances, the best thing you can do is enjoy the irony of it. This is an example of what Nietzsche calls the "gay science."

Warren Zevon's comedy noir masterpiece plays with the irony of being powerless in the face of a real human phenomenon. In his account of the history of the song, George Plasketes identifies Jackson Browne as being among those smart people for whom the dumb song was intended. In an interview at Zevon's memorial service in 2003, Browne ventured that the song is about aristocratic and high-powered men doing whatever they feel an impulse to do, especially cruel things:

> It's about a really well-dressed ladies' man, a werewolf preying on little old ladies. In a way, it's the Victorian nightmare, the gigolo thing. The idea behind all those references is the idea of the ne'er-do-well who devotes his life to pleasure: the debauched Victorian gentleman in gambling clubs, consorting with prostitutes, the aristocrat who squanders the family fortune. All of that is secreted in that one line: "I'd like to meet his tailor." (p. 50)

This is why Zevon refers to the werewolf's immaculate hair, insisting that he wants to "meet his tailor," thereby playing with the contrast between appearance and reality, which confirms that dangerous beasts can appear in the form of polished, high-class individuals, warning us not to get too close. What can we learn about such werewolves and about our possible relation to them?

In this chapter, we invite you to consider an interpretation of what these werewolves of London experience and symbolize, a reading captured best by the French philosopher Simone Weil, according to whom, in an act of force, there are two victims, because "Force is as pitiless to the man who possesses it, or thinks he does, as it is to its victims; the second it crushes, the first it intoxicates" (pp. 321–330). In other words, beyond the harm these werewolves cause to others, what further harm, we want to ask, is being done to them? Ultimately, we argue that they may well lose their freedom, while at once being alienated from the species.

They Are Not Aliens but Are They Alienated?

Alienation, in its most basic formulation, is the condition of being separated from something with which you ought normally to be united. For instance, those who are treated as the black sheep in their family may be considered alienated from those with whom, under better circumstances, they ought to be intimately joined.

But there are two main types of alienation, subjective and objective. For example, someone may feel alienated from her family, independently of whether she actually is. This is what philosophers call subjective alienation, the personal experience of feeling separated from some unified whole to which you nominally belong. On the other hand, you may not feel alienated from your family, even though, in reality, your family despises you, constantly enforcing a distance between you and them. According to David Leopold, this would be a case of objective alienation, in which, whether or not people feel alienated, they in fact are so. Which one do you think applies to these werewolves?

A case could be made that subjective alienation propels these beasts forward into action. Perhaps a personal sense of being separated from themselves or their human species leads to their destructive behavior. Surely, the sensation of subjective alienation may lead to unsavory behavior, as the alienated person desperately tries to capture, in the face of the experience of separateness, a sense of wholeness. However, if we were honest, this seems unlikely to apply to the were-wolves. We want to claim that these characters are, through their behavior and other mechanisms, objectively alienated, although their supreme self-confidence makes it unlikely that they are aware of their condition. So, what's happening?

These menacing figures are losing touch with the species as a whole. The imagery of becoming a werewolf perfectly captures the idea that these men stand somewhere between humanity and wild beasts. But they do not routinely incline in the direction of humanity. Instead, we propose, they are literally becoming a different species. There is a twist to this analysis. According to Karl Marx, alienation from the species is understood as a condition experienced by the lower classes, or, the proletariat. Marx argues that, after working inhumane hours in a factory, a human being is reduced to the condition of an animal that can merely eat and sleep.

Many of us have had this experience! At the end of the day, after exhausting ourselves laboring on someone else's project, we simply eat a juicy hamburger and fall into a deep sleep, or perhaps, on a good day, enjoy sex with a lover. Rarely, though, do we do anything that fulfills us in any fundamental way. Have we become brutes because we are bruised, beaten instruments of a capitalist system? Maybe, maybe not. The problem is that these werewolves, who undergo a metamorphosis that magnifies their distance from the species, are hardly members of the proletariat.

Here, modern distributivist philosophers may have something to say. Distributivism, which is most clearly articulated in the work of G.K. Chesterton, bears a curious relation to Marxism, insofar as it tries both to criticize and extend Marxist theory. In the act of extending it, distributivists point out that perhaps both workers and capitalists are dependent on the arbitrary will of another.

While the worker clearly bears the burden of working for someone else, the capitalist is dependent on the random will of the masses, who may or may not choose to purchase what they produce. So, the system, according to the distributivist, traps everyone. Perhaps we could say that these werewolves are subject to arbitrary shifts in the market, which limit their choices, including those concerning the use of their labor. But if this picture of servitude suits werewolves who work by day, it hardly seems to account for those who are privileged enough to inherit power. For at night, they turn into werewolves who exploit others, reducing themselves at once to mere animals acting on the impulse to terrorize London, or, of course, any other urban center.

Some might say, "they are not alienated from humanity, but are a perfect expression of our true nature!" Such an assertion, however, presumes that we are not naturally drawn to rarefied thoughts and enjoyments, but are trained to love, or pretend to love, those things against all our natural impulses. The English philosopher Thomas Hobbes suggests as much when he states that "man is a wolf to man," implying that selfish and belligerent tendencies precede civilized life. Expressions of the view that humans are fundamentally bad range from the doctrine of original sin to various representations in contemporary culture, including in the popular show *South Park*, where it seems to be a recurring theme. One vivid example of this commitment to human evil is in the first episode of the fourteenth season of *South Park*, titled "Sexual Healing."

The highlight of the episode focuses on a room full of political men who pretend to be confused and outraged about other, wealthy men having sex with a number of women. With furrowed brows, they ask themselves how this "new" behavior is even possible, at one point insisting that they "want answers!!!" Their eyelids constantly batting, they attempt to identify the source of what they regard as an anomaly in human behavior, and eventually come up with two potential answers: the water supply or wealth itself.

The humor of the scene derives from the assumption that these politicians, if given the chance, would act the same, as long as they were confident their wives wouldn't find out. The writers of the show are clearly mocking a widespread habit of reacting to our own less admirable actions. We are often eager to identify external causes of such actions, which, since they do not depend on us, free us, in a certain way, from any kind of responsibility or guilt. If concluding that our conduct comes naturally to us establishes our culpability, claiming that it is rooted in the failings of society absolves us.

This, however, is a mistake, since the question of how much control we exert cannot be resolved by determining whether the roots of action are natural or social. Even if awareness of the causal history of actions and occurrences can open up new strategies for correcting unethical behavior, it can hardly be said to liberate us. In any case, the assumption that our flaws are natural, and the influence of society negligible, has been challenged quite persuasively in the past.

Jean-Jacques Rousseau and, more than six centuries before him, the Arab philosopher Ibn Tufayl, reverse the equation. For it may well be the case, they suggest, that we were content in a state of nature, and that it is actually the pressure of the social world that heightens our tendency to behave badly.

We shouldn't forget that the werewolf isn't just a menacing creature, but also a transformed human. The force of Ibn Tufayl's and Rousseau's reflections is that such a metamorphosis is impossible without society. As Jacob Roundtree notes, the irony of the alienation of these beings is that it is precisely in the act of denying the humanity of others that they deny their own. Rupturing the common bond among human beings can entail a loss of freedom or amount to an expression of it. Which do you think it is?

Wanton Freedom

These werewolves are both free and not free at the same time, depending on how you look at it. In one sense, they are free to do whatever they want. Nobody can stop them. According to those who subscribe to this view, they enjoy unlimited freedom. In a popular conception of freedom, known as negative liberty, freedom and power are essentially identical. According to Hobbes, both are defined by the opportunity to do what you want without interference. But there are different types of power: there's power understood as the ability to accomplish a goal, power over yourself, and power over others.

Zevon's werewolves seem to enjoy unlimited power over others. They can mutilate "little old ladies," steal, even "rip your lungs out." They can abuse as they see fit and nobody can stop them. In other words, they can exhibit a childish attitude. Children, who are often assumed to represent humans in a state of nature, seem to crave this power over others.

Anthropologists and psychologists examine the behavior of children in order to better grasp human nature, but while they acknowledge some admirable aspects of it, it's an empirical fact that children can harbor tyrannical impulses. If you want to know whether or not original sin is real, St. Augustine would say, just look at kids. Surely, we've all seen what happens when a child wants something that another child has. The child who craves what belongs to another can cry, complain endlessly, or hurt the other child until he gets what he wants. And what he wants is power over others, because it's an instrument for the satisfaction of his own desires. Where negative liberty is concerned, as long as no one is physically stopping you from getting what you want, you are free, so the tyrannical child who steals or hurts other children is expressing a fundamental freedom in the context of enjoying power over others.

The only constraints on our power over others are those social conventions, including whatever ethical principles

prevail, that teach us to respect the freedom of others. As John
Stuart Mill says, your right to swing your fist ends at your
neighbor's nose. Mill calls this the "harm principle," the
conviction that your freedom is limited by the constraint that
you not interfere with the rights of others (p. 9). But these
werewolves, living a life of impunity, never have to operate
under this constraint, so they retain unfettered power over
others in pursuit of the satisfaction of their desires. But what
about power over yourself, or the power needed to accomplish
your goals, or even having a free will at all? Here, things get
more complicated.

Let's consider a thought-experiment to see if we can clarify
the phenomenon. Imagine that someone is driving. She takes a
left, then a right, then goes through a roundabout. By no
measure can anyone be said to be physically interfering with
her doing as she pleases. Imagine, though, that she's driving to
her crack dealer to feed her addiction. According to negative
liberty theorists, like Hobbes, she's simply free. But, according
to another conception of liberty, known as positive liberty, she
is not free at all. Since the addiction is controlling her decisions, she is unable to act autonomously. On this theory, you
can be enslaved from within. And if you're enslaved from
within, you lack power over yourself, no matter how much
power you have over others. You may even lack free will. But
how is that possible?

The philosopher Harry Frankfurt addresses the question of
what constitutes a person and how personhood, in turn, relates
to freedom of the will. Essentially, a person has both first-order
and second-order desires. For instance, he may have a first-
order desire to consume a drug he's addicted to and a second-
order desire not to do so. When he exhibits a preference for the
second-order desire, he could legitimately be said to have a
will. The addict, however, exercises no free will because his
freedom is undermined by the power of the first-order desire,
which overrides his will (pp. 5–20).

In any case, such a hierarchy of desires is distinctly related
to persons, whom Frankfurt distinguishes from what he calls
"wantons," who merely have first-order desires, or, if they
happen to have second-order desires, do not allow them to
generate a volition. In other words, to have a will involves not
only acting on whatever impulse we may have at a given
moment, but choosing to act or not to act on the basis of such
an impulse.

If you don't have second-order desires, then you lack a
distinct will, leaving you with just a string of impulses that

control you. If you do have second-order desires, but can't act on them, then you have a will, but are enslaved by your first-order desires. If you have second-order desires that motivate your actions, then you have a free will. A paradigm case of such a free will would be an athlete who's overwhelmed by pain in the midst of training, nurses a first-order desire to abandon training, but ultimately heeds his second-order desire to keep going.

Are our werewolves wantons or persons? Not only does it seem that they are entirely controlled by their first-order desires to do as they please, but there's every indication that they lack the reflective capacity to imagine their second-order desires. In this sense, these aristocrats and fancy werewolves, "walking with the Queen" and "drinking a piña colada at Trader Vic's," are wantons, and therefore cannot be considered free.

In more popular language, often captured in spiritual dialogues, this distinction between orders of desire can be equated with "higher" and "lower" selves. The lower self is governed by first-order desires to satisfy impulses that don't correspond to the image of who that person truly wants to be, whereas the higher self is disciplined and goal-oriented, more concerned about love and truth, and more determined to act in a certain way. We might think of the higher self as the soul or divine part of us and the lower self as the vital, animalistic part that threatens to overwhelm our higher self. According to some positive liberty theorists, if the lower self has all the power, then people cannot be free, because they are completely controlled by first-order desires. This issue of the struggle between higher and lower selves has a long religious and literary history. Goethe's *Faust*, for instance, illustrates what happens to a man when he abandons his higher self to pursue whatever passing desires bubble up within him. In the Christian context, the reflection, "What good would it be to gain the whole world if I lose my soul?", indicates a clash between lower and higher selves.

If you reject the idea of a higher and lower self, or of first-order and second-order desires, then of course Zevon's werewolves are perfectly free and powerful. There seems to be almost no limit to their freedom. If you see the value of such a distinction, however, then they are clearly unfree, as the lower self runs the show, while the higher self never even makes an appearance on stage. So, it seems safe to conclude that they lack a will, or, if they have one, it isn't free.

There are several ways to interpret this unfreedom. One is to conclude that there is a hierarchy of desires, with our higher-order desires reflecting what we truly want. The other relates to the philosophy of Simone Weil, for whom evil has an ontological force. When people are consumed by anger, hatred, or the need to hurt others, they're submitting to this force and, consequently, enslaved by it. However you look at it, according to the advocates of positive liberty, our werewolves are internally enslaved.

We remain neutral about whether Zevon's werewolves are truly free. However, we want to pose a very basic question that naturally emerges from our consideration of these terrifying, alienated, likely unfree characters. Should we show any sympathy for them? Is there space in our hearts not merely to forgive, but to care for creatures who've fallen so far away from their humanity?

Is There Another Option Besides Loving or Hating Them?

The game of turning others into villains can be dangerous. In "just war" theory, philosophers discuss the concept of *Homo hostilis*, the idea that humans join with each other by hating another group (Lazar). Is there any greater reason to hate another than by presuming that he or she is evil? As the American theologian Reinhold Niebuhr warns, turning people into villains can grant us a license to be as cruel to them as we wish (pp. 199–200). This is obviously true of Nazi psychology, which portrays Jews as scheming, evil villains who must be eliminated.

Time and time again, this habit of portraying a subset of the human population as evil leads to violent and dehumanizing treatment of them. Here, it's natural to think of many Quentin Tarantino films, concerning which Tarantino himself identifies the pleasure we get from watching them as the vicarious act of "victimizing the victimizers." In other words, in movies like *Django Unchained* and *Kill Bill*, we cheer fervently while watching people being kneecapped, sliced open, or killed, because we feel they deserve it. Villains don't deserve ethical treatment, we assume, because they themselves aren't ethical, or so the logic goes. We indulge our most outrageous fantasies of harm when we imagine ourselves inflicting it on an evil being.

Yet another way radically to dehumanize others, especially those we perceive as villains, is to absolve them of any responsibility for their actions. We don't criticize a lion for hunting, because we don't believe lions have anything other than first-order desires to account for their behavior. We're tempted to suggest that, despite the effects of alienation and the possibility of unfreedom, there is a way in which these werewolves may yet be responsible for what they've become. So, the most obvious way to reconcile not absolving people of responsibility with not turning them into mindless beasts is to show them mercy. Such a determination guides Father Gregory Boyle's mission with the renowned Homeboys Industries, which offers a second chance to gang members who have committed sometimes abhorrent crimes. At Homeboys, they offer therapy, jobs, and tattoo removal, so people who have gotten off on the wrong foot can take another stab at life.

Of course, the ex-gang members who join Homeboys Industries choose voluntarily to do so, suggesting that the process requires a readiness to change. We don't believe that these werewolves, comfortable and consumed by the glamor of power, would be particularly interested in becoming better people. They'd be unlikely ever to walk through the door of Homeboys Industries. It's such a complicated matter to try lovingly to tame the terror of the werewolves, which we believe is why, rather than offer a solution, Zevon invites us to enjoy the werewolves's company, to covet their hair and the attentions of their tailor, to laugh instead of cry.

There are no solutions that emerge from the thought-experiment presented in Zevon's song, only a comedy noir account of all that transpires.

Hugo's "Fun Club"

The French writer Victor Hugo presented the same thought-experiment a century before Zevon's hit song. Imagining what he calls the "fun club," a striking parallel to our pack of werewolves, Hugo likewise envisions rich Londoners running around and "having fun" at the expense of others. As he puts it:

> To break into a house, to break a prize glass, to scar the family portraits, to poison the dog, to put a cat in the aviary, is called "carving a fun piece." Giving out fake bad news that makes people take grief the wrong way is fun. (p. 288)

"Fun" shouldn't be misunderstood here. It's fun if rich people terrorize the poor, but a crime if the relation is reversed. That's how Hugo concludes his meditation. "If they were poor people," he writes, "they would be sent to prison; but they are nice young people." We have imagined and worried about such creatures for centuries, and they are still on the prowl, but, as Hugo says, it's just a "comedy" (p. 288).

There's another way to respond to the behavior of oppressors, apart from accepting this kind of comic injustice. There is the subtle response implied in Ralph Ellison's masterpiece, *The Invisible Man*. In the novel, a man oppressed to the point that he feels invisible assumes the role of spectator. Instead of laughing, crying or rebelling, the Invisible Man silently bears witness to all that happens.

When Zevon invites us to laugh with the werewolves, he is showing us that deep tragedy can be met with laughter. Eventually, however, the laughter must stop. When Hugo refers to the fun club and the innocence of its members, he is noting how inclined we are to punish the poor, rather than control those who oppress them. And that Ellison's Invisible Man lives in silent fear demonstrates how feeling powerless in the face of oppression may make a person feel less than human.

Objectively, Zevon's werewolves may be alienated, unfree beings who have lost their humanity under the guise of having fun. While we hesitate to demonize, the internal servitude to which they are subject leads us to conclude that they are indeed heartless bastards.

8
Looking for the Next Worst Thing

Zach Rubin and Hannah Rubin

There's looking for the next best thing, and then there's looking for the best possible thing. That's what utopia is: an imagined best-possible world. It's a portmanteau (two previously-independent words pushed together) of the Greek *outopos*—which means no place—and *eu-topos*—the good place.

It's the best of all worlds, made possible only because it is imagined and not found in the real world. The concept is ancient and found in different cultures across the globe, but today we associate it with Sir Thomas More's 1516 novel, where he invented the word as we now use it. In the novel, he describes a fantastical island in the recently discovered New World whose social, economic, and geographic arrangements were nothing short of ideal in the eyes of the Brits he was writing for.

Most observers interpret More's *Utopia* as a means of criticizing the tumultuous reign of King Henry VIII without directly confronting the power of the Crown, an indirectness that is a key characteristic of literary and artistic descriptions of utopias. The perfect world is a prop for exposing the failures of the present one, an imaginary alternative that must be located in a place just out of reach. For example, a lot of utopias involve stories of a past golden age from which humanity has fallen from grace, a future just out of reach from our present imperfections, or places so geographically distant that they can't be visited. As Ruth Levitas puts it in her book, *The Concept of Utopia*, "Utopia is the expression of the desire for a better way of being" (p. 9). It doesn't have to be as hidden or subtle as More's, because the target isn't always a power that the critic is afraid of. According to Lyman Tower Sargent, in his primer *Utopianism: A Very Short Introduction*, utopia can be a description of something desirable or undesirable, an extrapolation, a warning, an alternative to the present, or a model to be achieved.

Utopia scholars, however, tend to agree that the utopian impulse is a common feature of human societies. Because it can be regarded as an attempt to improve the society it critiques, it has taken many forms throughout history and across cultures. But the utopian impulse differs from other forms of social critique due to its focus on *perfection*: the ultimate transformation. Sometimes perfection is used as a rhetorical device to point out the most glaring flaws in a given society, while in others it's a means of setting the agenda for a better world. It can involve shooting for the Moon and landing among the stars, to paraphrase the adage of Norman Vincent Peale.

If you think this chapter is about utopia, then perhaps you should go back and listen to some more Zevon first, because it's definitely not something he believed in. Rather, his career is more clearly characterized by a preoccupation with *dystopia*: the worst place. Dystopia is a popular articulation of pessimism about or discontent with the direction of society, whose ultimate outcome is the opposite of utopia. In popular culture, we can see the ruling class of the Republic of Gilead in *The Handmaid's Tale* and those living in the Capital in *Hunger Games* as purveyors of dystopian authority. The enslavement of Offred for the purpose of childbearing and Katniss's fight for survival just to entertain the bourgeoisie of the Capital are, to the reader, the worst outcomes of a post-apocalyptic society gone wrong.

Zevon mastered a form of commentary that asserts that one person's utopia is another person's dystopia—all it takes is a change in perspective. Some of the characters in those stories cited above do lead wonderful lives that, from their perspective, are nearly perfect. But to readers of these modern fictions, perspective makes the difference as to whether these potential futures are the best or the worst. These concepts are, in fact, two sides of the same coin. For example, Zevon turned the wistful "Sweet Home Alabama" on its head by suggesting of the lifestyle idealized by the dead band that, in fact, "there ain't much to country living / sweat, piss, jizz and blood." Or, portraying a gorilla at the L.A. Zoo, who switches places with him only to find itself just as disappointed by a life of freedom as it was by captivity. As a consummate cynic, it's no surprise that Zevon was consistently drawn to themes of dystopia over those of utopia, turning the rest of society's optimism on its head.

Join Me in L.A.

Utopia and, by extension, dystopia, can exist in three types of places. First, in the future, where it has yet to be achieved. Second, in the past, suggesting that a fall from grace has knocked human society from its previously perfect perch. Finally, in a generic "elsewhere," a fictional geographic location that is far enough away that the current society has not yet reached it, but close enough that it seems feasible to imagine visiting someday.

Utopias and dystopias are supposed to be found outside the real world, in a world that's just distant enough from the one we live in to be unreachable, but close enough to be approachable. All of these locations can intersect with one another. For example, the *Star Wars* franchise is set "a long time ago in a galaxy far away," while the *Star Trek* franchise is set in humanity's somewhat-distant future. While neither of these is a complete utopia, both use time and the distance of space to illustrate through plot lines how our present society gets something wrong that could be rectified.

For the most part, we see Zevon as being focused on a future dystopia, sometimes set in general locations, but often focused in particular on Los Angeles. He critiques the world around him by pulling utopian dreams from parts of the society he inhabited and juxtaposing them with someone else's, and frequently his own, dystopia. He regularly pulled qualities or characteristics from one person's, or type of person's, utopia to describe the problems he saw in the world. Commonly, he would address war and fame to portray them as promising false utopias, describing their outcomes as damaging rather than salutary, as their boosters would. The most prominent theme throughout his music, though, is Los Angeles: a place with a reputation for boundless opportunity, but also, to his mind, endless exploitation and pervasive decay.

His troubled relationship with that city is a reality he shared with many other contemporary musicians and artists. But in his music, he creates an alternative vision of it that differs from those experiences and the popular imagination, and so creates the dystopia through the distance of perception. Zevon portrays the so-called City of Angels as a city of dark contradictions: what seems a land of opportunity for those who seek it out in their youth is, to Zevon, almost inevitably a place of disappointment that chews people up and spits them out. Though Los Angeles is real, and therefore precluded from counting as a dystopia, he portrays a not-too-distant future or alternative version of the present, ensuring that they are just distinct enough from current life to serve as a warning to anyone holding out hope that it will provide them salvation or fame.

Let's start with some examples that *don't* illustrate the concept, but that serve as a point of contrast. "Join Me in L.A.," a song about the real place he inhabited, is probably not a dystopian song, because it's so intimately linked to an interpretation of its present and to the personal problem, for him, of increasing drug use. In it, Zevon grouses that, though others say the city is evil, he's found something in L.A. "that will never be nothing," and that is why he stays. Here, L.A. is not transformed into an alternative version of itself. Rather, its present is explained through a personal experience of, as Zevon biographer C.M. Kushins describes it in his book *Nothing's Bad Luck*, a "'come hither' quality to the sin and promise of late-night Los Angeles" (pp. 69–70).

Likewise, in his epic "Desperados Under the Eaves," Zevon portrays a near-future where "California slides into the ocean / like the mystics and statistics say it will," though he suspects that the hotel he's staying in will remain standing until the debt he owes is paid. You would think that establishing this setting outside the present were sufficient, but the song also remains an intensely personal one. As Kushins notes, it reflects Zevon's many nights in California motels alone with nothing but his demons, adding that he "would later admit that 'Desperados' was, truly, the most autobiographical of all his songs" (p. 70). The song depicts a man doomed to live repeated lives in an increasingly chaotic world until he faces his demons and pays his bill. Is it a dystopia? Not really. It's a personal hell, rather than a larger world shot to hell.

A better indicator of utopian or dystopian thinking is when authors involve characters other than themselves and when relationships with those characters are couched in the larger structure of a society. These characters may be real or fictional, named or anonymous. They could even be non-human, like the gorilla in the L.A. Zoo. However, when they are real, an added element of unrealism is required to take them outside the space and time they actually inhabit. So, songs like "Bill Lee" and "Boom Boom Mancini" don't really fit the bill, as they describe the life and times of real people. "Suzie Lightning" could be, if she were intended as an archetype for relationships between men and women generally, rather than a composite of many of the women Zevon had been involved with over the years. Since those who inhabit a utopia or dystopia don't live in the same world we do, they need to be familiar to us in some way, while taking on some unfamiliar traits upon entering the best or worst place. And they need to represent social relationships or structures that go beyond the individual.

One type of utopia that uses time as a means of describing utopia is that of the "golden age," a trope as ancient as Greek and Roman philosophy. In many cases, the "ages" were cyclical, portraying humanity's fall from grace, struggle with hard times, and eventual salvation, to a restart of the cycle. The utopias of these times were temporary, the result of heroic efforts by humans that, after they were gone, could crumble along with the memories of what they had accomplished. They follow the pattern of natural cycles, such as those of good and bad crop years, or the whims of moody gods (though not the Hindu Love ones), which could bring either great abundance or famine. Either way, they lacked a strong concept of an afterlife, which influenced the way those societies thought about the best and worst places. With the advent of Christianity, Western writers who relied on the concept of utopia began to think about it more as an ultimate destination, like heaven or hell. Zevon, writing in an age dominated by this Christian ethos, adopted a dystopian view along these lines as well. Rather than cycle back through to a good (or best) time for humanity, it could only proceed in one direction—it could only run straight down.

When the narrator of "Run Straight Down" describes how, "walking in the wasted city," he started to think "about entropy," he isn't walking anywhere real. It's also not clear that this is the real or some alternative Zevon, leaving the identity of the unfamiliar protagonist up to the listener's interpretation. He might be walking in L.A., as in many of Zevon's personal stories, but there's no clear indication where he is, except in an unpleasant future. All the progress heralded by the technological innovations that occurred during his lifetime had promised a better standard of living for humanity, but all he could think about was the winding stream of indecipherable chemical names, floating like a discordant choral line behind him, being released into and poisoning the atmosphere.

This also illustrates how a future dystopia can serve as a warning about our current failings as a society. At least, it can seem that way from our present vantage point. The protagonist in "Run Straight Down" is likely walking through Transverse City, given the smooth progression of the initial trio of songs on the album of that name. In the title track, he tells his "little Pollyanna"—a name commonly given to someone of undying optimism—to follow him to a place "where life is cheap and death is free." In this dystopian city, he lists the sights and sounds, from the "shiny mylar towers" and "ravaged tenements" to the "test-tube mating call" and "poisoned waves of grain." The pace of progress and growing dependence on technology in Zevon's futuristic city has widened the gap between society's haves and have-nots. In the third song on the album, "Long Arm of the Law," he identifies with the latter, telling the listener that the first words he ever heard were, "Nobody move, nobody gets hurt." So, when his anonymous protagonist tries to remember the past, the present seems so much worse by comparison, ravaged by the inequalities of technocentrism run amok. He'd rather watch it on the news at eleven, sit back and watch it run straight down.

The Ideal Life, One for Desperados

Zevon composed quite a few songs that meditate on the human condition, a number of which help further explain the concepts of utopia and dystopia. But it's important to remember that these are *social* concepts, not individual ones. So, as much as he bemoaned being in the house when the house burned down, or the time his heart was broken in "MacGillycuddy's Reeks," those are really more musings about his own failings or inevitable pitfalls of the human condition than about the failings of a society.

Utopias and dystopias, then, are not about what happens to people generally as a consequence of the human condition, but what could potentially happen to people in the present society as a result of how it is arranged. For this, we can turn to the theme of fame, which so often recurs in Zevon's music: the pursuit of notoriety, or the pursuit of perfection, depending on how you look at it. If we recall that dystopia can serve as a warning, we can see many such examples in Zevon's songs about the consequences of fame.

In "Looking for the Next Best Thing," Zevon muses about how his efforts to please others persist, and yet are never satisfied. He also draws on a couple of well-known epic tales of uncompromising quests to illustrate the point that seeking fame is bound to disappoint, including Don Quixote's tilting at windmills, Ponce de Leon's "cruise," and Sinbad's many voyages. Like Zevon himself, these famous figures had probably been warned that they would be "all alone on the road to perfection," but foolishly pursued their goals anyway. Quixote's case, for instance, suggests that the pursuit of extreme ideals can lead us to create and attack imaginary enemies in a futile attempt to purify the world. In other words, the moral of that story is often taken to mean that, as long as people remain too dogmatic or rigid, they will never experience the satisfaction of creating the world they seek. De Leon, a historical figure, is most famously associated with his search for the fabled Fountain of Youth, itself a metaphor for an enticing but clearly unachievable dream. Modern scholars doubt that de Leon spent any significant time as a conquistador in search of the fabled fountain. Instead, the legend seems to have been born out of fictional retellings of his life by later authors.

Kushins describes the song as being about "a fruitless lifelong quest to find true love, then finally settling," but given the reference to characters long associated with utopian thought, it must also concern the determination to become an object of admiration and love (p. 173). The song itself is less than utopian in type, but it's the way that Zevon refers to other utopian tales that helps him illustrate why he might "appreciate the best," while "settling for less." The reference to *Don Quixote* (written in 1605) is especially poignant, as the novel takes place at an unknown point in the past not too distant in time from the period when it was written. The protagonist originates from a fictional village in the real region of La Mancha and is driven insane by the nature of his quest. Unless we're prepared to compromise, Zevon warns that, "all alone on the road to perfection," we might all share the knight's fate. So, we're reminded in these tales that perfection is folly, and that the next best thing is the more desirable, or more realistic, option.

Even the abiding desire for fame has its disadvantages. As Zevon's notoriety increased, everyone he knew in the city came out of the woodwork to mooch off his success and pick his bones clean, or so he implies in "Even a Dog Can Shake Hands." Is that what he expected? Maybe, or maybe not. Zevon never enjoyed the fame or commercial success that some of his closest friends and cohorts did, like Jackson Browne, Hunter S. Thompson, or David Letterman, so the song likely refers to the more general social phenomenon of the sort of cloying sycophancy he would witness when those friends were approached by "dogs" with an outstretched paw.

In a final example, Zevon's song "Porcelain Monkey" is an attempt to challenge the assumption that fame and renown are at all desirable. In this song about the death of Elvis, Zevon slyly mocks the fact that all the luxury Elvis had acquired and all the adoration he inspired over his career in entertainment could not save the King from a grim and embarrassing death on a toilet. By now, it's well known that the song was inspired by Zevon seeing a picture of the TV room at Elvis's Graceland estate, with a porcelain monkey on a table, which inspired him to re-tell the King's life from an alternative point of view. How absurd to spend your fortune on such a trinket! He threw it all away. Then, he died on a porcelain throne—the King of all us monkeys, and yet all that he had couldn't save him.

War or Splendid Isolation?

Let's consider one last characteristic of dystopian thought, that it provides a way to confront, without directly criticizing, power. Zevon, of course, was no Edward R. Murrow or Walter Cronkite, both of whom reported extensively on war from the anchorman's desk. Still, coming of age during the prolonged and unpopular Vietnam War, he expressed, like many of his contemporaries, a dismal view of the American empire. But, instead of a direct recitation of casualty figures or the weary salutation, "that's the way it is," he relied on dystopian story-telling through song.

If Sir Thomas More had some critical words for Henry VIII, he had to hide them in story-form for fear of being pursued by stern medieval justice. In Zevon's critique of war, however, story-telling is a way of amplifying his meaning. Songs like "Roland the Headless Thompson Gunner," "Jungle Work," and "The Envoy" describe various escapades of subterfuge and force, as well as what Zevon portrays as their pointlessness. After all, "Baghdad do whatever she please," he sings in "The Envoy," regardless of whether the President sends his top diplomat. Even artful subterfuge, diplomatic immunity, and a lethal weapon can't make for a peaceful world, as became apparent when the CIA got caught equipping paramilitary death squads. In this connection, he refers to the El Mozote Massacre of 1981, in which the U.S.-trained Atlacatl Battalion was found to have murdered over one thousand civilians in a single village, shaming the U.S. on the global stage. It's one thing to recite these numbers, quite another to convey the meaning in a rhyming stanza that can haunt the listener behind a progression of B-minor chords. Again, we return to the theme of how one person's utopia can be another's dys-topia. That's what makes this song dystopian in nature: it re-tells a dominant narrative of pursuing something admirable by revealing its shortcomings. Zevon notes that, in order for U.S.

foreign policy to establish peace throughout the world, the odd village must be wiped out from time to time. All the events retold in "The Envoy" really happened, but it's the way Zevon unites them in song and verse that makes this count as an instance of the dystopian genre.

"The Envoy" is reminiscent of another story that represents the utopian-dystopian dynamic, Ursula LeGuin's "The Ones Who Walk Away from Omelas." In this story, the reader is introduced to a perfect little town, described in very few specific details, beyond the suggestion that it is pure bliss to live there. In fact, LeGuin encourages the reader to imagine it "as your own fancy bids," because the details of the society are less important than the unsettling tradeoff that makes it possible. In order to live under such a blissful regime, the town keeps a ten-year-old child locked up in a squalid basement somewhere in the village. Somehow, it is only through the suffering of this child that everyone else is able to achieve such unsurpassed bliss in their lives. It is a tradeoff between everyone's perfect happiness and a single innocent child's unimaginable suffering. Those who "walk away" are the ones who come to learn the secret and decide that the tradeoff is not worth it, and instead trade utopia for the great unknown.

"The Envoy" essentially asks us to confront a conundrum similar to that confronted by the people of Omelas: is it okay to cause suffering elsewhere in order to improve our own condition? And, knowing about such suffering, should we accept it? Of course, despite all the rhetoric, the US is not a utopia, so the song does not concern an actual tradeoff, but rather how the commitment to utopian peace through strength runs through US foreign policy. Once again, Zevon takes one person's utopia and transforms it into another's dystopia.

This theme of dystopic US diplomacy is most apparent in the middle of Zevon's career, bookended by other themes like those of romantic relationships and death. There are a couple of reasons for this. For one, the Vietnam War had ended, and many of the diplomatic endeavors Zevon wrote and sung about, like the El Mozote Massacre or shuttle diplomacy ("whoa-oh, Jerusalem"), were too esoteric for the American public. In a related way, the commercial failure of *The Envoy* led him to pursue a different artistic direction. Other than "Ourselves to Know," a song about the Crusades on *Life'll Kill Ya*, "Turbulence," a song about the futility of the Cold War on *Transverse City*, and "Disorder in the House" on *The Wind*, Zevon seems to have steered clear of the themes of war and diplomacy after the early 1980s. In any case, those songs aren't really dystopian in nature, because they are about real events, thereby failing to represent a major re-telling of those stories in an effort to flip their meaning.

Disorder in the House

What are we to make of the cynic dystopian, Warren Zevon? Above, we outlined how the concept illuminates his thoughts on technology, fame, and foreign policy, though an astute listener will probably detect many more examples in his catalogue. Arguably, he was the storyteller we needed, but whom too few wanted to hear.

As is often the case, audiences can be turned off by stories that portray their society as being on the wrong track. We can respond to stories of personal struggle, addiction, and heartbreak, because they seem possible to overcome, whereas social problems often seem too big for any single individual to grapple with. Or, once identified, such stories seem almost like personal insults when addressed to the whole of the society to which we pledge allegiance. Even as he sorted among the reasons behind it and the various contexts in which we might observe it, Zevon continued throughout his career to insist upon one central theme: one person's utopia is another's dystopia.[1]

---

[1] Rubin and Rubin would like to thank Larry Rubin and Rich Rubin for their good influence on our musical taste, as well as feedback on this chapter.

IV

Don't Let Us Get Sick

9
Shit's Fucked Up

HANNAH RUBIN AND ZACH RUBIN

L et's break it on down, it's the fucked-up shit. Disease is inescapable; it happens to everyone, even the best of us. Or, as Zevon says, the rich folks suffer like the rest of us—it'll happen to you.

And that's not just lyrics, it's a view of the world. To Zevon, it's both cavalier happenstance and inevitable absurdity that afflicts all of us, treated with a mix of humor, defiance, and resignation. This stands in contrast to how many in society view health and illness as simple states of being, binary and easy to diagnose. Many philosophers argue about the very definition of what it means to be in good or ill health. Disease and disorder, while sometimes seemingly simple to describe— "the shit that used to work, it won't work now"—are actually, once we get down to it, as complicated to define as Zevon's attitude towards them.

We often think of disease and disorder as malfunctions: some part of the body is behaving abnormally, or not according to its particular purpose. But our attitudes toward behaviors and conditions, how we think things ought to function, matter to what we call healthy and what we call diseased more than we might think.

Should we, as Zevon seems to do in "Excitable Boy," treat someone rubbing pot roast all over his chest with the same cavalier attitude as that same person building a cage with the bones of his murder victim? These are both abnormal behaviors, but one might be harmless, while the other may indicate something seriously wrong.

I went to the doctor; I said, "I'm feeling kind of rough"

There are many questions we care about when it comes to health and disease. We might want to know how to cure an illness, whether a disease is hereditary, or how a disorder will affect our life (or the life of a loved one). But lurking behind all of these is a more fundamental question: what does it mean to be healthy or unhealthy, to characterize some state of being as a disease or disorder? Of course, there are many medical distinctions drawn, and lots of terminology—disease, disorder, pathology, syndrome—but let's not get too bogged down in these. Let's just focus on the concept of disease, the general state of being unhealthy.

You might be wondering how we're going to fill a whole chapter describing what it means to be healthy or diseased. Surely, you know when you're healthy because all the shit that's supposed to work, works, and you know when you're diseased because the shit that's supposed to work, won't. As you will soon see, though, defining what it means to be healthy or diseased is tricky if we want our definition to rely only on scientific facts.

One main question here is whether our notions of health and disease are *objective*, or free from personal bias, opinion, preconceptions, and so on. Someone might want to claim that there are facts about the human body that we can come to know by doing science, and we can build our concepts upon these facts. Anyone who understands the facts will understand and agree on when people are healthy and when they are not.

One way to argue that our concept of disease is objective in this way is to talk about "malfunction." Scientific research allows us to discover the proper functions of various body parts or systems, and tells us when those things aren't working like they should. These scientific facts, once understood, will then let us determine when someone is healthy or diseased. But, we might ask for some elaboration of this: how do we know when something has malfunctioned? It can't just be that "the shit that used to work, it won't work now," since many diseases are present from birth. It turns out, there is no single answer to this question that all experts agree on.

None of this is to say that there are no facts of the matter, that medical research doesn't uncover truths, that science is all a matter of opinion or that you should avoid going to a physician for twenty years (which Zevon concedes that, for him, might have been a "tactical error"). Instead, the idea is that how we label particular conditions—which we can describe scientifically, or learn more about through research—depends on factors other than just the facts of the matter.

She gazed only at my chart, the valleys and the peaks

Here's one way—one very influential way—to try to answer this question, to say what it is for something to malfunction: Christopher Boorse's Biostatistical Theory. The basic idea is that we can say something is malfunctioning when it's functioning below the statistically normal level of function. For instance, we might say that a person's lungs generally are able to extract a certain amount of oxygen from the air when she breathes, and if her lungs can't achieve that, they are malfunctioning and she has some sort of disease.

Sounds plausible, but we need some more information to apply this in particular cases. For instance, we can't just say "normal level of function" and be done with it; we have different kinds of people in our human population and what's statistically normal for some isn't statistically normal for all. An infant should not be expected to have lungs that can hold as much air as fully grown adults, and someone living up in the mountains needs to have larger lungs than people living at sea level. (This is before we even think about disease in non-humans, where there are clearly different things that count as statistically normal.)

So, we have to qualify what we mean by statistically normal and identify who we are comparing these people (or their lungs) to. Generally, the thought is that we should compare organs (or whatever it is we're talking about) to other organs from others of the same species, same sex, and same age. This is what's known as the "reference class." Who all are we referring to when we're talking about what's normal for a population?

Don't let us get sick, don't let us get old

This need for a reference class leads to all kinds of problems, though. For instance, sure, age matters when it comes to whether or not something is functioning normally. We all know life'll kill ya. The same things that are normal when you're old, aren't when you're young. To take Scott DeVito's example, osteoporosis is normal for women after a certain age. If our reference class is women aged seventy to seventy-one, osteoporosis is not a disease, but is statistically normal. But there's no particular reason to restrict the age-group so much. We could just as well have said that we cared about women aged seventy to eighty, or women twenty to seventy-one.

How we define the age-range determines whether osteoporosis is a disease, and yet these are arbitrary or subjective choices (DeVito, p. 546). They are driven by what we think is important; no scientific fact will tell us that we should have a cut-off point at sixty or seventy or any other particular age. And just because life'll kill ya, do we not want to say the various ailments that come with age are diseases? (And what about the disease called death?)

In "Disorder in the House," Zevon evocatively describes (what we might interpret as) the experience of a body failing, coming to terms with the end drawing near. That the "tub runneth over" and plaster falls "in pieces by the couch of pain" suggests that it's time "to duck and cover," that there's a "fly in the ointment" that's going to bring the whole system crashing down. Most people don't have to deal with this kind of bodily disorder in their fifties, as Zevon did. We might justifiably think it is more tragic to experience this at a young age, when you have plenty more left to give to the world. But, would dealing with more and more disorder in your body, even later in life, be something we'd want to call healthy?

Another thing: you may have already noticed that just talking about the same age, species, and sex doesn't allow us to separate out people living in the mountains from people living at sea level, but surely that is an important distinction to draw when it comes to determining whether a certain lung capacity is normal. So, it seems we need to make a choice in this particular example, and we might want to say that our reference class for lung capacity would be people of the same species, age, and sex, living at the same altitude. That might make sense so far, but the more choices we have to make about the reference class, the less straightforward this way of defining disease becomes. As it turns out, there are many such choices we're forced to make, and having to make them should lead us to be skeptical of this definition of disease.

For instance, in the lung-capacity example, environmental differences seem pretty clearly to affect what's needed to function normally. Do we feel the same about an example where the "environment" is socially constructed, or made by humans? Let's consider an example that Quayshawn Spencer discusses in an interview with Shelley Tremain: lactose intolerance. In the

USA, lactose intolerance is considered an impairment (which basically means that a function is diminished or lost), despite the fact that 65 percent of adults worldwide are lactose intolerant. How can we make sense of this according to the Biostatistical Theory? It seems the digestive system's function of digesting lactose cannot be statistically normal for adults if a majority of adults' digestive systems can't do it.

You might want to appeal to a particular reference class. For instance, Northern Europeans, South Asians, and people whose ancestors came from those regions tend to be able to process lactose in adulthood, while Native Americans, people from West Africa, East Asia, the Middle East, and many other regions tend to be lactose intolerant. But do we appeal to reference classes based on ancestry or based on where a person currently lives? Some people are better at digesting lactose than others, and some of the more severe forms of lactose intolerance cause considerable problems in certain countries, for example the USA, where products with lactose are hard to avoid (lactose makes its way into a surprising number of foods, many of which don't even have any milk products in them) and where they are the main source of Calcium and Vitamin D for people. The USA views lactose intolerance as an impairment because of the country's history, its current cultural practices, and its racial composition; the reference class in this case, understandably, seems to be people living in the USA.

Run Straight Down

It's weird to call people of certain ancestries impaired because of some historical contingency (that dairying—raising animals for consumption of their milk—was and remains uncommon in their region of ancestry) when their digestive systems function just fine in other contexts. It is only in certain environments, which humans have created, where there's any issue. This line of reasoning has often been emphasized by disability scholars: we call something a disease, disorder, disability, and so on, because society has been constructed in a particular way, such that certain people struggle. Maybe you think dairying is firmly established enough that it's fine to consider it a standard part of the environment, but what about new changes we introduce to an environment?

Let's imagine humans in the wasted city described in "Run Straight Down," where the ozone layer is so thick with fluorocarbons that water and wildlife are threatened. Would you function well when the water's gone, and there's not a creature stirring 'cept the robots at the dynamo? Would the same people who thrive now also thrive in that environment? Probably not. At what point do new environmental changes become just the new normal, so that people who can't function as well as others are designated as diseased? It seems hard for scientific facts to settle these questions. At some point, we have to make an arbitrary decision.

We can take it too far the other way and blame the environment for our suffering, in ways that seem inappropriate to distinguish health from disease. As biographer C.M. Kushins describes, Zevon had a tendency earlier in life to blame his surroundings for his struggles with addiction, often picking up and moving, looking for a "fresh start" or "new beginning," moving away from the temptations in L.A. to find somewhere more secluded, moving back, retreating to Hawaii, always finding a new place to live. Environmental factors can certainly be relevant to addiction, but this seems like a very different case from the high/low-altitude and large/small lungs examples in terms of there being an environment in which a person with certain features will thrive. However, we have to draw a line somewhere indicating whether an environment should count as part of the reference class or not, and that line will be drawn arbitrarily, based on our intuitions about where it should go, and so won't be based on scientific facts.

It's Shot to Hell

The reference class is one qualification that needs to be made in order for the Biostatisical Theory to be applied to particular cases, but that also ensures that it runs into trouble. That seems bad enough, and you might already be prepared for the next section, where we introduce a different definition of disease, but there's another qualification that needs to be made to the Biostatisical Theory: not all "functions" matter when it comes to health and disease. For instance, we probably don't want to count left-handedness as a disease, even though left-handed people generally have right hands that function below a statistically normal level. Again, we need to be more specific if our definition of disease is to make any sense. Maybe we don't care about sub-par performance when it comes to certain goals, things like writing with your right hand or the ability to saw a woman in two for a magic trick (at least not when it comes to defining disease). But we can't just make a long list of what kinds of goals don't count; we need to say what the relevant goals are.

For the Biostatistical Theory, the relevant goals are reproduction and survival (or things that contribute to reproduction or survival). So, we care if below-average functioning leads to increased chances of death or decreased rates of reproduction. But, why choose these goals? They are important, sure, but other things are important. If, as Zevon describes in "Quite Ugly One Morning," it's a "hollow triumph" just to "make it to the bottom of another day," reassuring him that his reproductive and survival capabilities are not compromised is unlikely to convince him, or anyone else, that everything is fine. Most people would say that, at the very least, quality of life ought to count for something when it comes to your health. Zevon tells us to "enjoy every sandwich"— what's life worth if we can't do that?

On the other hand, does it matter if "You've got an invalid haircut" or "It hurts when you smile"? Possibly not. You might think those things don't really belong with health-related problems in a song about how life'll kill ya. While reproduction and survival are clearly inadequate to capture all the relevant goals of functions we care about when it comes to health and disease, the question remains, what should we say those goals are? We can pick and choose which things are important to us, or try to come to some sort of agreement, but notice that when we do we're no longer basing things on just the science.

Even if we try to amend the Biostatistical Theory to try to incorporate other relevant functions that lead to other relevant goals, like those affecting quality of life, we have to make some kind of arbitrary decision as to which functions and goals are relevant and which are not. We can all agree about the facts of the matter, discovered by scientists, but disagree about whether something counts as a disease because we disagree about what goals are important to a life well lived (or whether a life well lived is even a goal). There's no way to make this an objective definition of disease, one that doesn't depend on personal biases or whims.

The shit that used to work—It won't work now

Okay, now it's probably time to move on from the Biostatistical Theory and try out a different definition. Another way to talk about malfunctions is to say that something is failing to fulfill its purpose. So, we ask, "what is it for?", or, "what gives the parts or systems in our body purpose?" Some people answer that question by turning to evolutionary theory, as Jerome Wakefield does in his account of disorder. So, when we ask "what is it for?" or "what is its purpose?", what we really mean to ask is, "what did it evolve for?"

Wakefield takes a bit of a different approach to Boorse in trying to come up with a scientific or objective definition of disease. You might take Wakefield to be saying, what matters is that this thing used to work in evolutionary time, evolving to work for this purpose, but it won't work now, for me. In other words, he looks to the past (evolutionary history) to talk about functions, whereas Boorse looks to the future (how something affects future lifespan or reproduction). He also outlines what is really a "two-part" definition of disorder, where one of those parts (he argues) is objective, based purely on facts and science, while the other is subjective, based on our evaluations and feelings about whether something is harmful. (Actually, Boorse has a "two-part" theory, too, but his second part comes in defining illness rather than disease; he says that a disease is an illness when "it is undesirable, entitles one to special treatment, or excuses bad behavior.")

This first part, the part that's supposed to be objective, is intended to define *dys*function, where something is not performing the function for which it evolved. The second part, which goes beyond just facts and lets our feelings in, is that we as a society judge the dysfunction to be harmful. So, *mal*-function, or disorder, needs both things: dysfunction plus our judging it to be harmful (Murphy). This doesn't quite give us an objective definition of disorder or disease, but it does tell us that our judgments concerning health and disease are built on an objective concept of dysfunction. It might be comforting to think there's some objective concept that underlies our notion of disease, even if we can't completely get rid of personal biases or other subjective feelings.

All the salty margaritas in Los Angeles

Again, this sounds plausible, but there are reasons to think it can't be right. For one thing, there are many situations where the evolutionary "what is it for?" question doesn't apply. When evolutionary biologists talk about adaptations, they are concerned about how something helped some organism survive in a particular environment. Or, if you want your phrasing to be closer to how Darwin described it, you'd talk about "fittedness" to an environment. (Like, for instance, how larger lungs evolved to take in more air, helping to breathe in high altitudes, versus smaller lungs at lower altitudes.) When we take people away from the environment their ancestors evolved in, there's often no way to answer the question whether their bodies are functioning according to their evolutionary purpose. Is something behaving as it's supposed to in the environment? Well, I don't know; it's not *in* that environment.

When a novel environment arises, the idea of dysfunction does not apply. DeVito demonstrates this point with an example of mixing Rubber Cement into the ink in a fountain pen, and noticing it won't write anymore. It does not function, but it would be weird to accuse it of not functioning according to how it was designed. The manufacturers didn't design it to handle Rubber Cement. In other words, "not functioning" isn't the same as being dysfunctional.

DeVito uses this example to talk about disorders related to substance use, such as alcohol intoxication delirium. In such a case, are a person's mental mechanisms behaving in a way consistent with their evolutionary purpose? We can't answer this because our mental mechanisms did not evolve in an environment where they were regularly exposed to large quantities of alcohol. It just seems wrong to say they are dysfunctional. In fact, as David Letterman quipped regarding Zevon's tendency early in his career to drink a couple quarts of vodka a day, this demonstrates, if anything, "the resiliency of the human system" (*Nothing's Bad Luck*, p. 143).

DeVito concludes that *no* disorders related to substance use can count as disorders on Wakefield's definition of disorder, and so Wakefield's definition can't be right. But, even beyond this, there are a lot of things in our environment that didn't exist in our evolutionary past. In some sense, this complements the problem we had with Boorse's theory, when we asked, at what point do new environmental changes become the new normal, and possibly count towards what we think of as "normal function"? In this case, our current environment can never be the one that's relevant to distinguishing between health and disease, unless it's sufficiently similar to the environment of our evolutionary past.

Don't the trees look like crucified thieves?

It's clear that normative judgements, those concerning how things ought to be, play a role in determining whether something is harmful. But why society's judgements? People's attitudes toward and perspectives on conditions vary. Zevon adopts many of these perspectives in his lyrics, including those of humor, defiance, and resignation, as well as a cavalier attitude towards seriously deranged behavior. These extend from a perhaps sarcastic view of death, or a false bravado ("I'll sleep when I'm dead"), which he adopted when younger, to a more mature view, after dwelling on the subject in *Life'll Kill Ya*, to final reflections as he came to terms with his mesothelioma diagnosis in *The Wind*. There are too many to list, so here are a couple of examples of his contrasting viewpoints.

First, "Life'll Kill Ya" is a straightforward acknowledgement of the inevitability of death that appears to mock the profound struggles many contend with when confronting their own mortality in its extreme bluntness and simplicity. Compare this to "Don't Let Us Get Sick," a practical prayer for avoiding sickness, on the very same album, that might strike some as a strange way to communicate love. How we view a state of affairs, how bad we think some condition is—whether we in fact think there's any harm in, for instance, rubbing a pot-roast all over your chest—is a matter of perspective, of our values, our viewpoint. So, the notion of "harm" incorporated into an account of disease can depend on how you look at things, what attitude you take on a particular day. Or, it might depend on your own, rather than society's, goals. As Dominic Murphy points out, Wakefield's definition tells an infertile woman who doesn't want children (so much so that she would have a hysterectomy were she fertile) that she is disordered because society judges her life to be harmed by her infertility, though her views may simply be deviant.

Classically in the social sciences, deviance is viewed as something essential to and recognized by any given society. In fact, according to nineteenth-century social scientist Emile Durkheim, societies need deviance because it serves three major functions: when someone deviates and is punished, it reminds everyone else where the boundaries of right and wrong are; it creates social solidarity among either the majority or the deviant minority (or both); and, rather than reinforcing current norms, it can be, alternatively, a source of social change through the innovation of new norms. To apply this to Zevon's life, we might see, on the one hand, how his aversion to doctors led to a late-diagnosed and fatal case of mesothelioma, and as a reminder to the rest of us of the importance of regular checkups. On the other hand, his struggles with substance-abuse early in his career resonated with many fans, who either struggled with that themselves or could at least empathize with the experience.

Deviance, in this context, concerns either how a society reminds itself what's normal or how it develops new norms. And, as we know, what society considers bad or harmful is subject to change. Left-handedness used to be considered a disorder, and a sign that someone had sinister intentions. Drapetomania, the compulsion to flee, used to be considered a disease that affected enslaved peoples. The evolutionary function-versus-dysfunction debate aside, it seems like this definition allows too much room for society's judgments to sweep in and answer these questions. Surely, those past judgements were wrong?

It has to happen to the best of us

We all have *something* wrong with us. As Zevon reminds us: sentimental hygiene—it's so hard to find it—and it's hard to keep from fallin' apart. Even when we know some shit's fucked up, it may be hard to evaluate relative to the whole—the whole person, the whole life, overall function. Consider, for instance, sporadic episodes within an overall life well-lived, a diseased kidney that brings down an otherwise extremely healthy person's overall level of health to the norm, or, like Zevon, hurling yourself against the wall in an attempt to avoid relapse. We may know how to evaluate the particular but not the whole. Are those individuals healthy despite a disease or disorder? Are those behaviors healthy in balance?

The complications regarding our attitudes toward health and disease are reflected in the life and lyrics of Warren Zevon. And our complicated attitudes toward assessing them in an overall relation to the whole may be reflected in how we think about Zevon himself: genius, cynic, sporadically violent in his early days, strong enough to master his demons, passionately lonely, and surprisingly sentimental. As Steven Hyden writes: "What listening to Warren Zevon songs tells you is that good and bad co-exist and remain present in us at all times, amid idealistic gestures that crash into daily disappointments. Then you wake up the next day hoping for another chance."[1]

[1] Rubin and Rubin would like to thank Larry Rubin and Rich Rubin for their good influence on our musical taste, as well as feedback on this chapter. Thanks also to Mike Schneider for comments.

10
Zevon and the Prigs

JOHN E. MACKINNON

In "Jackson Cage," Bruce Springsteen sings about a woman who returns home from work, only to draw the blinds against the ravages of the outside world. The song powerfully captures the tone and pitch of the woman's desperation. How can she ever find solace when trapped in this job, this routine, this town?

In "Sentimental Hygiene," Warren Zevon addresses the same issue of conflict in the public world, in particular the workplace, as well as our strenuous efforts to contain it and avoid harm. James Campion describes the song as among those "exclamations" of Zevon's about his own "turmoil and resurrection" (p. 139). I suspect this is true, but, whenever I hear the song, it's never Zevon, or any man, that I picture. No doubt because of the theme it shares with "Jackson Cage," it's always a woman I imagine, struggling to steady herself against the gales of interpersonal turmoil, just trying to get along.

Even with Neil Young on guitar, "Sentimental Hygiene" lacks the raw propulsion of "Jackson Cage." With its soft keyboards and therapeutic appeal, it's a California homage to Springsteen's harrowing Jersey jeremiad. Unlike "Jackson Cage," though, "Sentimental Hygiene" at least hints at a solution to the problems that beset the embattled citizen. As a matter of fact, sentimental hygiene itself is the proposed solution. But what exactly is it?

George Plasketes describes the title phrase as "unusual," C.M. Kushins as "ambiguous," and Campion as "wonderfully evocative." But Zevon himself isn't particularly helpful when it comes to illuminating that oddness or ambiguity, or elaborating what exactly makes it so evocative. According to Peter Gallagher, Zevon appears not to have given the question of meaning all that much thought, quoting his response to an interviewer's question that one of his tasks as a songwriter was "trying to think of interesting phrases," and "trying, whether deliberately or not, to make a lot of interpretations possible and a lot of meaning available" to listeners (p. 60). "Sentimental Hygiene," he added, was "one of those titles that just come to mind unbidden" (*Nothing's Bad Luck*, p. 228). Concerning the title of "Mohammed's Radio," George Gruel claims that Zevon simply "loved the sound of those two words together . . . the mellifluousness. That's it" (*Warren Zevon*, p. 30). Could "Sentimental Hygiene" be as arbitrary, as inconsequential?

In his contribution to this book, Heinrik Hellwig refers to how "coy" Zevon could be when it came to addressing questions about the significance of his titles and lyrics, describing how determined he was, for instance, to dispel the impression that "Boom Boom Mancini" was in any way socially conscious. Hellwig quotes Zevon's half-hearted explanation that the "main purpose" of the song was to sound like the Rolling Stones' "Start Me Up," that "Boom Boom Mancini" is simply "about saying the guy's name. None of it is very conscious." This isn't just being coy, but downright obstructionist. It hardly amounts to the stout defense of lovingly-wrought language that we would expect from him. Eventually, Zevon proved a bit more co-operative, agreeing that the song was about keeping your "feelings so clean you can eat off of them" (*Accidentally Like a Martyr*, p. 138). Beyond that, writes Kushins, "he kept his true inspiration to himself" (*Nothing's Bad Luck*, p. 228).

I hope to clarify the "true inspiration" behind Zevon's concept of "sentimental hygiene." Much of what I want to argue is that it's not just a title, nor just an appealing or evocative combination of words, but a concept of potential significance. In this respect, my intuition shares much with that of Jarkko Tuusvuori, who, in his chapter, elaborates what he calls the aphoristic element in Zevon's song-writing. In the same way that, according to John Gardner, simple "physical detail pulls us into a story," creating "a rich and vivid play in the mind," and that, according to Matthew Specktor, particular sentences can by themselves "pull the weight" of entire novels, so snatches of lyric and simple images often prove most powerful in the songs of Warren Zevon (Gardner, p. 30; Specktor, p. 133).

In the lyrics to "Sentimental Hygiene," it's not as if we're confronted by finely crafted poetry, and whatever drama is hinted at is muted by the promise of therapeutic intervention.

A tale is told, a problem identified, and a solution, however elusive, proposed. The title, however, and the concept that it picks out, invite commentary, of a sort far more robust than Zevon himself was willing to provide. How are we to make sense of it? To what interpretation of the concept are we entitled?

zevon politikon

When I urge that sentimental hygiene be recognized as a potentially significant concept, I have in mind its serving as a tool of political, or more broadly cultural, criticism, as a move within, or possibly even against, our political culture.

In his *Politics*, Aristotle famously characterizes man as *zoon politikon*, or, a "political animal," not in the sense that we are natural-born pamphleteers or door-to-door campaigners, but in the simpler sense that we are born into communities, and that our identity is therefore rooted in the network of connections we enjoy with and responsibilities we assume among our fellow citizens. Although other species are capable of collective action, human beings remain the paradigm case, excelling at cooperative behavior (Book I, Chapter 2).

What interests us is what we might call *zevon politikon*. What kind of political animal was Warren Zevon? At first, the possibility of answering this question may not seem all that auspicious, since Crystal Zevon insists that he "was not a political being" (p. 259). Concerning his participation in a series of "Save the Whales" benefit concerts in Japan in the 1970s, she insists that he "had no political commitment to the cause—nor any other cause, for that matter . . ." (p. 134). This verdict is hard to reconcile, however, with his obvious fluency in history and geopolitics, which Zach and Hannah Rubin so ably address in Chapter 8 of this volume.

Even if we manage to establish that Zevon had political commitments, though, it remains difficult to locate him on the political spectrum. There is, for instance, plenty of evidence of conservative sympathies in Zevon. To Crystal, he declared himself "to the right" of, not just her conservative father, but none other than Ronald Reagan, then proceeded to rage against one or another "Communist hippie" (p. 190). When a former girlfriend objected to dependably left-wing Hollywood actors presuming to address matters of national interest, his pleasure, she reports, was obvious (pp. 267–68). Later, at a show in Austin, Texas in 1983, when a member of Special Forces bluffed his way back stage to present Zevon with his Green Beret pin, Zevon wrote in his journal, "I was totally overwhelmed . . . I could barely talk." The soldier, he wrote, had given him "the greatest honor of my life" (p. 183). And to musician and composer Matt Cartsonis, who joined Zevon on his last couple of tours, he vehemently challenged those "pointy-headed bleeding hearts" who were campaigning to keep the Pledge of Allegiance out of public schools. "Tell that to the men who died defending your right to speak," he huffed (p. 386).

At the same time, Danny Goldberg reports how, when he told Zevon that Ann Coulter, the "flamboyant right-wing writer," had shown up at an event that he and his wife hosted, announcing that she was "a huge fan of Warren's," Zevon had "blanched," finding the anecdote "depressing" (p. 260). And it's well known that "Disorder in the House," his Grammy-winning duet with Springsteen on *The Wind*, was intended as an indictment of George W. Bush (p. 409). "If you asked five people what his political positions were," writes Crystal, "they would give you five different answers" (p. 259). It's rumored, she says, that he voted for Ross Perot; he told his friend Ryan Rayston that he was a Republican; and he played at the gubernatorial inaugural of Jesse Ventura, a Reform, then an Independent, candidate. But he also campaigned for then-Tennessee Senator, and current Congressman, Steve Cohen, accompanying him to the 2000 Democratic Convention.

It's probably most sensible to conclude that Zevon was a centrist, whose political passions turned, not on whatever party happened to endorse a particular view on a given issue, but on the issue itself. Billy Bob Thornton describes himself and Zevon as "moderate radicals" (*I'll Sleep when I'm Dead*, p. 259).

Granting that his songs "are all about fear," Zevon observed that there are nonetheless "things more insidious than violence," among which is what he calls "hypocritical optimism" (*Accidentally Like a Martyr*, p. 122). What makes an optimist hypocritical? Presumably, if his optimism isn't well-grounded, if it's thoughtless or conceals darker urges. Even though sentimental hygiene is presented in the song as a curative of sorts, a means of dulling life's hard edges, so that we can tame fear and cope more ably and cheerfully with life, it identifies, for Zevon, a potential threat. "If you looked up the word 'autonomy' in the dictionary," he quipped, "it would be a picture of me with a fishing cap on" (*Nothing's Bad Luck*, p. 293). But whether the autonomous individual wears a fishing cap or not, the sentimental hygienist is no ally. To see why, we have to reflect on very different song of Zevon's, "Life'll Kill Ya."

The Empire of the Ants

Whereas "Sentimental Hygiene" is a "big, bold beast of a song," according to Gallagher, "Life'll Kill Ya" is "surely popular music's most jaunty and delightful song about death," the title song on an album that Zevon himself insisted on calling "a folk record" (pp. 60, 92, 93). And yet, these two songs must be heard together. We can't understand what sentimental hygiene is without appreciating the wisdom of "Life'll Kill Ya."

As much as I warmly recommend Gallagher's book, a thoughtful and witty overview of the Zevon catalogue that's generous and admiring, without ever being fawning, he misses virtually everything that's important about "Life'll Kill Ya." He describes the line, "You've got an invalid haircut," for instance, as a "bizarre but undoubtedly cruel insult," and concludes that the lines, "It's the kingdom of the spiders / It's the empire of the ants," jointly refer to "a pair of ropey 'nature strikes back' sci-fi horror flicks," a "nod," he supposes, to William Shatner, who starred in *Kingdom of the Spiders*, but was also Zevon's boss when he composed the theme music for Shatner's *TekWar* (p. 93). But the significance of the reference is hardly so trite.

When Zevon refers to invalid haircuts and warns of a regime under which we have to register our nicknames, insults are the furthest thing from his mind. He's describing a society where regulation has run rampant, where the most personal and picayune of details are strenuously monitored, where control is so pervasive that you need a permit just to walk around town and a license to dance. When he likens this sort of society to a kingdom of spiders or an empire of ants, he intends to do far more than invoke frightening images or recall a couple of "ropey" sci-fi horror flicks. Spiders, like bureaucracies, entrap, just as ants, like captive, pliant citizens, swarm.

The image of ants and anthills has a noteworthy pedigree in the history of literature. In his *Essays from the Nick of Time*, Mark Slouka recalls his parents reading him Aesop's fable, "The Ant and the Grasshopper," in which the idle grasshopper plays his fiddle in the sun, while the ant industriously toils (p. 97). In *Prometheus Bound*, Aeschylus, whom Zevon described as his favorite author, describes human beings as "new gods," whose "privileges of honor" were assigned "in full complement" by Prometheus's gift of fire. Before receipt of that gift, however, they were "mindless" creatures, acting "without intelligence," incapable of mastering their wits. They had eyes, but couldn't see, and ears, "but heard not . . . They lived beneath the earth like swarming ants" (lines 439–457). And in *Notes from the Underground*, Dostoyevsky invokes the image to suggest the perils of a socially engineered utopia, where happiness of a sort is secured, but only at the expense of freedom. When a human being is treated like an ant or a cog in a machine, "a sort of piano key or a sprig in an organ," he is no doubt spared difficulty, his path smoothed over, but so too is his range of choice narrowed, his very nature impaired (p. 24).

Slouka reports that, as a child, he confounded both Aesop and his parents, since he "bore away the wrong moral" from the fable, favoring the free-spirited grasshopper to the obsessively dutiful and "perpetually busy" ant (*Essays in the Nick of Time*, pp. 97–98). And yet, in our time, Slouka laments, "the dominion of the ants has grown enormously," leaving us "less citizens than cursors, easily manipulated, vulnerable to the currents of power" (pp. 98, 100). It is in the dominion, or empire, of the ants where rules and regimentation prevail, where, in the interest of uniformity, order, and productivity, people are urged to maintain valid haircuts, register their nicknames, keep current their licenses to walk or dance, and to bear these impositions with contentment, their expressions frozen in a rictus of rectitude.

The New Puritans

In *The Uses of Disorder*, Richard Sennett addresses many of the issues that concern us here. The title of his book alone confirms Sennett's interest in how we contend with and respond to upheaval, or more, how we can manage to anticipate and avoid it. His analysis includes an examination of what he calls "the purification mechanism," the motive behind which is a "fear of losing control" (p. 98). Sennett finds evidence for this impulse in a fascinating array of cases, including those of Puritans, revolutionary leaders, young psychiatrists, and urban planners. Common to all of these is a determination on the part of individuals and communities to forge a "purified" or "absolute" identity that constitutes a "fearful defense against the unknown future," a "means of evading experiences that can be threatening, dislocating, or painful," leaving them in "a state of bondage to security," enslaved to "cowardly ideas of safety" (pp. 8, 9, 24, 34, 134, and 180). Hidden in this urge to purify, says Sennett, is a distinctly "conservative tendency," whereby the "known" in any given "scheme of identity" is so insistently taken to be true that those "unknowns" that don't fit are excluded (p. 10). What binds together these various groups amounts, he claims, to a "truly reactionary force" (p. 11).

According to Sennett, the "darker desires" that we harbor "for safe and secure slavery" have a common source, which he traces to the transition from adolescence to adulthood (pp. xvi–xvii, 30). Although horizons of possibility expand significantly during adolescence, so too does the interest of adolescents in "tactics of evasion," so they can avoid "unknown, painful experiences" (p. 13). Only this can explain their wariness of their own strength, their suspicion of what is "vital" and "messy," their pursuit of ideal men or women, rather than of loving, if flawed, real people, and their attempt to create for themselves an aura of "invulnerable, unemotional competence," a sort of "professionalized expertise" in the finer points of navigating the social world (pp. 13–15).

Resolving to steer clear of the new and unexpected, of whatever can't be controlled in advance, ensures that there can be no exploration, no tolerance of ambiguity, "and so no inner growth" (p. 15). In such circumstances, says Sennett, the "basis of community order is sameness," the consequences of which are, not just a studied avoidance of all possible pain and discomfort, but a reliance upon and eagerness to display outward signs of conformity, and an attendant commitment to the "repression of deviants," to expressing scorn for those who are different (pp. 41–44). In these ways, an otherwise enviable age of affluence, our very own latter-day anthill, manages to create successive generations of "adult puritans," who engage in self-repression, not for the greater glory of God, but out of fear "of the unknown, the uncontrolled" (p. 83).

Puritans or Prigs?

The opening section of *The Uses of Disorder*, which consumes roughly half of Sennett's book, is called "The New Puritanism," a label that, in the intervening decades, has appealed to a number of authors in their efforts to diagnose more recent manifestations of the pervasive human urge to avoid risk and control conduct, including expression. The Oxford political philosopher John Gray, for instance, writes that those with unhealthy habits "have been afforded no protection from the New Puritanism," which is inspired, "not by ideas of right and wrong, but by a weakness for prudence that expresses itself," specifically, in "an obsession with health and longevity" and, more generally, in the conviction that all human problems, rather than being "sorrows to be coped with or endured," can be solved (pp. 30, 28). Likewise, the historian Anne Applebaum describes as "New Puritans" those who, scornful of the liberal values of ambiguity, nuance, and tolerance of difference, mount on-line campaigns that are designed to "punish and purify" perceived moral transgressors. Allan Stratton has examined a recent instance of the very sort of campaign that Appelbaum has in mind, namely, the on-line mobbing of the comedian Dave Chapelle by a band of "umbraged souls" he calls "the New Puritans."

We naturally think of hygiene in relation to physical health, but as Sennett's account implies, and as these subsequent attacks on the New Puritanism confirm, it's a disturbingly elastic notion. Among the first to notice this was G.K. Chesterton, who, in *What's Wrong with the World*, characterized the effort to treat social and moral problems on the medical model as "the medical mistake" (p. 3). Just as, according to Sally Satel, the medical profession has become more deeply ideological, as its ranks have swelled with what she calls "indoctrinologists," so an increasing number of areas of public life have become "medicalized" (p. 59). Jeffrey Schaler notes how readily applicable to any human activity the metaphors of sickness and health are, and how, today, these metaphors are "increasingly used to extend the boundaries of public health" and "to legitimate the intrusion of governmental or private bureaucratic power into individuals' private lives" (p. 63). Schaler refers to this ideological obsession as "moral hygiene," the metaphor of which, he concedes, can prove "bewitching" (p. 64). Not only does "the ideology of moral hygiene" view health as "the supreme value," but moral behavior itself as "'healthy' or 'sick,'" so that "under the banner of moral hygiene, coercion for moral and religious motives is dressed up as coercion for public health reasons" (pp. 67, 68).

It's important, here, to acknowledge Marilynne Robinson's efforts to defend Puritanism against the common charge that this "highly elaborated moral, religious, intellectual, and political tradition" is somehow uniquely harsh, narrow, and intolerant (p. 150). Although she, too, wants to challenge the prevailing "hypertrophic instinct for consensus" and the round of denunciations in which it finds expression, she prefers to call the culprits, not puritans, but prigs (p. 153). Whereas the belief among Puritans that we're all sinners "gives us excellent grounds for forgiveness and self-forgiveness," writes Robinson, the modern rejection of sin strengthens the priggish view that social engineering and "intellectual eugenics" can produce a good society full of good people (p. 157). The first commitment in such a society, she says, is to weed out bad ideas and replace them with socially useful ones, then identify the bad people, especially those who are "carriers"—note the epidemiological metaphor—of bad ideas (p. 156).

In *Profession of Medicine*, Eliot Freidson observes that a society "so obsessed with physical and functional well-being as to be willing to sacrifice civil liberty and moral integrity" is likely to "press for a 'scientific' environment similar to that provided laying hens on progressive chicken farms," hens that "produce eggs industriously and have no disease or other cares" (quoted in Zola, p. 502). Freidson's hens are simply Dostoyevsky's ants, just as those who administer, and those others who accede to the demands of, such a regime are Sennett's New Puritans and Robinson's prigs. But they are also Zevon's hygienists. What remains for us to ask, then, is, what makes a hygienist sentimental?

The Second Tear

Any worthwhile human life, we assume, must be rich in sentiment. But sentiment is not the same as sentimentality. If sentiments are emotions, sentimentality is more a way of experiencing them. According to Anthony Savile, it is "properly seen as a mode of feeling or thought, not as a feeling of a particular kind" (p. 237). Displays of sentimentality are "always open to criticism," he adds, since the thought in which, say, grief or pity is grounded "will always be defective in some way…" (p. 337). For instance, it may be false, or it may well be true and yet lack evidentiary support. In either case, though, the sentimentalist will resist any correction of the thought, since his desire "is not a desire for truth and knowledge," but "something else," a kind of desire that can be satisfied only "by seeing the object in a false light" (p. 238).

If sentimentality is thought to misrepresent the world in some significant way, the sentimentalist himself is eager to do so, if only to generate and sustain certain feelings about himself. What he desires, Savile argues, is less "a gratifying feeling" than "a gratifying image of the self," which he is able to sustain through a fabricated, or at least falsely colored, emotion (p. 239).

One of the finest analyses of the concept of sentimentality is developed by Milan Kundera in his novel *The Unbearable Lightness of Being*. Sentimentality, or "kitsch," as Kundera prefers, is an aesthetic ideal that involves the "absolute denial" of the unpleasant. Kitsch, he says, "excludes everything from its purview" that it regards as "essentially unacceptable in human existence" (p. 248). Where kitsch is concerned, "the dictatorship of the heart reigns supreme," so that the mind's quibbles are dismissed, not simply as confused or mistaken, but as "indecent" (p. 250). That the feeling induced by kitsch is the kind that "multitudes can share" confirms its daunting political potential. It counts, in fact, as "the aesthetic ideal of all politicians and all political parties and movements." Whenever a single political party, movement, or set of attitudes prevails, to the point that it can count on going unchallenged, we are caught in the grips of what Kundera calls "totalitarian kitsch," a "world of grinning idiots," where all displays of individuality, expressions of doubt, and hints of irony are "banished" (pp. 251–53).

Later, Kundera declares that we "all need someone to look at us," and proceeds to identify four categories of people "according to the kind of look we wish to live under" (p. 269). Those in the first category long for "the look of an infinite number of anonymous eyes," the second for the look of "many known eyes," and the third for the look "of the person they love," while the fourth long to "live in the imaginary eyes of those who are not present" (pp. 269–270). What's striking about this overview is that it ignores a possible fifth category, one that otherwise proves vital to Kundera's account of kitsch, namely, those who long to be the object of their own attention, luxuriating in their own high self-regard.

Oscar Wilde memorably describes sentimentality as the urge to enjoy "the luxury of an emotion without paying the price for it," implying that what matters to the sentimentalist is not emotional investment, but display (p. 501). In this sense, the sentimental self is the performative self, which is why Savile emphasizes the sentimentalist's ultimate interest in sustaining a gratifying self-image. One of the most valuable aspects of Kundera's analysis is his elaboration of this idea. Sentimentality, or kitsch, he says, "causes two tears to flow in quick succession," the first as the heart swells in response to some stirring scene, while the second falls in response to that initial response, as if acknowledging how nice it is to be moved, to be the kind of person who is moved, together with all other suitably sensitive people. "It is the second tear," writes Kundera, "that makes kitsch kitsch" and the sentimentalist sentimental (Savile, p. 251).

According to Savile, "any emotion can on occasion be sentimentally entertained," for once we understand its "structure," it's clear that it need not be restricted to those emotions that are sweet and tender (p. 241). Although they're hardly pleasing, anger and indignation, jealousy and hatred count among those emotions, he says, that we can sentimentally indulge (pp. 239–240). But Macalester Bell is unconvinced. Precisely because sentimental responses are not just reflexive and self-sustained, but self-congratulatory, the idea of sentimental fear, for instance, seems incoherent. "It is difficult to imagine a case," she says, "in which one experienced one's fear in a reflexive and self-congratulatory manner" (p. 25). But if I'm right about Zevon's notion of sentimental hygiene, Bell's skepticism is unwarranted. In our current cultural condition, rather than projecting "an exaggerated vulnerability and innocence" on children and domestic pets, we project them on ourselves and each other (*The Test of Time*, p. 239). Sentimentality still serves its "protective function," not by filing down the world's "uncomfortable edges" in order to portray it as falsely reassuring, but by sharpening them in order to portray it as exaggeratedly fraught, steeped in untold sources of harm to which the model citizen can only respond with the obedient, self-congratulatory caution of a wheezing convalescent (p. 240).

Knowing and Naming Your Enemy

In his book *Doing and Deserving*, Joel Feinberg, citing the near-universal agreement among us about the proper working order of the human body, concludes that, "in general, our culture identifies bodily health with vigor and vitality." At the same time, he says, "we can imagine a society of mystics or ascetics who find vitality a kind of nervous distraction," even to the extent of coming to regard it "as a sickness," just as they regard "certain kinds of vapidity and feebleness" as signs of "exemplary health" (pp. 254-55). In the half-century since Feinberg wrote these words, we appear to have arrived at the very cultural condition that he intended to pose as an exotic, if not exactly wild, hypothesis. At issue here is no mere medical disagreement, but a conflict between radically different conceptions of value.

How should we describe a cultural moment where, as Feinberg predicted, vitality discomfits, vapidity and feebleness are celebrated as exemplary, and the prevailing order, like Sennett's New Puritans, "makes impotence a virtue"? (p. 83) Mark Wegierski christens such an order "the managerial-therapeutic state" (pp. 169, 173), since it aims, by means of a wide array of bureaucratic interventions, to "reconstruct collective consciousness," while Robinson prefers "the tyranny of petty coercion," since it manages to enforce, through the instruments of "aspersion and ridicule," enough like-mindedness in the population to "demoralize politics, debilitate candor, and disrupt thought" (*The Death of Adam*, pp. 256, 262, 263). Zevon shares these concerns. But while it's important in public life not just to know, but to name, your enemy, the fact remains that neither Wegierski's nor Robinson's label has stuck. Perhaps "sentimental hygiene" will.

V

The Songwriters'
Neighborhood

11

A Hard-Rocking Aphorist

Jarkko S. Tuusvuori

"He was a poet and a storyteller." This description of Warren Zevon, uttered by David Letterman, has reached the widest of audiences. The popular talk-show host was also a long-time fan who, in the artist's words, was "the best friend my music ever had."

But was Letterman right in ascribing that double identity to Zevon? His verdict makes sense, as long as we're happy to stress our high valuation of a life's work that's not as widely acclaimed as it deserves to be. Letterman no doubt wanted to broadcast the view that Zevon was no garden-variety minstrel boy or clueless pop star, but the real deal: he had something to say and the means to get it said. But Letterman's preferred epithets are too general, and even misleading, if we want to achieve a finer appreciation of Zevon's artistic output.

There are many others who are prepared to describe Zevon similarly. Take Gabino Iglesias, who emphasizes that Zevon "was a poet with a knack for using popular culture and his own imagination to craft songs." Or check out Jonah Raskin, who adds that Zevon "was an original poet with a vivid imagination who drew inspiration from newspaper headlines and from popular myths and legends."

Perhaps poetry is invoked here simply to establish that Zevon's lyrics can't be dismissed as boilerplate. He could do wonderful, unexpected, stirring things with language, but calling a lyricist lyrical hardly illuminates matters all that much. In any case, there are others, like Joni Mitchell or Patti Smith, whose writing overshadows Zevon's songs in this respect: their work even more convincingly bears the poetic stamp.

The same goes for that other category Letterman mentioned. Just as Iglesias attributes "lasting storytelling power" and Raskin "narrative power" to Zevon's work, so Hadley Freeman declares that it is "highly literate and based on storytelling." According to James Campion, Zevon's songs are "chapters in the great American novel" (p. xi). The headline of Zevon's obituary in *The Wall Street Journal* even read, "Song Noir Storyteller of Wit and Irony." But the overwhelming majority of Zevon's songs simply aren't stories, at least not in any straightforward sense. And there are better tellers of tales—for instance, Bruce Springsteen or Tom Waits—in the songwriters' neighborhood.

What makes philosophical inquiry critical is the art of carefully comparing the object of our concern with related phenomena, so that we can come to grips with whatever aspect accounts for its distinctive character. The Greeks had a word for this special thing, *eidopoios diaphora*, or, in Latin, to which Zevon himself sometimes resorted, *differentia specifica*. What, we want to ask, are the peculiar features of his songwriting?

To the Dramatic

Consider Bob Dylan. He is by far the most influential singer-songwriter on Earth, as well as the greatest inspiration to Zevon. What is less well known, though, is that Dylan is a great admirer of Zevon (and was perhaps nudged by him to pursue the hardboiled kind of writing typical of Dylan's mature work). In the BBC documentary *Getting to Dylan* (1987), he declared that his songs are not stories, since "my things are more like short attention span things." Dylan associated this with what, "in a group or a crowd of people," is "going down very quickly," so that the "normal eye wouldn't even notice it."

Although we should be wary of accepting uncritically what comes from the horse's mouth, the claim here is convincing. It really is better to treat Dylan's songs, not as poems or tales, but as dramatic pieces in which settings, scenes, characters, and dialogue steal the show. His mastery is displayed in drawing from the reserves of both popular and folk music, which abound in *personae* and bits of conversation. His songs are able to capture the excitement of interpersonal exchanges happening swiftly, the intensity of shifting constellations, and to capitalize on how, "In the dime stores and bus stations / People talk of situations."

Dylan's artistry helps us get beyond the two basic options identified by Letterman. Zevon certainly wrote songs with strong poetic, narrative, and dramatic elements to them. He was very accomplished at all of these. In an interview, Zevon remarked that "There's more of an exchange, a human exchange of ideas and feelings to be had at the bus stop than over the phone with your accountant" (Denberg intervew). This was his way of separating "issues of being rich and famous" from real life, adding that he was happy and lucky for having dodged overwhelming success and wealth. But his comment serves to illuminate his songwriting too.

The foremost reason for not treating Zevon's songs as primarily poetic is that he was so good at what is called the prosaic. No, "commonplace," "unexciting" and "unimaginative" do not work as synonyms here, although they're not totally out of place. Rather, without spurning humor, invention or bravado, Zevon's lyrics excel in their everyday sense of the real, to the extent that this outweighs those aspects of his work that approximate poetry. In any case, there are those other singer-songwriters who are more skilled at producing poem-like tracks.

The principal reason for not characterizing Zevon's songs as primarily narrative in nature is that he neither favors traditional (folk or country) styles of telling tales nor concentrates on delivering complete stories. Rather, he impresses with more situational creations, with dramatic facets standing out. Again, there are other songwriters who surpass Zevon as storytellers.

The chief reason for not regarding Zevon's songs as primarily dramatic is that, in them, he doesn't seem to foreground dialogue or habitually develop conflicts between people. And Dylan, at least, is a greater champion of drama.

The Aphoristic

We need a fourth alternative to make room for Zevon in the tower of song. And the aphoristic approach to songwriting is what emerges as his particular strength. I don't mean that Zevon's LPs resemble collections of winged sentences. This wouldn't be true any more than it would be to proclaim that Mitchell's songs are poems, Springsteen's songs are tales, or Dylan's songs are (scripts for) theatrical spectacles or movies. His compositions are and remain popular songs, and surely echo one another far more than they do specimens of those other art-forms. But whereas Smith, Waits and Dylan compose songs that, respectively, convey lyrical, narrative and dramatic force, Zevon's achievements distinguish themselves for their aphoristic strength.

He clearly inherited, or at least shared, Dylan's allegiance to the endless talk going on at coach stations and bus stops. Zevon seems especially to have taken to heart the power and role of the quick but weighty sayings that crop up in people's interactions in such settings. Proverbs contribute to "the social construction of meaning" as "discursive tools" used in arguing and entertaining, furnishing advice and establishing rapport, with important implications for both language acquisition and heightening metalinguistic awareness (Domínguez Barajas 2010). The above excerpt from Zevon's interview with Jody Denberg is itself an excellent aphorism concerning language as collective action.

The Beat poet Michael McClure drew a contrast between the "multilayered, multidimensional imagery" of mid-sixties Dylan and the stunning fact that his mature lyrics are "composed entirely of figures of speech" (Sounes, p. 415; Heylin, p. 733). This valuable insight should be further examined. I would say that, from the 1980s onwards, Dylan has indeed inclined toward the aphoristic, possibly under Zevon's influence, yet he retains the essentially dramatic style, while Zevon honed to perfection the art of concise expression. These might both have been fueled, in part, by writers like Raymond Chandler, who were able not only to narrate a complicated plot in a riveting fashion, but to conjure with a few words both memorable characters and definition-like crystallizations of people and things. Dylan and Zevon were also no strangers to philosophical nonfiction.

It shouldn't be too far-fetched to speak of epigrammatic style in the work of someone who has recorded albums entitled *My Ride's Here* and *Life'll Kill Ya,* or songs entitled "Even A Dog Can Shake Hands" and "You're A Whole Different Person When You're Scared." But how should we portray the manner in which such tracks are constructed? Moreover, can it really be said to apply to Zevon's whole enterprise?

We could have a long talk about what an aphorism is or what counts as aphoristic style. For example, the difference between folk proverbs passed by word of mouth, on the one hand, and learned sentences drawn from philosophical books, on the other, might be important. But let's not get into that. Popular songs cannot amount to anything terribly exclusive, since enjoyment of the medium itself requires no background education. Talking about aphoristic writing here can only refer to the habit of succinctly employing a variety of witty remarks as parts of songs. The crux of the matter is that, in Zevon, such elements seem to be the most significant units. This is magnified by the way his texts are sung, lines delivered, and stanzas phrased. It was always Zevon's long suit to be able, all at once, to sing and to say, to croon and to clinch. "I say it best musically, if I say it at all,"

Zevon once confessed. "Songwriting is designed for the inarticulate" (Read interview).

How do some of his best-known songs appear when considered from this angle? "I'll Sleep When I'm Dead" lends the most obvious support to my claim, since it certainly builds everything up for the zinger. "Lawyers, Guns, and Money" provides less direct, though still strong, evidence of the aphoristic by introducing a new catchphrase for being in a messy situation. The same could probably be said of "Poor, Poor, Pitiful Me" repurposing the conveniently terse psalmic line, "woe is me."

By contrast, "Werewolves of London" does not seem to support, and perhaps very nearly thwarts, the reading I am suggesting. The song patently attests to undergoing something wild, rather than articulating anything we might conclude from such experiences. "Werewolves of London" does, however, include the line, "I'd like to meet his tailor," which is a readymade phrase utilized in a way typical of Zevon. And the title line itself can be taken to coin, or rework, a concept for reckless and uncontrollable events taking place. In Zevon's case, "the aphoristic" is a term covering diverse instances. Oftentimes, his turns of phrase are smart and captivating enough to settle a given case at a blow, and yet keep the listener coming back for more.

The Beginnings

In the first monograph written about Zevon, George Plasketes states that his debut album, *Wanted Dead or Alive* (1969), already "revealed an abundant songwriting palette and lyrical depth that was sophisticated, intelligent, detailed, dark, romantic, poetic, psychological, geographical, historical, sly, and sardonic" (p. 37). Listening to the record may go a long way to refining our thoughts, not only about these and other moods of songs, but also specific modes for crafting them. We can, for instance, perceive how beautifully poetic "Tule's Song" is, or how "Traveling in the Lightning" begins by assuming the form of a story. "Gorilla," in turn, arrestingly exploits the nonsense *ad lib* typical of pop tunes, just as the borrowed song "Iko-Iko" does.

The track "She Quit Me" perhaps most nearly approaches the artistry Zevon would later come to know inside-out, since it relies on the potency of the stripped main clause, the impetus of unequivocal statement. Apart from somebody's having walked out on the narrator of the song, there is a more general lesson learned: life is like this, capricious, full of hazards, so that one of the few tangible first-hand discoveries we can make about reality is that it effectively resists our aspirations. This is apparent in the method of writing, since the idiomatic "up and do something" structure further enhances both the upsetting abruptness of the couple's break-up and the need to communicate nothing but the bare facts.

The title track, "Wanted, Dead or Alive," although not written by Zevon, is also important. A crucial spot in its lyrics is the phrase "they say," referring to common speech. We encounter this again in a number of Zevon's later compositions, including "Join Me in L.A.," on *Warren Zevon* (1976). One of the most notable qualities of that album, however, is that, in numerous songs, narrative prevails. "Frank and Jesse James" and "Mama Couldn't Be Persuaded" are largely stories. In the former, it's only the repetitive lines in the chorus and the culminating reassurance that the James brothers "do the best they could" that open the song up to other possibilities, while, in the latter, the cheeky meta-poetic jab, "If they heard this song, which I doubt they will," draws our attention to what the songwriter is doing (rather than to the incidents the singer is recounting and the issues he is addressing). Listeners conclude that there's something exciting in these tales, which may well be found in their dramatic dimensions.

The third song, "Backs Turned Looking Down the Path," contains the line, "Some may have and some may not," which appears to anticipate the character that would eventually emerge as distinctive of Zevon's writing. In "Hasten Down the Wind," the lyrical aspect comes to the fore again, yet this track, concluding with a conversation between lovers, inclines strongly toward the dramatic. On a still closer look, it combines downright banal or worn out (but no less real) clauses, like "nothing's working out the way they planned" and "keep him on the limb," that help propel the title line to its almost hyper-lyrical effects (and allude to "Red River Valley"). The same technique is found in "The French Inhaler," where the narrator enumerates the shortcomings of its main character (who isn't "cut out for working," "just can't concentrate," and "always shows up late"), thereby demonstrating how everyday expressions can gain a new vigor when transformed into parts of a song and, in this case, joined with the surprising title.

"Carmelita" has an obvious poetic allure, but what's all the more striking about it is the blatantly unpoetic declaration, "I'm all strung out on heroin," along with the verse, "The county won't give me no more methadone / And they cut off your welfare check." Beautiful love songs can apparently be constructed in a plain style. The album's other heartbreaking ballad, and Letterman's favorite, "Desperados under the Eaves," starts off story-like, but is soon a full-blown drama, amplified by a vision of the Golden State falling into the Pacific. All of a sudden, the adage, "Except in dreams you're never really free," is incorporated, accompanied by "Heaven help the one who leaves." And the three "don't the X look Y" lines allude to the second verse of Dylan's aphoristically named, "It Takes a Lot to Laugh, It Takes a Train to Cry."

From at least this album on, Zevon's predilection for expressly aphoristic writing comes through. He can be poetic and dramatic, and he knows how to tell a story, but he seems to prefer good one-liners, being most comfortable with, but also cunning about, set phrases and introducing more or less novel sayings in order to formulate a point or determine the nature of things. He trusts that it's perfectly fine to spit out just a few words at a time to cover big issues or events, throw in quotations and unusual combinations for atmospheric purposes, to color a whole song, while drawing attention to how he delivers the momentous line. This is a talent he developed early.

Excitable Boy (1978) opens with "Johnny Strikes Up the Band," which sounds like the most harmless rock song ever. Still, it boasts the sort of features that we associate with a cultivated songwriter. In the verses, we find a commercial tagline ("guaranteed to please"), a high-literature allusion to Ben Jonson ("keeper of the keys"), and an eloquent yet humorous phrase ("jubilation in the land"). Zevon rehearses the so-called literary style, which we might think too fine for ordinary contexts, except that he manages to integrate the literary into day-to-day, often shabby or shady settings, where it embraces vulgarity. This could perhaps be regarded as a popular song's searching for its limits.

In "Roland the Headless Thompson Gunner," which includes a rundown of the exploits of quite a noteworthy character with comic-book vibrations, the story-mode triumphs, as it does in the title track. And yet, "Excitable Boy" centers not on the youth himself, but on those who talk about him. And the star of the song is the refrain, "'Excitable boy,' they all said." The verses serve to illustrate the definition of the word "excitable," as "capable of the being readily roused to action," or "easily influenced, changed, and damaged." Both songs, though quite different, lean on the dramatic, but with a twist.

In "Accidentally Like a Martyr," we once more find an allusion to Dylan, who would add off-hand adverbs to his song titles. The difference is that he never actually sings any of those words, whereas Zevon puts a lot of weight on singing *ac-ci-dent-'ly*. The track climaxes in the aphorism, "the hurt gets worse and the heart gets harder."

Searching High and Low

Zevon once advised that the trick in his line of work is, first, to recognize that "all those songs you've written have probably got a couple good lines in 'em." The next thing to do is to "throw out everything but those and start over," and then to "build those up on a couple of songs" (Reid interview). Two brilliant examples are "Searching for a Heart" and "Fistful of Rain," both of which exploit noted literary bits, thereby greatly enhancing the songs' weight and memorability.

In the former, "love conquers all" is drawn from Robert Browning's tragedy *A Blot in the 'Scutcheon* (1843), the same line that George Barlow's poem "Love's Victory" (1890) quoted a hundred years before Zevon. Whether the American himself had either of these English authors' works in mind when composing his piece is irrelevant. What matters is that they furnish the subtext of his lyrics. That Zevon prefaces the citation with "they say," suggests that he doesn't want to take all the credit: his proficiency is not in exploring some fantasized *terra incognita*, but in arranging or synthesizing the legacy of writers before him, which may indeed be as searching as ever. And he keeps it all conversational and approachable.

We could even say that the introductory part of his line suggests a meta-level of meaning. While "X conquers everything" is at least structurally a simple phrase about the power of X, placing "they say" before it shifts it into a double construction, where certainty or conviction is converted into something more like an allegation, an inference, or hearsay. It's like the neighbors whispering about the excitable boy. The words serve to mark Zevon's awareness of the fact that he is recycling a notion set down by someone else, thereby making us aware, in turn, that he is taking advantage of available formulations, rather than creating everything from scratch.

In "Searching for a Heart," the line appropriated from the literary archives precedes an original, and decidedly twentieth-century, one that asserts, "you can't start it like a car / you can't stop it with a gun." This tendency to mix the strikingly novel with the historically entrenched is precisely Zevon's original take on his chosen artform.

"Fistful of Rain" also draws from Browning. "Ah, but a man's reach should exceed his grasp," the Londoner wrote in the poem "Andrea del Sarto" (1855). The standard interpretation of the remark is that we ought to strive even for the unattainable, because such an endeavor brings out the best in us. "When your grasp has exceeded your reach," Zevon sings, spinning the line to fit not only the bitter monologue of one Renaissance painter, as in Browning, but also the sentiments of his compatriots, contending with the American nightmare. He goes on to sing: "and you put all your faith / in a figure of speech." This is a paraphrase of the refrain's "grabbing a hold of" water droplets. All these lines refer to the dangers of empty rhetoric (of, say, demagogues) and hollow exhortations (of, say, life-coaches), while at the same time affirming Zevon's credentials as a true believer in figures of speech. This representatively poetic number embraces the aphoristic, both in its use of a time-honored phrase and its ability to cause us to reflect upon and analyze its nature.

The majority of aphoristic instances in Zevon's writing differ from these two. When he sings, "Life is fragile, we are frail," in the song "Bujumbura," the line carries evident literary overtones, even though it lacks an exact historical source. On the subject of human vulnerability, a line like "Most accidents happen at home" is more distinctly Zevonian in its witticism, and, whether he knew it or not, had also been featured in a book, namely, Harold Q. Masur's pulp fiction detective story *Make a Killing* (1964). Overall, his aphorisms sound less literary and more streetwise. Consider the following nine excerpts:

> "I'd rather feel bad than not feel anything at all"

> "Love can cut right through your heart"

> "The name of the game is be hit and hit back"

> "Only the dead get off scot-free"

> "Life is cheap and death is free"

> "The rich folks suffer like the rest of us"

> "Everybody needs a place to stand / And a method for their schemes and scams"

> "Nothing matters much but love and money"

> "When you're living in a four-letter world"

This is a handsome selection of perceived truths. Still another set of cases might be termed semi-aphoristic elucidations or other apposite one-liners. We'd have the likes of "You buy everything you want and then you want more," which expresses, simultaneously, a local truth about a given situation and a more general picture of an entire way of life.

Finally, there are certain idiomatic expressions that, when fused into song lyrics, verge on the aphoristic. While "Trying to run before she can walk" might well be included in the previous group, "like father, like son" exemplifies a common phrase elevated by Zevon to a passage in a suspense thriller or tragedy. In songs like "Finishing Touches" and "For My Next Trick I'll Need a Volunteer," this type of *objet trouvé* is used inventively, like a pun.

Ultimately, classifications are not all that pivotal here. What counts is that, in his songwriting, Zevon put his faith in aphorisms in a variety of ways. More often than not, he deploys worn-out sayings to set the stage for one that is fresh. It's central to his art that Zevon didn't shy away from trusting clichés. As evidence of his appetite for the aphoristic, he experimented with how even they could indirectly heighten the force of his lyrics and the pungency of his songs by preserving their credibility and inclusiveness.

Living Aphorisms

Of the four types of songwriting, it is the aphoristic mode that is most amenable for philosophical purposes. Yes, Voltaire wrote blazing satire, Sartre composed several plays and novels, and Chekhov, Dostoevsky, and Tolstoy churned out powerful prose that is routinely accepted as philosophy. In any case, academic journal articles and book-length treatises aside, aphorism is most commonly associated with wisdom, as an especially effective means of conveying important thoughts that we have inherited from the greatest luminaries.

"Philosophy in the West starts with the fragment or the aphorism," Guy Elgat reminds us. The surviving splinters of the tracts written by the Pre-Socratics "expressed in an oracular fashion their insights about the cosmos and human life that opened the space for all subsequent philosophical thinking." When early modern thinkers, such as Bacon, Pascal and Lichtenberg, adopted similar literary means, they seemed to exercise the freedom of this form to impress their readers. As for the first truly modern philosophers, like the two Friedrichs, Schlegel and Nietzsche, it was more about reflecting in their writing the newly found "snapshot, disjointed character of reality." In Elgat's view, since the aphoristic approach is anti-systematic, it amounts to an "experimental and provisional" way of thinking, where trial-and-error is the key. The "particular voice of the author" becomes decisive, while the mode itself also "engages the critical capacities of the reader."

In the words of poet Irving Layton, an aphorism ought to "be / like a burr: / sting, / stick, / and leave / a little soreness / afterwards." In short, it should be both catchy and scratchy. It needs to be strong and memorable enough for the reader or listener to undergo a change that is not necessarily all that congenial, but amounts to an education of sorts. According to Kostas Boyiopoulos and Michael Shallcross, "modernity is, itself, constructed upon aphoristic premises." This is precisely what their co-edited anthology, *Aphoristic Modernity*, seeks to outline, while at the same time trying to do justice to both the long history of aphoristic expression and the claim that it somehow characterizes the "fractured and fragmented experience" of our present condition (Sandy, p. 37).

Kierkegaard's *Either/Or* already equates "living aphoristically" with the modern predicament. Searching in vain for contact and association, we're doomed to be atomistic "aphorisms in life." Renowned for his writing so many songs about loneliness and mortality, Zevon carries the Kierkegaardian torch forward. The funny but chilling idea of us moderns as walking aphorisms strikes an echo in many of his songs, most unmistakably "Empty Hearted Town."

It would be too facile to assume that Zevon preferred aphorisms in order either to highlight the claim that our contemporary human reality is curiously, perhaps disturbingly, shattered or to concede that this is all he can do, given his own status as a late-modern artist. It's much more likely that he simply enjoyed close-to-the-bone one-liners and was skillful enough to develop his musicianship by pursuing this very enthusiasm. These literary means make it possible to comment upon, or conclude on the basis of, the language that precedes them, thereby altering the way the rest of the song is received.

Aphorisms could presumably be seen as a poetic, narrative or dramatic device that allows, respectively, the lyricist, storyteller or playwright-type of songwriter to move from one line in her tune to the next. Zevon's take on words of wisdom suggests a more intrinsic value: they stand almost freely in his songs, and serve as the focus for all eyes and ears, while vouching for, and even electrifying, the more forgettable lines.

"Remarks" were Wittgenstein's chosen mode of philosophical writing. He's known to have cherished early on the notion of a book "honest" enough to contain "a record of separate mental events" or an "extremely compact presentation" of what has "occurred," with no amendments or distortions, all diligently jotted down by the author. On the other hand, his later thinking is full of discussions about how a given simple utterance functions in human discourse as an act, the meaning of which is to be found in its use. Perhaps he envisioned a text that would consist of a full catalogue of descriptions of somebody doing this and saying that in such-and-such circumstances, while at the same time registering thoughts, feelings and urges before and after each deed and utterance. It's safe to assume that several modern or postmodern novelists—though presumably far fewer autobiographers—have tried something like this, yet Wittgenstein himself held fast to his pattern of relatively short and more or less discrete or independent notes.

As with Wittgenstein's favored genre, Zevon's served him well. It's hard to imagine how he would sound if he weren't intelligent and amusing. Rather than coming across as someone who is determined to avoid torturing us with unnecessary blather, he appears to have concluded that his appetite for pithiness resonates with much in our philosophical and literary traditions in general, and in the world of popular song in particular. In a late interview, Zevon cut right through the murky spheres of inspiration:

> Generally, songwriting starts with lyrics. It starts with some kind of weird phrase. The creative process is sort of goofy and mysterious and impossible to explain, and if it's not those things, it's something else, it isn't the creative process. That's the craft we spend our lives learning. That's the technique we learn to figure out what to do with those wacky ideas. (Read Interview)

Recognizing the centrality of the aphoristic helps us bring form and content together. Zevon's approach was fruitful for ruminating on themes such as isolation, splendid and not so splendid, urban, late-modern and perennial. That he operated aphoristically shouldn't be taken to indicate a preference for a lofty or austere style: just as, for all his dedication to stock phrases, he wasn't phraseological, so his view that songwriting wasn't in constant need of more words is not about celebrating scarcity or the primacy of the parsimonious. He did seem to enjoy almost every sandwich, with a penchant for pursuing all kinds of sidetracks and adding touches of lyrical grace notes.

Very rarely did Zevon simply rehash platitudes, but instead found ways to revitalize old materials and accommodate in his songs a wide spectrum of tones and hints. And for all the rage and mockery expressed in many of them, his brand of life-philosophy is far more placid than grim, because it breathes such understanding, humor and even moderation. We may be all alone in this world, but our lives both depend on, and are enriched by, those of others, and it would help if, as living aphorisms, we learned how to walk and talk with each other with a clearer sense of reality. Sweetness is no less a trait of the real than bleakness.

Hostage-O

"We do not think with a part of ourselves," writes L. Susan Stebbing. I've always found this statement both intellectually appealing and experientially true. Her subsequent remark, however, is more difficult to digest. "Our thinking," she says, "involves our whole personality." To me, this involves far too much psychologizing, and so is a tad disappointing. But I've come to conclude that "personality," here, refers to our situation at large, to the way the world passes through us, offering a vast array of alternative views and materials that serve as the basis for all kinds of possible conceptions. After all, it was Stebbing's mission to advance critical thinking by preparing us for different "prejudices which are an effective bar to thinking," in order that we be able to deal intelligently with our problems, personal and social (pp.18 and 31).

Zevon's contributions to this cause are remarkable, though typically reversed or roundabout. His "Disorder in the House" refers to a state where "the less you know, the better off you'll be," which I'm confident has already prompted many to know a lot more. As Elgat claims, aphoristic writing awakens our critical dispositions. In the world of popular music, this involves a markedly social setting. The art of critical thinking is a general one, thriving in long-term practices and participatory activities, and proving absolutely vital for democracies that depend on enlightened citizens. And yet, we're probably all in need of individual voices to interrupt our dogmatic slumber.

William James once described Walt Whitman as being committed to material that was within anybody's reach. Explaining the poet's devotion to the grassroots, he claimed that Whitman "abolishes the usual human distinctions, brings all conventionalisms into solution, and loves and celebrates hardly any human attributes save those elementary ones common to all members of the race." This applies to Zevon as well, albeit with important qualifications. Like the lone pioneer Whitman, popular musicians today feel "the human crowd as rapturously as Wordsworth felt the mountains, as an overpoweringly significant presence" ("On a Certain Blindness in Human Beings," p. 26).

Zevon celebrates common, elemental things, not by dissolving conventionalisms, but, rather, by making the most of them. In this way, he is a true popular artist, because he takes seriously the concept of "the popular," as that which concerns the general public, without dumbing it all down. What is familiar shakes hands with any number of oddities and curiosities, "weird phrases" and "wacky ideas," shifting angles, poses and lightings, with impressive results. His artistry or handiwork reflects an ability to come up with rewarding new insights that are apt to enlarge listeners' horizons. When popular music took him hostage, we got lucky.

There is nothing wrong in commending him as a poet or a storyteller. For example, if the aim is to tell his life story, his songs may indeed be routinely referred to as tales, narratives, or "poetic journal entries" (*Nothing's Bad Luck*, p. 251). But should we try to catch the *differentia specifica* of those songs, we must be resolutely discerning and attentive to fitting comparisons.

Make no mistake, not every track by Zevon is a fine display of wit. "Jungle Work" borders on stupidity. "Down in the Mall" is a run-of-the-mill satire, suggesting very little of the refined selection we expect from Zevon. And of the most evidently aphoristic numbers, "Never Too Late for Love" includes the power line "everybody hurts"—predating the R.E.M. hit by a full decade—but quickly deteriorates into the most insipid litany of self-help tips ("try to let the past slip away," "live for today," "don't stop believing in tomorrow" . . .). Successful Zevon compositions may occasionally rely on trite, overused sayings, and yet, given the uncommon depth and breadth of his artistic commitments, avoid becoming uninteresting.

His love songs are a case in point, since they achieve prowess even when his lyrics remain highly accessible. But Zevon upped the ante by calling songwriting itself an act of love, since it's about passing on a fascination with something that caused the song to be composed in the first place. Or, as he also said, we can acquire certain interests (from who knows where), which then begin to develop on their own (Read Interview). Public artworks, such as first-rate popular songs, transform those interests into everyone's concerns.

According to Iris Murdoch, the essence of both morals and art is love, understood as "the extremely difficult realization that something other than oneself is real." By openly betting on recovered material, Zevon never lets us forget that he sees us as emerging from social interplay and being forever in the hands of one another. When Murdoch writes that "love, and so art and morals, is the discovery of reality," she speaks at once for Zevon, that American virtuoso of concise, weighty sayings (p. 51).

12

Warren Zevon and the Sonic Death-Punch

ROSS CHANNING REED

There is not one Warren Zevon album that does not have at least one song about death, and in almost every instance, the subject is masked in dark humor . . . Zevon chose time and again to at the very least chuckle at the existential enormity of nonexistence.

—JAMES CAMPION, *Accidentally Like a Martyr*

Back in the mid-Eighties, between stints in grad school, I worked for a southern rock band out of Baltimore. Every night between sets—and I mean *every* night—the sound engineer would play Warren Zevon's album *Excitable Boy*. From "Johnny Strikes Up the Band" to "Lawyers, Guns, and Money," I knew every song by heart. Who the heck could forget "Werewolves of London"? Being a musician and philosopher myself, I recognized a kindred spirit, and I spent a lot of time thinking about the music, the lyrics, and the guy behind both.

Nobody would ever confuse Warren Zevon with Elton John. Or would they? Zevon is paradoxically unique, yet camouflaged. There is always something evanescent about him. He's a stand-up comic who uses music as his foil. He's a sonic magician who uses lyrics as his trick. This guy is dark, weird, humorous, sardonic, perceptive, sensitive and, did I mention, dark? He observes the human condition from a perspective that is both detached and poignant—an extraordinary combination that is indeed rare to behold. His work categorically articulates what is generally left unsaid. He sees through the graft and gimmicks and glamour of life. Warren Zevon, in short, is the existential troubadour.

Like most existential troubadours—particularly those with a penchant for gonzo literature—Zevon's life was a crisis-in-progress. Just listen to the music and it's right there, up close. And that's evident even when he's writing about gorillas and werewolves and headless Thompson gunners doing unspeakable things in exotic places. It seems that he never lets a crisis go to waste. Thus, a significant body of work.

I went to Sweden in 1989 and there was Zevon on his solo world tour. Solo world tour? That in itself sounds like enough to spawn an existential crisis. Nothing like playing "Splendid Isolation" to a packed house.

Back in the States in the early 1990s, I managed to see Zevon in concert a few times, the last of which was at the Village Night Club in Lancaster, Pennsylvania. Zevon was again on a solo tour. While the place might be (yes, it *is* still there) big by Lancaster standards, let's just call it intimate. He played grand piano and amplified acoustic six- and twelve-string guitars (not at the same time). And it was a solo tour, all right. Just him up there. I was able to get close, real close, to the man himself. And he looked just like he did in the photos. Cynical, sad, maybe, lonely––who knows?—and intense. He peered out from behind those round wire-rims, cigarette smoke wafting across his visage. *Splendid Isolation . . . I don't need no one . . .*

Sure, this is just a character, a persona, I thought. He's a performer. But being a performer and philosopher myself, I noticed something else. A clandestine presence, a translucent transparency, a visionary transcendence. Jean-Paul Sartre with a sense of humor? Really, the more I stared at him and the more he stared past me, the more I realized that I just couldn't think of *anyone else anywhere* like Warren Zevon. He was articulating in no uncertain terms the existential crisis of our age, but he was doing it in translation, with a saturnine style *and* a trace of levity. It was gallows humor through and through. The hopelessness. The desperation. The fatalistic, almost sadistic take on the hopelessness and desperation. Yet, the glint of a moral compass shone forth from beneath the façade. The voice of a prophet, crying aloud from the wilderness?

What wilderness, you ask? The wilderness of Los Angeles, California? Sure, L.A. exudes its own beau-monde barbarity, astutely captured by the prophet. But ultimately the place of which the prophet spoke was darker, more macabre. I peered back at the unshaven poker-faced figure and listened. Up there on stage, alone, Zevon was staring down his—and our—mortality—and the sense of meaninglessness that can metastasize from the realization that everything you've ever loved is going to die.

Splendid Isolation . . .

Reflective Transcendence

That's always been his humor, you know . . . death has been a pervasive theme in everything that he's ever done.

—READ interview

Zevon's hallmark is reflective transcendence. You can see it; you can feel it. You can *hear* it. Wherever he is, he's there, and he isn't there. He's simultaneously laughing and serious. He's giving life the finger *and* he's diving in. There is something palpably inescapable about the fact that it's his nature to escape. Why would he want to escape unless he didn't quite feel comfortable? How could he feel comfortable when he's fully aware that at some point, whether he likes it or not, he's going to be forced to leave?

The concert's going to be over, the after-party's going to disband, and he's going to be left to his own devices to face his very imminent demise. The problem for Zevon is that he's facing his own very imminent demise *during* the concert, *during* the afterparty. He can't get away from it. He transcends the scene, whatever the scene, and goes beyond, beyond to his own nonexistence. And who the hell wants to think about that all the time?

Transcendence is all about being there and not being there. It's about being rooted in the here and now, in time and space, but somehow going beyond, rising above, seeing through. It's flying above the housetops, above the trees, way up into the sky, and looking down, carefully surveying all that is before you. It's recon, man. And to do that, you've got to step back, get away, keep your distance. You're on the lookout for the next best thing. Or the next worst thing.

Yeah, it's recon. And in Zevon's case, involuntary recon. If you think the age of the prophets is over, just listen to the music.

What's worse—or better—than life? Death? Or is it the other way around? When you check out Zevon's body of work, you might just be left with one big question mark. That's what makes him a philosopher too—that question mark. It permeates all of his writing. So, it's no wonder he's such a magnetic character. Isn't *philosopher* right up there with *rock star*?

It's not like Zevon is taken in by any of it. His jaundiced eye surveys all, Don Quixote and his windmills, Ponce de Leon, who took his cruise, and Sinbad, who needed seven voyages to see it was all a ruse.

Zevon gazes into, through, and beyond what appears on the surface. It's a metaphysical thing. If that's how you roll, you'd better get creative. Or suffer from major depression. You've got to work with that transcendence. Ironically, you've got to *go beyond*. So, how the hell do you do that? This might be *the* question of the ages. A popular route is to drink and take drugs. Yes, Warren did all that. And he did it in an epic way. Like most, he found that, in the end, drinking and drugs didn't really help him deal with the blessing and curse of transcendence.

It's in taking a point of view on his own transcendence—as a songwriter and performer—that he finds his voice. Through his voice, he shares his healing powers with us. He gives us the momentary ability to rise above the quotidian, the everydayness of everyday life. Every good rock song shares a dream. And we believe that dream, if only for three minutes and fifteen seconds.

Transcendence is the quintessential aspect of art. It's the reason we gaze at an artist's representation of a flower or a landscape or a person even longer than we gaze at the thing itself. The allure, the appeal, the inestimable value of a work is its ability to transport us *somewhere else*. And so, we recognize the inestimable value of the work of Warren Zevon. He's already *somewhere else*, one foot in the transcendental world, beckoning us to come along. Every good song invites us to take a journey. The listening is the journey itself. The voice, the six-string, the twelve-string, the piano, lead us as a Sherpa guide up the mountain and into the heavens. As the air thins, we trust the voice.

Reflection is a form of transcendence, if not its original form. It's a stepping back from your stream of consciousness and occupying a point of view on that stream of consciousness. In a Buddhist tradition, this may involve absence of judgment. But for mere mortals, stillness may only be possible on the other side of art. As an artist, Zevon rises above, describes the lay of the land, the universal aspects of consciousness, the opacity of his own psyche. He reflects his way from beginning to end, from birth—to death. One may have the capacity to reflect one's way *to* one's mortality, one's own imminent demise, but what can it mean to *understand* it?

This confrontation with absence is a presence in Zevon's work from beginning to end. Imbued with absence, he sings the wistful song of one who knows of the impermanence of all things, an impermanence grounded in a permanence that is as timeless as the music itself. Antoine Roquentin, the protagonist in Sartre's novel *Nausea*, has this very feeling while sitting in a café listening to jazz on a gramophone. He experiences the jazz as fleeting and absent, while also timeless and present. The music rings out, and is gone. The performance is everything. The recording itself is ungraspable; it transcends even the artist. So too the flower of the field.

And so it is with life itself. When you think your way to the end, you might be hard pressed to figure out what to do in the meantime. Warren Zevon sounds like a man who has thought his way to the end, and then thought his way back to tell us—in a singular, oblique, often dolorous manner—all about it. And he does it in a concentrated, distilled way—like every good musician—in a pungent, short, couple-hundred-word song—and that includes plenty of repetition. Like life, every song has a refrain, a meandering bass line, harmonic and melodic motion. Then, there is always that sonic undercurrent. Most of us don't want to face our mistakes, our sins, our wasted time. It is all too painful, laced with loss and regret.

But then you keep listening, like a gawker at the sight of a gruesome accident. You can't turn away. The tenor of Zevon's baritone exudes a wistfulness and wisdom that traverses your internal topography, following the vagus nerve from the mind, through the heart, and right down into the viscera. The listening becomes an offering to the ancient, implacable gods of antiquity, an obeisance to the Earth from which all things come and to which all things return. The weeping is held in abeyance as the chords progress from tonic to dominant and, finally, back to tonic.

You find yourself singing along. In the midst of suffering and confusion, there is an ontological calm. The cyclical harmonic progression contravenes the lyrical heart of chaos. The circle of fifths articulates the natural order of things, an order that even Arnold Schoenberg and the like failed to upend. Dissonance can no more be emancipated than the cycle of nature can be replaced by the linearity of Western logic. In a quantum world, not even chaos and order are necessarily antithetical. And so you keep listening.

Salvific Tonality

He who fights with monsters should be careful lest he thereby become a monster. And if thou gaze long into an abyss, the abyss will also gaze into thee.

—FRIEDRICH NIETZSCHE, *Beyond Good and Evil*, Aphorism 146.

Darkness forever forms the backdrop for all that is luminous. Between the ages of thirteen and fifteen, Zevon had the rare opportunity to have a series of talks with the aging classical composer Igor Stravinsky. Stravinsky had already traveled to the edge of the tonal precipice, utilizing extended compositional techniques that included bitonality, polytonality, polyvalence, and polymetricality. His illumination of being played at the edges of darkness, hovering over the abyss. Zevon listened, but with the exception of a few compositions—particularly in string arrangements like those found in "Genius," "Interlude #1" and "Interlude #2," and the short piano solos on "Calcutta" and "The Long Arm of the Law"—did not venture beyond functional, tonal harmony. Why?

First, let's address a few obvious questions. What is tonality? What is functional harmony? Here's a thumbnail sketch. If you need to skip a couple of paragraphs, these might be the ones.

Western music theory begins thousands of years ago with Greek modes. Modes are essentially scales—a series of pitches going from one octave to another—that constitute the foundation for musical compositions. Pythagoras, circa 570–495 B.C.E., was the first important musical theorist to note the *mathematical nature of harmony*, or, the relations between pitches.

Mathematically based theory continued to evolve through the Medieval, Renaissance, Baroque, and Classical eras to develop a series of major and minor scales, each scale beginning and ending on the tonic note or "home" pitch. Knowledge of the mathematical relations between notes allows for the construction of musical instruments—if a string is halved, the plucked note will sound one octave higher, and so forth.

With a home pitch and a scale, *functional harmony* could develop, which simply means that a composer could utilize various techniques for traveling away from the home center—creating tension—and traveling back to the home center, releasing tension. The *progression* or movement of chords, therefore, "makes sense," so to speak. Harmony is said to be functional because the tension and the release of tension create *motion* in a composition. Tension creates interest, but at the same time feels like a temporary suspension that needs to go somewhere, much like going on a vacation. Everything is bright and different and new and exciting, and you may like it very much, but after a while, you're ready to go home. Back at home, the piece "resolves" on the tonic pitch or chord. Music that has a tonic pitch or chord from which one can travel and to which one can return is said to be *tonal music*.

Stravinsky challenged tonality and pushed the boundaries of functional harmony in ways that Warren Zevon did not. Perhaps this is why Zevon was unable to complete the symphony he so wanted to write. He carried his uncompleted symphony around with him for years.

There may be many reasons why Zevon did not *challenge* the tonal structure of music, but instead invested his *challenge* into the lyrical content of his songs. The most obvious reason is that he wrote in the pop-rock-folk idiom, so he remained tonal for commercial reasons. Even the commercial viability of much of his lyrical content has been mixed. Nevertheless, his sustained critique of the emptiness and violence of post-modernity is cogent and compelling. This lyrical challenge, if combined with a sonic challenge, would have undoubtedly relegated Zevon to somewhere between obscurity and invisibility. As Sun Ra was to jazz, Warren Zevon would have been to pop-rock-folk. American composer and pianist Sun Ra (1914–1993) led a working band for decades and recorded over a hundred albums. Sun Ra? Exactly. The prolific invisibility of Sun Ra makes Warren Zevon appear . . . popular.

But then, of course, there's also the example of the heralded American composer, musician, and bandleader Frank Zappa (1940–1993). Zappa found critical acclaim, and a significant measure of commercial success, while challenging the gamut of musical and lyrical conventions, although, unlike Zevon, Zappa relied heavily on scatological and salacious humor. Zevon and Zappa in concert? It never happened, so one can only speculate. Love, sex, death—and feces? It would have been an explosive combination. But this is an aside. We'll leave that to the spinners of alternate histories. Let's continue our exploration.

A second possible reason why Zevon didn't push the boundaries of tonality is that he simply didn't have the training, interest, mental acuity, or aptitude to challenge the tonal structure of Western music. Based on the available evidence—his extant compositions, his own words, and the observations of those who knew him best—I am inclined to rule this out without further discussion. Zevon himself has written that he "was writing avant-garde symphonic music by thirteen." Zevon's friend and early manager Chris "Kit" Crawford remembers that when Warren was young he "was always working on some kind of twelve-tone [atonal] or serial [atonal] music inspired by Stockhausen or Bartók" (*I'll Sleep When I'm Dead*, pp. 23, 25). Many others have weighed in on Zevon's training, aptitude, and skills, offering similar observations and drawing similar conclusions.

So where are these avant-garde compositions? And why didn't his music continue in this direction? Let's keep going.

Another possible reason may both address and fail to address the question: the construction of the instruments themselves. The piano, for example, divides each octave into half-steps, with a total of twelve half-steps in each octave. The same is true for the fretted guitar. Fretless instruments (violin, fretless bass, etc.), trombone, and electronic instruments (beginning with the theremin and moving through various synthesizers) allow for an *infinite division* of the octave, which allows for the possibility of new scales based on something other than half-steps (such as microtones). This opens up the possibility of a *completely new world of sound* not available to keyed and fretted instruments, even if they are retuned or have extra valves (a four-valve quarter-tone trumpet, for example).

This possible explanation both answers and fails to answer the question because keyed and fretted instruments *could* be utilized to create *some* types of pantonal or atonal music, music that lacks a tonal center, that has no home to which to return. (Some might point to an elementary school band rehearsal as an egregious example of this, particularly a rehearsal early in the school year, after a summer of kids not touching their instruments. This, of course, would be inadvertent pan-atonality.) I harken back to Sun Ra. He was a piano player just like Zevon. So this doesn't really answer our question. Let's go further.

The fact remains that Zevon didn't have to write in the idiom in which he wrote. And, being a piano player, he could have switched to electronic keyboard and soared into a microtonal, pantonal, atonal world. So, why doesn't he push the boundaries of tonality? Given his temperament, his unique training and life experiences, he seems like the very guy to do it, but he appears to swerve from the course.

We'll leave aside the question of the economic exigencies of making a living as a composer and musician. Sure, it's an important and potentially fruitful line of questioning, and, in the end, might offer the most plausible reason he relegated himself to pop-rock-folk. But I suspect that there are other psychological and philosophical reasons as well. Economics alone doesn't sound particularly *Zevonesque*, if you catch my drift.

Let's go a bit further. To speculate: Zevon is *already* peering into the abyss in daily life; he simply can't do it in his music as well. It would be too much. Music, for him, is a salvific force. Tonality is a guardrail, a hedge against chaos, darkness, and the final entropy of death. Utilizing a framework of tonality, Zevon skirts, if only momentarily, this ultimate entropy. On this theory, he *must* write music that is tonal, music that makes sense, because if the music doesn't make sense, *nothing* makes sense.

And yet, as noted, contained within his music is a conspicuous bifurcation. While it may be unabashedly tonal, with plenty of dissonance, it resounds, as it were, within a tapestry of linguistic enigma, paradox, satire, loss and death. Linguistic atonality, as it were. We hear the clear yet arcane voice of the existential troubadour calling out to us. We listen because there's something there that we need to hear, but we can't quite make it out. So we keep listening.

Death Tango

Warren lived his whole life expecting death, so he was ready for it. Maybe more than most of us who are trying to live clean and decent lives. I'd say he kicked death right in the balls.

—DAVE BARRY, Pulitzer Prize-winning writer, humorist, friend

Sonic tonality allows us to hover over the semantic abyss. We continue to listen, to make the journey. There are sonic landmarks, but the meaning of it all is unclear. From the vantage point of distance and time, we see the unfolding thanatology that is the work of Warren Zevon. The direct, oblique, and interstitial message is a message of death. Yet, it is a death mediated by the comfort of tonality, that is to say, home.

Still, in the end, absence looms larger than presence; mortality becomes the absurd Sisyphean struggle to reach the heights. And if, in the end, the end is all there is, why the journey at all? Why light the candle, if, in the end, it will be extinguished and there is nothing, absolutely nothing, you or anybody else can do to stop it? While embracing the end, the music of Warren Zevon makes you want to burn the candle.

Zevon's music is always a tango with death. The backstage pass says it all: a skull smoking a cigarette. The rock band Heart put it succinctly: *You gonna burn, burn, burn, burn, burn to the wick. Barracuda.* Yeah, barracuda. Life is all about running away from the flames. And sometimes *being* the flames. *Barracuda.*

What is death, anyway, when every static object comprises molecules forever in motion? And subatomic reality could be particles *or* waves *or* one-dimensional strings? The reality before us remains forever elusive, even as we labor intently to grasp its truth. And so, the planet waves of music.

The sonic blast of the music batters the gates of death. Is death the illusion? Or is life the illusion, pure samsara, merely an opaque facet of infinite cyclical permutations of the material world? Or is it both? Or neither? Is ultimate truth found in the *kokoro*, the abyss of absolute nothingness? What could be the meaning of such truth? Absolute seriousness can drive us to madness. Zevon transcends with a grin. It is the grin of the skull, transcending the life of mere mortals.

But no artist wants to show his cards. He may flash them for a second, as is inevitable with a purposive unconscious, but generally, even in a creation that effuses candor, the cards remain close to the vest. Sure, you're up there, on stage, belting it out, but all performance is at the same time a form of hiding. There is a mise en scène within a mise en scène, a setting within a setting, a play within a play. The essence of the thing is somehow—beyond. Or so it is when art reaches the apex of beauty, when the music and lyrics fuse into a paean to the existential reality of impermanence and the inevitability of pain, loss, and death. Without awareness of this triumvirate, there would be no Warren Zevon. Absence infuses his work in ways both resigned and celebratory. He is climbing the mountain, regardless. Sure, the weather might change. In fact, you can count on it.

In his most significant work, *Being and Nothingness*, Sartre argues that consciousness is the *nihilation of being*. My rough translation: consciousness nothing-izes being. Stay with me here. Consciousness "is" freedom and freedom alone, something that is absolute and has no essence. Consciousness is nothing other than the gap, the space, the lacuna in what would otherwise be a plenum of being. This space allows us—in fact, *forces* us—to take a point of view—in fact *to be* a point of view—on being. This gap that we call consciousness is not any *thing*; "it" is, rather, *no thing*, or in Sartre's words, *nothingness*.

Feel free to exhale. Okay, let's keep going.

Becoming aware of the (non)essence of consciousness (nothingness) is fraught with difficulty (Exhibit One: Zevon's protracted existential crisis). Thus, Sartre's famous line in his popular essay, "Existentialism is a Humanism": *Man is condemned to be free.* Consciousness can't accept its own elusiveness, even though this very elusiveness is its own indelible nonbeing. It is evanescent in the best of cases: 1. because consciousness cannot capture itself as such, since to do this it would have to *be* the thing it seeks to take a point of view on, and 2. it cannot be this thing—or any thing—even in principle, because "it" is, in essence, no-thing. Absence is the fundamental presence of human being. Nothingness, it turns out, is a necessary precondition for the (elusive) possibility of being. (If a tree falls in the forest . . .) Put differently, absence is the basis of presence. Consciousness itself is absence *as* presence. Or presence as absence? Particle, wave, or one-dimensional string?

But who wants to think about all this stuff? For some, it never even crosses their minds. Which could, undoubtedly, be a major blessing. For others, they just can't let it go. You know exactly who I'm talking about. His curse turns out to be our blessing.

Zevon's work exhibits the sustained—in fact, lifelong—*centrality of absence*. It's no wonder that his work gets our attention. He may flash his cards for a second but no longer, lest our eyes linger for too long and we must look away. Thinking about nonbeing is, let's face it, abstract. But experiencing your own nonbeing is anything but. It's precisely what can unexpectedly happen when you're listening to the haunting work of the existential troubadour.

Sherpa Guide

Zevon spun his near-death tales into scores of darkly comic songs. The Grim Reaper made a cameo in most of 'em.

—Billy Bob Thornton (Read interview)

Warren Zevon was unique in that he was not only a musician. He was also an intellectual. This is obvious from anything more than a cursory glance at his lyrics. The god of rock is, arguably, Dionysus, the god of frenzy, revelry, loss of self, transcender-god of fear. There is much that is Dionysian in Zevon's corpus. But as an intellectual, he is also concerned with the auditory and linguistic form of his compositions. And so, the god of Apollo enters the picture, with light, music, and poetry.

The fusion of the Dionysian and the Apollonian produces a loss of self during which it is possible, if only momentarily, to stare with an averted gaze into the black hole of non-existence. Frenzy and revelry induce a state of connectedness, oneness, communion. For a mere *Augenblick*, or blink of an eye, you peer into the abyss. The paralyzing terror of nonexistence is stayed, if only until the overtones of the final chord are silent.

The most misunderstood philosopher of all time (and that's saying something, what with Hegel, Heidegger, and Derrida in the mix), Friedrich Nietzsche, talks quite a lot about the Dionysian and the Apollonian in his first book, *The Birth of Tragedy out of the Spirit of Music*. This work is ostensibly a general critique of Greek culture, art, music, and philosophy. But, in fact, Nietzsche spends a great deal of time attacking the guy who has become something of a patron saint of Western philosophy, Socrates. The problem, as Nietzsche sees it, is that Socrates was *too damn rational, too damn Apollonian.* He wanted to light up every corner, every dark space, every nook and cranny until they all shone brightly in the noonday sun. So annoying. And not only to Nietzsche.

Do you know anybody like that? Maybe you wanted them to . . . just go away? Concealment, the unknown, the unknowable, these have always been hard things for intellectuals, TV evangelists, and anybody who works for the Internal Revenue Service. And so it is with Socrates, according to Nietzsche. What's good about Socrates, the narration continues, is that he asks the questions. He just can't accept *not knowing the answers*. And so it is with the Apollonian intellect, refusing to admit the fundamental unknowability of existence—and even of your own self.

Enter Warren Zevon. In bridging the divide between the desire to know and the desire to accept the unknown, he throws down the epistemic gauntlet, leading like a Sherpa guide up the treacherous mountain. Pain, loss, and death will be a given. All will not be form and light. There will be confusion, the unknown, the unknowable. And still, the music will go on. Every song tells a story. It has a narrative construction that takes us *somewhere else*. But understanding? We cannot yet fathom existence. How could it be that we could withstand the knowledge of nonexistence? Yet what is life but a journey up the mountain? While mourning the loss of the illusion of permanence, we can still celebrate the ephemerality of all that is.

Sure, there will be the inevitable regrets along the way. Every dead-end trail, mirage, switchback, may fill us with remorse. In the light of non-infinite time, all these sidetracks may feel like impediments. By what does it mean to get sidetracked when the main trail itself ends abruptly, without justification or explanation? Maybe those dead-end trails, those mirages and switchbacks, are the trail itself. This is the message of the deadpan troubadour. When we get to the end, will it be any different from the journey? If not, why choose the main trail? Why use the guidebook? Why not look and smell and listen and wonder and follow that wonder wherever it goes? Especially if, no matter how hard you try, the sirens of fate will beckon until finally you are consigned, with or without consent, to the murky depths? Even the love of Dido and Aeneas was insufficient to deflect the will of the gods.

And what's your hurry, by the way? The words of the darkest of dark crooners ring out loud and clear: "Enjoy every sandwich." And so it was that Warren Zevon spoke these timeless words of wisdom while appearing for his last time on the *Late Show with David Letterman* on October 30, 2002. Shortly before this appearance, he had learned that he had only months to live. *Enjoy every sandwich*. He died of peritoneal mesothelioma less than a year later, on September 7th 2003. "I might have made a tactical error in not going to a physician for twenty years. It was one of those phobias that didn't pay off," he said during that same show. Why is it that we seldom want something more than when we feel it slipping away?

Back at the Village

Warren Zevon's music is a sonic temple for the electrically evolved, inciting exciting filth, sass, and sincerity, blowing from a horn that shouts: you are not alone. . . . His music is a part of my life's sound-track, pointing fingers and laughing along at all the Wonder Bread shoppers. . . . His songs are musical bubbles that hold laughter, foxiness, and tears, making a spectacle that feels like an inside joke.

—ROB WOFFORD, guitarist and lead vocalist, Bobby Skulls and the Yowl

I harken back to Lancaster, Pennsylvania. The visceral memory is still there. Zevon's solo performance at the Village Night Club poignantly exuded absence as presence. He was there and he was *not there*. For me, it was a double absence, as I thought about my dad playing jazz trumpet and trombone on that very stage back in the Fifties and Sixties. Warren and Jim. Both performers, smokers, drinkers, each enigmatic in his own way, struggling to articulate what they didn't want to know, and which turned out, in the end, to be unknowable. They flew high above terra firma, transcending life by creating a fictional reality within which they could live, if only momentarily.

I don't know if I could have spoken with Zevon that day, now over thirty years ago. I don't know because I didn't try. I've regretted it ever since. He tried a lot of things that I didn't, and that's one of the reasons I'm writing about him rather than the other way around. Even an eagle can't transcend when perched alone on the ground.

The Song Goes On

Existentialism has become such an important theme in modern life, and Warren Zevon has a sort of gift for acknowledging the crippling fear of existence and finding catharsis in it, usually by being funny or earnest, which are qualities that remain eternally relevant."

—SAMMY "VANILLA THUNDER" SWINDELL, rock aficionado, Ozark Mountain Writers Guild

Warren Zevon had an ambivalent relationship with death, a *sympathetic antipathy* and an *antipathetic sympathy* well described by the considered father of existentialism, the melancholy Dane and proto-hipster Søren Kierkegaard, in his masterpiece, *The Concept of Dread* (pp. 37–42). Sweet dread entangled both Kierkegaard and Zevon in ways neither could understand or surmount. Each tormented soul sought to write his way out of his tenacious tango with nonexistence. Zevon had the additional ability to sing his way to the surface—and beneath the surface. Both are remembered for what they have left us.

Kierkegaard tells us that freedom is infinite and arises out of nothing. Holy cow, that's a mouthful, especially if you're just trying to enjoy every sandwich. Freedom may be infinite, but temporality is not. When you've already thought your way to the end, you understand that infinitude is a nonlinear concept. You've got to choose to embrace the infinite by making a finite choice to live in the only moment that is or ever will be.

Absence is the ground bass of the musical form that was the life of Warren Zevon. His life was his song, and his song was his life. His guitar, piano, and voice blended mellifluous and beautiful descants above an indelible cantus firmus. The sound may have ended, but the song goes on.

VI

The Vast Indifference of Heaven

13

Accidentally Like an Existentialist

NICHOLAS WERNICKI

Warren Zevon managed to be a lot of things in his relatively short life. During an interview with long-time friend David Letterman, Zevon said he got to be Jim Morrison a lot longer than Morrison himself did. In addition to living like Morrison for a good portion of his life, he crafted some of the most raw and honest lyrics ever written about what it means to be a human being.

He was an abusive and unfaithful husband, a terrible father, lousy and jealous friend, Olympic-caliber drunk and addict, ruthless bandmate and performer, and world-class womanizer. He was all these things, until one day he wasn't. There was a period of almost twenty years of sobriety near the end of his life that marked a real turn in who he was as a person and artist, even if his voracious appetite for women remained constant until the very end.

Women would come into his life for an hour, a weekend, sometimes for years. Sometimes more than one at a time. His drinking was legendary and poisoned nearly every meaningful part of his adult life. Perhaps the only saving grace was that he rarely remembered any of the terrible things he did. Warren Zevon did not get rock'n'roll drunk; he got *Leaving-Las Vegas*-drunk. It was a recklessly-shooting-his-.44-magnum-pistol-in-the-streets-and-falling-off-piano-benches-while-performing kind of drunk. It was only after a flurry of interventions, trips to rehab, and damaged relationships that he achieved sobriety. Despite it all, his estranged wife Crystal remained a lifelong friend, supporter, and confidant until the end of his life. Perhaps no one in Zevon's life knew him better than she did. For this reason, one of Zevon's last wishes was for her to write his biography, which she did, publishing it under the title, *I'll Sleep When I'm Dead: The Dirty Life and Times of Warren Zevon.*

Zevon was also a lovable curmudgeon, redeemable friend, and loving father and grandfather. In his later, sober years, he was a gracious and gentler bandmate and collaborator, especially with those who stuck by him during those dark and vicious years fueled by drugs and alcohol. Despite the well-catalogued list of seemingly unforgivable things he did, especially as a spouse, friend, and father, Zevon was the kind of guy you couldn't help but root for. His persona was that of the carefree, reckless, and fearless rock'n'roller. He could be violent and wildly unpredictable one moment, but tender and vulnerable the next. Zevon was the quintessential movie villain who everyone hopes will redeem himself in the end. And, in some ways, he found that redemption, both personally and musically. Even though the wake of his destructive behavior was deep and far-reaching, he was beloved by so many over the course of his life, especially by Crystal. He was all of these things and, in a way, a bit of a philosopher.

Music, Philosophy, and Knowing the Unknowable

Philosophy is like science in that there are different kinds of philosophers who try to solve different kinds of problems. If we were interested in how the cells of a frog work, we would ask a biologist, as the physicist probably wouldn't be much help. Likewise, philosophy boasts specializations of its own aimed at solving particular problems or answering particular questions. Philosophers are, in the most basic sense, problem-solvers who seek the truth. They do their best work on problems that science isn't equipped to solve, like whether or not God exists, how we can know right from wrong, and the most fundamental questions about the meaning of existence.

Like songwriting, much of philosophy begins with trying to explain or describe the seemingly inexplicable. In his case, Zevon was vexed by the inexplicable human experience of death. Throughout his touring days, the coveted backstage pass for his shows was a simple laminated graphic of a skull smoking a cigarette. This is the perfect visual representation of Zevon the thinker.

Zevon released over fifteen albums over the course of his abbreviated career. He wrote about love, contempt, fate, resignation, and death. His songs were much more than folk and rock musings about these seemingly inexplicable human experiences. Like a philosopher, he was really asking: this is what life is, right? Zevon had an uncanny way of putting you on the hook to answer him.

Philosophers are keen on developing complex arguments and offering rational proofs in an effort to solve problems and better understand the world. For many philosophical problems, this process is reliable. For those that are not solvable through logical proofs, human beings often reach what the philosopher Karl Jaspers called a "limit situation." A limit situation is a moment where reason begins to falter, and the truth begins to mask itself. We know there is more to know, but we just can't get there through rational thought. For Jaspers, "we react meaningfully to limit situations not by planning and calculation in order to overcome them, but by an entirely different sort of activity: namely, by *becoming the Existenz possible within us.* We become ourselves by entering into the limit situations with our eyes open. To experience limit situations and to be *Existenz* are one and the same" (p. 97). By *Existenz*, Jaspers means one of the possible ways human beings can be-in-the-world. It's an actualization of the self, brought on by being open to what transcends our everyday awareness of what is true. This is accomplished through the expressing of our will to communicate with others concerning what is out of reach or beyond our limit situation. We can consider reading existential literature or listening to Zevon as participation in *Existenz*. In either case, we are open to that which is out of reach of human reason.

Since the ancient period, philosophers have been concerned with the question of what it means to be human. It wasn't really until the second half of the nineteenth century and into the 1970s that a group of philosophers called existentialists confronted the unique aspects of the lived human experience. This is how existentialists are distinct from other kinds of philosophers, since they are primarily concerned with whether it's possible to assign meaning to the lived experience. They ask: what should we make of all of this? How do we deal with the fact that there is no apparent reason for us being here and that someday we will simply be gone? Death is certain, for all of us. How should we face the almost cruel situation of springing up in the world, existing for a few brief moments, and living with the certainty that the self will someday be annihilated into nothingness? Perhaps more importantly, because human existence is so temporary and uncertain, existentialists worry about what to do *in between* our inexplicable birth and certain death. How is it that we *should* live?

In the existentialist's view, the traditional method of relying on rational arguments and philosophical proofs to understand the human experience falls short. For the existentialist, and for Zevon, comprehending the human experience is an irrational pursuit. How could we possibly rationalize the irrational? *Life simply doesn't make sense.* Many existentialist thinkers relied on simply describing the human experience by writing short stories, novels, and plays to try to reveal through creative expression what is universally true about human existence.

Perhaps the best the existentialist can hope for is an accurate description of life itself, while offering some thoughts on what to do with it. This describes Zevon's rich catalogue of songs on life, death, and the few human experiences in between that matter. Perhaps it is no small coincidence that he was creating his music around the same time that the twentieth-century existentialists were producing some of the movement's most important philosophical works, plays and novels. Zevon, like the novelists and playwrights of the existentialist movement, was an exceptional storyteller. He regularly commented that he saw himself as a lyricist and storyteller first, and a musician second. Zevon was an avid reader and intellectual, who read existential philosophy and literature by Martin Heidegger, Samuel Beckett, and by Arthur Schopenhauer, who could be read as a precursor to existentialism.

Zevon recognized songwriting as a blend of fiction and nonfiction, which is a perfect description of existentialism. He was a self-taught guitar player, who hardly counted among the guitar gods of his era. On the other hand, he was a classically trained and much more accomplished piano player, although even he recognized that his piano-playing would not be his legacy. His work as a lyricist is another matter. According to critical accounts and the testimony of fans alike, Zevon is regarded as a master songwriter, even though *Rolling Stone* magazine unfathomably omitted him from their "100 Greatest Song Writers of All Time" list.

In response to this omission, NPR's music reviewer Tom Moon wrote, "this list—which was sponsored entirely by Apple Music (raise eyebrow over editorial independence here)—has generated its share of dissonance. Howls of outrage can be heard over certain regrettable omissions: No Jim Morrison! No Nick Drake! No Warren Zevon! No Public Enemy! No Pink Floyd! No John Mellencamp! How could they?"

One hypothesis for these exclusions is that, when Roger Waters and David Gilmour of Pink Floyd or Chuck D of Public

Enemy tackle fundamental human problems in their songs, they offer no corresponding resolution. They put these problems in your lap and say, "Now this is your problem too." It creates an empathetic encounter between artist and listener, which establishes a meaningful reciprocity between the two. The same can be said of Warren Zevon. These artists confront the listener over existential problems about what it means to be human. Their songs are not merely sad.

That's the primary difference between this category of artists and songwriters like Taylor Swift (#97 on the *Rolling Stone* list). Swift writes touching lyrics and beautiful melodies, but we always get the sense that things are somehow going to be okay, no matter how sad the song. Like the existentialist philosopher, however, Zevon stops short of offering a resolution. He forces the listener to reckon with the harshest of realities, which for most of us is something we are naturally inclined to avoid.

While Zevon never wrote a philosophical text or even a work of existential literature in the traditional sense, his lyrics engage existential themes. Lyrically, he was trying to work through philosophical problems about the human experience. Good songwriting, like good philosophy, puts the listener in conversation with the artist. For existentialists, the conversation can be dark, hopeless, inspiring, empathetic, and, yes, even funny. The focus of Zevon's lyrical genius was almost always death. Much of Zevon's life is catalogued in his personal diaries, parts of which Crystal Zevon includes in the oral biography of Zevon. The diary entry on August 28, 2002 reads: "Rough day. I went to the Doctors. They tell me I have terminal lung cancer."

Zevon had been diagnosed with a rare lung cancer called mesothelioma and given only a few months to live. The news of his terminal illness came two years after he released his 2000 album *Life'll Kill Ya*, which includes, along with the title track, the song "Don't Let Us Get Sick." The album also includes a track called "My Shit's Fucked Up," which is a dark, comedic lyrical anticipation of his subsequent diagnosis. Mere months before he became aware of his illness, he released his 2002 album *My Ride's Here*, which includes songs about loss, absence, and a search for answers to existential questions.

These themes were constant touchpoints of philosophical thought throughout Zevon's career. In his song "Sacrificial Lambs" he took a lyrical swipe at popular spiritual movements and mystics, such as Madame Blavatsky, co-founder of the Theosophical Society, and Jiddu Krishnamurti.

Zevon and the Existentialists

Existentialism occupies a unique corner of philosophical thought because it relies on so many fields outside of philosophy to respond to questions about what it means to be human. These include psychology, theology, art, and literature. This is especially true of philosophers who deal with the problem of death. Zevon is no different.

When existentialists confront the problem of death, they're not simply talking about the moment when life is wrenched from the body. Instead, they have in mind a specific way in which human beings are in, or oriented to, their world. When they are alive, they exist as unique individual beings-in-the-world, but once they have died, they simply no longer are. They participate in what philosophers call non-being. In other words, they lack existence. The individual or "self'" is annihilated, at which point there is mere nothingness, or no-thing-ness. This produces a special kind of anxiety, called existential anxiety, which cannot be medicated or, in Zevon's case, drunk away.

Existentialists are deeply concerned about how to live with the knowledge of this eventual reality. Zevon's preoccupation with death was not relegated to his final years. He was always conscious of these existential problems, so they seeped into his lyrics from the beginning of his career through his final and perhaps most acclaimed album, *The Wind*. The job of the existentialist is not only to describe the human situation and remind us that life is fleeting, but also to offer some insight into how to deal with this absurd and impossible situation. Most existentialists agree that to be a human being is to be in anxiety over our eventual lack of existence. On this point, I am sure Zevon would agree.

The concept of existential anxiety is a recurring theme in existential philosophy and literature. The Danish philosopher Søren Kierkegaard was one of the three founders of the existentialist movement, along with Friedrich Nietzsche and Fyodor Dostoevsky. For Kierkegaard and Nietzsche, existential anxiety is rooted in an overall loss of a world and sense of being. This is manifested in various ways. One way might be the experience of a kind of homesickness, even though you may be in your own cozy environment. Kierkegaard's perspective, which is grounded in Christian theology, takes this position one step further and traces our existential anxiety to the origin of the human's paradoxical position of being simultaneously *in relation to* and *estranged from* God. For Kierkegaard, this can be traced back to original sin.

For the existentialist, fear is different than anxiety. When we are afraid, we're always afraid of some specific thing, some object that we can ultimately reason away. I could be afraid of being diagnosed with a rare disease, but I can overcome that fear by reasoning that the odds of contracting the disease are vanishingly low. Or I could visit the doctor, who would assure me that my fears are unfounded. Going to the doctor was something Zevon feared greatly. In fact, he had not been to a doctor for almost twenty years prior to the diagnosis of his illness. His friend and dentist, Dr. Stan Golden, was his only doctor. Zevon would say that if Dr. Stan couldn't fix it, he was screwed. Ultimately, it was Dr. Stan who dragged Zevon to a specialist, who diagnosed his fatal disease.

Kierkegaard and Nietzsche were the primary influences on the twentieth-century existentialists, such as Sartre, Heidegger, and Jaspers, each of whom offered his own treatment of existential anxiety. However, it was two lesser-known thinkers who brought theology, philosophy, and psychology into productive dialogue over the problem of existential anxiety. Paul Tillich and his student Rollo May produced some of the most important work of the twentieth-century, while May himself was largely responsible for introducing existential psychotherapy to the United States.

Existential anxiety is the anxiety we experience over the sheer lack of being, which is not something human beings can even imagine, for even in our imagination we can only conjure the concept of total darkness, which is at least something. Existential anxiety is anxiety over an individual's eventual participation in something of which we all lack experience. It is the anxiety of the experience of nothingness, or the absence of experience altogether. According to Tillich:

> The anxiety of fate and death is most basic, most universal, and inescapable. All attempts to argue it away are futile. Even if the so-called arguments for the "immortality of the soul" had argumentative power (which they do not have) they would not convince existentially. For existentially everybody is aware of the complete loss of self which biological extinction implies. (*The Courage to Be*, p. 42)

Existential anxiety is the awareness that, eventually, the self will simply be gone. According to some existential thinkers and psychoanalysts, if we fail to confront this type of anxiety, it can manifest itself in all kinds of destructive neuroses.

Early in his career, Zevon lived in the same apartment building as actor and musician Billy Bob Thornton. They met, in part, because of their shared struggles with obsessive-compulsive disorder (OCD). Much of Zevon's life was ruled by his OCD rituals, as well as his superstitious, yet steadfast, faith in luck. Thornton describes their first meeting like this: "I went to my mailbox one day, opened the thing up, and I took my mail out, put it back in, closed it, pulled it out again, closed it . . . I did it like three times in a row. And Warren was standing next to me watching me do this thing and he says, 'You have that too!' And I said, 'Yeah.'"

Those close to Zevon knew all too well how deep his phobias and superstitions ran. He had lucky colors, which changed over the course of his life, that would control his behavior and choices. He had an extended grey period near the end of his life, during which he wore and collected exclusively grey Calvin Klein T-shirts. Some existentialists might recognize this behavior as a neurotic response to the threat of non-being. The neurosis takes the threat of nothingness and turns it into an object. The thinking runs as follows: "As long as I honor the compulsive behavior, stay with the lucky colors and lucky numbers, I will be okay."

Existential anxiety then becomes fear, which can only be temporarily escaped, so the anxiety eventually returns. When Zevon died, there were stacks of grey Calvin Klein T-shirts found in his home, still in their original packaging. He would buy them compulsively in every city that was a stop on his tour. Tillich claims that the only way to avoid the kind of neurosis associated with existential anxiety is to face it courageously and thereby affirm the self, however temporary that self is. According to Tillich:

> The neurotic is more sensitive than the average man to the threat of non-being. And since non-being opens up the mystery of being he can be more creative than the average. This limited extensiveness of self-affirmation can be balanced by greater intensity, but by an intensity which is narrowed to a special point accompanied by a distorted relation to reality as a whole. Even if pathological anxiety has psychotic traits, creative moments can appear. (p. 67)

Zevon's life and lyrics creatively exemplify the struggle of the human spirit that courageously investigates the abyss in one moment, while fleeing it in the next. Zevon's song "The Indifference of Heaven," from his album *Mutineer* (1995), poignantly captures the existentialist sentiment of self-affirmation and courage in the face of non-being, noting how, as a gentle rain falls, all life "folds back into the sea," while we contemplate eternity, "beneath the vast indifference of heaven." This theme is also apparent in his song, "Don't Let us Get Sick," in which he implores his friends not to get sick, old or stupid, but to remain brave and "play nice," so they can all "be together tonight."

Tillich would say that Zevon's articulation of the experience of peering into the abyss of nothingness only to face the indifference of the universe lies at the core of authentic human existence. From an existentialist perspective, the heavens are, indeed, indifferent. Confronting this fact requires the courage to be an authentic self.

Life, Death, and the Art of Tragic Comedy

The existentialists were not *all* doom and gloom. Well, okay, it is *mostly* doom and gloom, but sometimes things are so terrible that we can't help but laugh. Some existential philosophers even had a healthy sense of humor about the fact that existence was, at best, meaningful but temporary or, at worst, totally meaningless and absurd. In either case, existentialism honors the sheer wonder and finality of it all, while recognizing that sometimes we just can't help but laugh. Zevon was a master at introducing humor into the most dreadful and difficult themes, especially toward the end of his life. His longtime friends Bruce Springsteen and Jackson Browne shared their admiration for Zevon's ability to thread a sharp sense of humor through rock'n'roll songs that also addressed tragedy. Browne once said, "It's not easy to write a rock'n'roll record about mortality, because so much of rock'n'roll is spent eluding it. But he does it with a humor and appetite for what life is really like. His work has always been characterized by a comic kind of courage."

In some ways, Zevon's lyrical genius is reminiscent of absurdist existentialists like Samuel Beckett, who would in one breath draw out the panic and horror of the certainty of death, then shrug it off in the next with the kind of biting humor that defined their genius. The sentiment of existentialist philosophers, playwrights, and poets, including Zevon, is that there is nothing to be done. We are human, finite, and stuck with it. Browne is quoted as saying that Zevon "could satirize and mythologize all in one stroke." Examples of this kind of comic resignation run consistently throughout his catalogue, including in his more popular sing-a-long songs, like "Werewolves of London" and "Excitable Boy." The songs are so clever that it's easy to forget they're about rape, murder and getting your lungs ripped out by a perfectly quaffed Werewolf.

Perhaps Zevon's best depiction of the existentialist temperament, which is focused on the temporary nature of human existence, is "Desperadoes under the Eaves," which encapsulates the seemingly dissonant emotions of wonder and despair. While existentialist humor brings a certain levity to the notion that we exist without any real explanation, it also prompts the question of whether we are responsible for who we become. For some existentialists, the sum of our choices is synonymous with who we are. At every moment, our entire existence is at stake. And yet, the constant need to choose who we are is a source of anxiety. Should we radically affirm the self and say, "to hell with morality"? Should we rely on faith in a god or gods to save us? Or perhaps, like Albert Camus, the best we can hope for is to live courageously in contempt of our existential situation. Camus recounts the myth of Sisyphus, who was damned by the gods to roll a rock up a hill endlessly, only to see it roll back down again. Yet, Camus sees Sisyphus as happy.

> I leave Sisyphus at the foot of the mountain! One always finds one's burden again. But Sisyphus teaches the higher fidelity that negates the gods and raises rocks. He too concludes that all is well. This universe henceforth without a master seems to him neither sterile nor futile. Each atom of that stone, each mineral flake of that night-filled mountain, in itself forms a world. The struggle itself toward the heights is enough to fill a man's heart. One must imagine Sisyphus happy. (p. 78)

Zevon was happiest in a state of struggle. He was, in many ways, a modern-day Sisyphus. Utter contempt for the gods of fate? Check. A certain resignation over his lot in life? Definitely. A realization that, while he wanted desperately to control his environment and the course of his life, it was mostly not up to him? Absolutely. Zevon was certain that his many superstitions and rituals could, in some way, control what was going to happen. In reality, of course, they controlled him.

Camus recognizes Sisyphus as the absurd hero. And yet, despite his absurd and impossible situation, he keeps rolling the rock, out of sheer contempt. It's the ultimate upward thrust of the middle finger to the gods. Zevon was a lot of things in his relatively short life, and heroic was one of them, especially in the face of his many failures. With the exception of a few popular hits like "Werewolves of London" and "Lawyers, Guns, and Money," Zevon never received the popular acclaim he deserved. He was not a regular on the charts, and has only recently been nominated for the Rock'n'Roll Hall of Fame. His career experienced major swings, from playing with some of the most accomplished musicians of his time, like Dylan, Browne, and Springsteen, Neil Young, Bonnie Raitt, and R.E.M., to playing solo gigs for a handful of loyal fans at local clubs. He was signed and dropped by record labels with regularity, and record sales in the middle of his career were lackluster at best. Perhaps all of this was punishment for telling it exactly how it is, which is both exactly what he did and what existentialism is all about. As fun and raucous and touching and heartfelt as his music is, he never lets you forget that the last laugh is always on us.

Zevon's Curtain Call

When Warren Zevon was diagnosed with cancer, he did two things almost immediately. He rushed to the studio to record his final album, *The Wind*, and he started drinking again after seventeen years of sobriety. Along with the booze, which he would mix with morphine, like a cocktail, came an army of friends and musicians to support his final burst of creativity. This included his dear friend David Letterman, who appears on Zevon's song "Hit Somebody (The Hockey Song)."

Zevon was a regular guest on the *Late Show* with Letterman and even filled in for Paul Shaffer as the show's band leader from time to time. On hearing the news of Zevon's diagnosis, Letterman decided to devote an entire show to him, which would be his last appearance. When he asked Zevon what he had learned about life and death since his diagnosis, he answered that he now knew how much you should enjoy every sandwich. This perfectly summarizes the existentialist's perspective on the temporary nature of the human experience. There is nothing to be done about our existential situation; it is temporary, fleeting, so perhaps the best we can do is enjoy life's small but tantalizing pleasures.

With the help of some his closest friends and supporters, like Jackson Browne, Billy Bob Thornton, Dwight Yoakam, Tom Petty, Ry Cooder, Jorge Calderón, Don Henley, and Bruce Springsteen, Zevon returned to the studio in November of 2002. As he got sicker and weaker, he raced against the clock to finish the album. While the creativity came easier than at any other point of his career, the stamina required to play and record the songs took every ounce of Zevon's will.

Like Sisyphus, existential contempt may very well be what drove Zevon to finish the record. He died at home on September 7th 2003 from lung cancer. His last recording was "Keep Me in Your Heart" and he lived to finish *The Wind*, which, shortly after his death, was certified gold. It was nominated for five Grammys and won Best Contemporary Folk Album. His duet with Springsteen, "Disorder in the House," was awarded Best Rock Performance by a Duo or Group with Vocal.

Zevon often recited Hemingway's famous observation that "All good stories end in death." Zevon's lyrics, from his first album to the last, were essentially works in existentialism. He responded to life's most fundamental problems with courage, honesty, and wit. Perhaps that explains why he didn't enjoy more popular acclaim. Existentialism requires a good, long look into the abyss. Zevon pointed the way.

14
Warren Zevon and the Absurd Universe

RICHARD JONES

In the bluesy "Rub Me Raw," one of the last songs written, or in this case co-written, by Warren Zevon, we get this line: "I don't share your need to discuss the absurd."

We know what he meant. He'd been diagnosed with terminal mesothelioma, and there were, quite reasonably, plenty of times when he sought to withdraw into himself rather than to be reminded yet again of his mortality. And it's not like we hadn't seen this before, in songs like "Splendid Isolation" and his cover of "Laissez-moi Tranquille."

Still, there is more than a little irony at play here, for two reasons. First of all, there were also moments when he absolutely did want his medical condition to be front and center. The private and often reclusive Zevon urged his marketing team to go full throttle in exploiting his illness to boost sales of his final album, *The Wind*, on which "Rub Me Raw" is the penultimate track. Nor can there be any doubt that songs like the closing ballad, "Keep Me in Your Heart," or a cover of Bob Dylan's "Knockin' on Heaven's Door" would resonate in a particular way with fans who knew of his illness, and virtually all of them did. More importantly for the purposes of this chapter, however, is the simple fact that Warren Zevon had been writing and singing about the absurd for decades.

Camus and Absurdity

Unquestionably, the most famous articulation of the absurd universe comes from Albert Camus. He opens the volume *The Myth of Sisyphus and Other Essays* by noting that there is "but one serious philosophical problem, and that is suicide" (p. 3). He has already provided his conclusion in the book's preface, declaring that "even if one does not believe in God, suicide is not legitimate" (p. v). He subsequently defines the contours of the absurd, describing how,

> in a universe suddenly divested of illusions and lights, man feels an alien, a stranger. His exile is without remedy since he is deprived of the memory of a lost home or the hope of a promised land. This divorce between man and his life, the actor and his acting, is properly the feeling of absurdity. (p. 5)

The title essay of the volume examines the case of Sisyphus, who, for the crime of cheating death, is condemned by Zeus to forever roll a boulder up a hill, only to have it roll back down the slope again. This enforced tedium is, to be sure, a remarkably effective punishment for a mortal as clever and life-loving as Sisyphus. Camus, however, presents a different perspective, arguing that "Happiness and the absurd are two sons of the same earth" (p. 90). Sisyphus rises above his fate not by fighting against it in a battle he cannot win; rather, he recognizes it and embraces it, especially but not exclusively in the moments he descends from the summit to start the process anew:

> Sisyphus, proletarian of the gods, powerless and rebellious, knows the whole extent of his wretched condition: it is what he thinks of during his descent. The lucidity that was to constitute his torture at the same time crowns his victory. There is no fate that cannot be surmounted by scorn. (p. 90)

The essay concludes with one of the most famous lines of twentieth-century philosophy: "We must imagine Sisyphus happy" (p. 91).

In his play *The Misunderstanding*, Camus also suggests that even if there is a higher power that governs, or even influences, our lives, such a "god" is uncaring, amoral, and whimsical. In the play's final scene, a young woman has just learned that her husband has been murdered by his mother and his sister. The sister, admitting to the murder, offers advice: "Pray to your God to make you like stone. It is the happiness he claims for Himself, and is the only real happiness. Be deaf to all cries, become a stone while there is still time." She leaves to hang herself, leaving the wife alone on stage.

She cries out, "Oh! God! I cannot live in this desert." Falling to her knees, she continues, "Yes, it is to you I appeal. Have pity on me, turn towards me! Hear me, give me your hand! Have pity, Lord, on those who love each other and are parted." The

Old Manservant, a hitherto silent and rather creepy figure, complicit in the murders, appears, asking, "Did you call me?" Maria begs him, "Help me, for I need help! Have pity and agree to help!" He responds, in a tone that is "clear and firm," simply "No." Final curtain. (*Le Malentendu*, pp. 253–54; translation mine). "Vast indifference of heaven," indeed!

To the average person, however, when the term "absurd" means something other than simply "weird," it is linked to the Theatre of the Absurd, a coinage employed by the critic Martin Esslin in his ground-breaking book of that title. Esslin stresses that the "Theatre of the Absurd has renounced arguing *about* the absurdity of the human condition; it merely *presents* it in being—that is, in concrete stage images" (p. 6). Thus, it was not Camus and Jean-Paul Sartre, both of whom wrote several plays, but, rather, later dramatists—Samuel Beckett, Eugène Ionesco, Arthur Adamov, Jean Genet, and Harold Pinter, among others—who ushered in a new dramatic movement.

With these plays, no less intellectual than those of Camus and Sartre, albeit in a fundamentally different way, we get further explanations of the absurd universe. The most important of these is the detachment of events from intentionality, an abnegation not merely of the acting theories of Konstantin Stanislavsky at one level, but also, more importantly, of the notion of an ordered universe. Things happen at random, often without context, and completely independently of any benevolent deity, if such a thing even exists. Meaning is often indecipherable, or at the very least ambiguous. This notion of a disordered, indiscriminate, and often brutal world manifests itself especially in an unemotional and objective fascination with death and its repercussions. In particular, violence becomes morally and ethically neutral. Accompanying this disruption is a blurring of the lines between the serious and the comical, or perhaps more accurately between the tragic and the farcical. Finally, whether we view this vision of the absurd as a version of existentialism or as a sort of philosophical stepchild, it certainly maintains the notions of angst in the face of an unknowable world and of the focus on the individual as a free and responsible agent.

Violence and Amorality

The notion of amoral violence is particularly prevalent in Zevon's songs. We are more intrigued than repulsed by the antics of the rapist-murderer Excitable Boy, not least because in true absurdist fashion the jaunty tune belies the sordidness of the lyrics. Similarly, we remain undisturbed even if the blood on his hands referred to by the narrator in "Indifference of Heaven" is literal. Frank and Jesse James are "misunderstood," embarking on a mission to "clear their names." We see nothing wrong with the fact that Jeannie needs a shooter (or that the "shooter" is himself shot). The perfectly-coiffed titular characters of "Werewolves of London," capable of mutilating little old ladies and ripping the lungs out of adult males, are simply a fact of life: destructive, but, especially because of the apparent randomness of the attacks, more a force of nature than a manifestation of evil. Indeed, we rejoice when Roland the Headless Thompson Gunner gives the traitorous Van Owen his well-deserved comeuppance, blowing his body from Mombasa to Johannesburg. The subsequent references in that song to Ireland, Lebanon, Palestine, Berkeley, and Patty Hearst carefully avoid taking sides, simply noting events in recent history in which violence has been employed. The listener may believe in the perfidy of one side or the other in, say, the Palestinian conflict, but, by extension, that also means that the other side is ethically justified in using violence.

It may be, however, that the two narrative sports-related songs, "Boom Boom Mancini" and "Hit Somebody! (The Hockey Song)" serve as the best examples of amoral violence among Zevon's works. In the former, from the 1987 album *Sentimental Hygiene*, the listener is implicated in the excited anticipation ("hurry home early!") of the upcoming bout between real-life lightweight pugilists Ray Mancini and Bobby Chacon. We're encouraged to view the carnage of the boxing ring almost as play: "the name of the game is be hit and hit back." Zevon emphasizes the brutality of the sport by referring to the death of Korean boxer Duk-Koo Kim, who died from a subdural hematoma suffered in a bout against Mancini a little over a year before the Chacon fight. But he also absolves Mancini of ethical responsibility: others made "hypocrite judgments after the fact"; "someone should have stopped the fight, and told me it was him." The song also connects back to the notion of withstanding punishment, central to Sisyphus's triumph: "if you can't take the punches, it don't mean a thing."

In "Hit Somebody!," from 2002's *My Ride's Here*, our hero is Buddy, a Canadian farm boy hoping to fulfill his dream as a hockey player. Alas, "he wasn't that good with the puck." He was big and tough, however, and, despite the fact that "his heart wasn't in it," he became a "goon," charged with remembering his role: not to score himself, but to protect the "fast guys" who do. Perhaps predictably, in the last few seconds of his final game, he gets off a shot a fraction of a second before being "coldcocked . . . on his follow-through." The lyrics then take an ambiguous, one might almost say absurdist, turn: "The last thing he saw was that flashing red light. / He saw that heavenly light." Perhaps the flashing red light that signals a goal seems heaven-sent to Buddy. Conversely, perhaps it is actually a *heavenly* light, suggesting entry into the afterlife following what was literally the last thing Buddy (ever) saw. Sports journalist Mitch Albom, who wrote the lyrics, favored the former reading; Zevon himself, the latter. Either way, Buddy, like Boom Boom Mancini (and presumably like Buddy's Finnish antagonist), has been trapped in a long-term cycle of inflicting and sustaining injuries in order to fulfill expectations of him. The ethics (or lack of them) associated with the job are never up for debate. After all, "what's a Canadian farm boy to do?"

Zevon's dabbling with Eastern religion and philosophy would inevitably have included a consciousness of the Taoist concept that X cannot exist without not-X. Therefore, classifying certain forms of violence as morally or ethically neutral is merely redundant unless other forms of violence are indeed immoral. Thus, "Veracruz," on the 1978 *Excitable Boy* album, refers to an actual event in which American troops invaded that Mexican city after the arrest of nine U.S. sailors during the Mexican revolution. The invocation of "Woodrow Wilson's guns" serves as more than just the proverbial exception that proves the rule. Rather, the juxtaposition of the military forces that can be mustered by a U.S. president with the plaint of a single woman ("I heard Maria crying") underscores a power dynamic not altogether different from the plight of a single mortal cursed by the king of the gods.

Repetition and Tedium

The most direct parallel between Camus's Sisyphus and the characters in Zevon's songs, however, comes in the notion of tedium. "Trouble Waiting to Happen" features the line, "just when I thought it was safe to be bored," suggesting that even the apparent security of stultifying familiarity is illusory at best. Sometimes, the oppressive sameness comes from continuous activity, as in the hum of the Hollywood Hawaiian Hotel's air-conditioner in "Desperados Under the Eaves," the incessant precipitation in "Stop Rainin' Lord," or the inability of the Rosarita Beach Café to change a million-dollar bill. Occasionally, the phenomenon manifests itself as a predictive future, as in my favorite Zevon lyric, from "Desperados Under the Eaves,": "And if California slides into the ocean / Like the mystics and statistics say it will / I predict this motel will be standing / Until I pay my bill." Notice, also, the mordant humor associated with these (and so many other) lyrics.

More relevant to this discussion, however, would be a few songs in particular which relate to repeated, rather than continuing, action. Two of them were released on the same album, *Sentimental Hygiene*. Side One offers "The Factory." This tale of proletarian life, backed by Bob Dylan on harmonica, is the first-person account of a factory worker who inherited his job when his father went on disability. He and his wife "get by the best [they] can do"; luckily, there's at least "a good medical plan" thanks to the union. Still, the monotony of daily life is palpable, as reflected, for instance, in nine lines in a row that end with "the factory": "Kickin' asbestos in the factory / Punchin' out Chryslers in the factory / Breathin' that plastic in the factory, and so on." Talk about repetition!

In this song, which gestures to the working-class consciousness we associate with Zevon's friend Bruce Springsteen's early work, the narrator is constrained by the monotony of working "in the factory." That he presumably took over his father's job at Pontiac, but himself is "punchin' out Chryslers" and "making polyvinyl chloride" seems more an attempt at universalizing the experience than an error in the story-telling. Even as a "union man," the narrator works six-day weeks (his wife does, too, apparently) and rises early every morning. "Yes sir, no sir," chanted a total of six times (two sets of three) in the song, certainly underscores both the repetitious nature of the work and the enforced conformity expected of workers. This isn't exactly Sisyphean labor, but it is as mind-numbingly monotonous even if not quite so physically taxing.

"Bad Karma" appears on side two of *Sentimental Hygiene*. The song brings together allusions to Eastern religion with Zevon's well-documented belief in a form of luck akin to superstition: former girlfriend Merle Ginsberg calls him the most superstitious person she ever met (*I'll Sleep When I'm Dead*, p. 223). Thus, an individual's actions—drinking from this Coke can instead of that one, for example (pp. 2, 335 and elsewhere)—can influence one's "luck," but karma is visited on someone who not only cannot undo the past, but can't really be held responsible for events "in another life." What occurs, then, is simultaneously a completely random occurrence and a retribution for volitional acts, albeit not those under the conscious control of the present-tense individual.

Again, it is the repetitive action that oppresses: "I can't run. / Can't hide. / Can't get away / It must be my destiny / The same thing happens to me every day." Significantly, the protagonist does not face specifically new hardships: it's *the same thing* every day. "Bad Karma" is "killing me by degrees," a more torturous fate than a swifter oblivion.

"Studebaker" was written sometime prior to 1976, but was apparently never played in concert or released in a complete version (*Accidentally Like a Martyr*, p. 19). It's unclear why not; the obvious conclusion that Zevon wasn't that fond of it is undercut by C.M. Kushins's observation that he was "particularly proud" of the song, at least in its work-in-progress stage, and even contemplated using a line from it as the title of what would ultimately become his self-titled second album (p. 40).

The bare-bones rendition that appears on the posthumously issued *Preludes* album stops not merely in mid-song, but literally in mid-word. A much more fully realized recording by Jordan Zevon, Warren's son, ranks with Bruce Springsteen's cover of "My Ride's Here" as one of the standout tracks on the tribute album *Enjoy Every Sandwich*.

If we take the lyrics literally, the song is about another victim, in this case one who pours good money after bad into his "misbegotten car." The manifold blows, and an axle breaks as he steers the Studebaker off the road. By the time we get to that specific information, however, the listener has already understood that this song isn't really about vehicular transport. Rather, it's a metaphor made more explicit in a Jim Steinman/Meat Loaf song, "Objects in the Rear-View Mirror May Appear Closer Than They Are": "If life is just a highway, then the soul is just a car."

The chorus tells the story: "I'm up against it all like a leaf against the wind / And the Studebaker keeps on breaking down again." (It's a "damn Studebaker," by the way, once on the version on *Preludes*, thrice on Jordan's rendition on *Enjoy Every Sandwich*.) Of particular note is the use of both "keeps on" and "again"; either would be sufficient to indicate repeated action. Using both does more than make the scansion work; it underscores the unrelenting frequency (as opposed to the severity) of the breakdowns.

Delighted Resignation

But if we're comparing these songs to Camus's Sisyphus rather than to Homer's, we must look to the perspective of the protagonist. Significantly, all these narrators seem to have very much come to terms with their plight. The bad karma may not be permanent, but there's nothing the individual can do to precipitate the change. Nor is there any attempt to find another job or to trade in the Studebaker for a Ford. The situations are what they are. None of these figures necessarily achieves Sisyphus's scorn, but neither are they in deep despair. Zevon once described his philosophy as, "life is a very rough deal, a very unforgiving game, but people kind of do the best they can" (*I'll Sleep When I'm Dead*, p. 421). That attitude is foregrounded in many of his songs.

"The Indifference of Heaven," which appeared first on the 1992 live album *Learning to Flinch*, then on a studio version on 1995's *Mutineer* album, covers much the same ground, but slightly differently. This may be both the quintessential Warren Zevon song, while also furnishing the closest connection to the absurd. We can start with the fact that Zevon himself attributed its impetus differently at different times. He describes it both as "a song about the looting in Los Angeles" in the aftermath of the not-guilty verdict in the 1992 Rodney King case (*Accidentally Like a Martyr*, p. 180) and "the first of many depressing songs about the departure of my flaxen-tressed fiancée" (his former girlfriend Julia Mueller). It was, of course, both, and the transition from the looter with his "hands in the till" to the forlorn lover who "had a girl / Now she's gone" lends the song a particular poignancy.

The song also features the ambiguity that characterizes many Zevon songs: is "Time to kill" simply a rephrasing of "Time on my hands," or is it a declaration that the moment to engage in killing has now arrived? And there are these lines which serve as the bridge between the introspection of the petty criminal and that of the abandoned lover: "They say 'Everything's all right' / They say 'Better days are near' / They tell us 'These are the good times' / But they don't live around here / Billy and Christie don't / Bruce and Patti don't / They don't live around here." These lyrics, skewering the trite aphorisms of the comfortable, are sung at a considerably faster tempo than the rest of the song, thereby catching our attention, while adding a little wit in the form of a perhaps not-so-gentle dig at Springsteen, whose credentials as a voice of the working man had been eroded more than a little by his multi-millionaire status.

More importantly, we once again note the emphasis on repetition: "Same old sun / Same old moon / It's the same old story / Same old tune." Here, the protagonist may or may not have entirely worked through his condition. Lapsing into melancholy about a failed romance is not the stuff of heroism in the absurd universe. But even as we understand that our narrator may not have yet risen above his fate, he provides what may be the most succinct encapsulation of the absurd universe ever written: "We contemplate eternity / Beneath the vast indifference of heaven." Achieving this level of consciousness of the nature of absurd existence doesn't mean our story-teller has reached his goal of transcending his bonds, but he's certainly well on his way.

Speaking of being "on one's way," in "My Ride's Here," which highlights what James Campion describes as "the composer's obsession with the vagaries of the universe manipulating mere mortals through life as if chess pieces," Zevon and co-writer Paul Muldoon invoke a host of striking referents (p. 206). There is Christian imagery ("wrestling with an angel," seraphim) and the Hollywood version of Judeo-Christianity ("Charlton Heston with the tablets of the law"). Hollywood's representation of the Old West also appears in a reference to the classic movie "3:10 to Yuma" and in the person of John Wayne (his real first name, Marion, also appears). Added into the mix are the Romantic poets Keats, Shelley, and Byron, writers known for their interest in imagination, the sublime, and freedom from artificial restraints. Thus, art (or Art?) becomes central to any legitimate contemplation of life, death, or the prospect of an afterlife.

The "world beyond" is not, at one level, a topic of much interest for either Zevon or Muldoon, who was to win a Pulitzer Prize for his poetry collection *Moy San and Gravel* a year after his collaboration with Zevon. But Muldoon argues, "it's not so much about what we thought or what we believed: it's the milieu of the song. It's not sad. I'd say, if anything, there's a kind of delighted resignation to it" (p. 209). Is there a more perfect phrase than "delighted resignation" to describe the attitude of Camus's Sisyphus?

To be sure, it may be Zevon's life rather than his songs that tells the more complete story. Asked about having to play "Werewolves of London" and "Lawyers, Guns, and Money" at every concert, he responded that "Getting on stage is always novel to me . . . In a lot of ways, I'm like the goldfish in the Ani DiFranco song; you know, they go around the bowl and every time they see the little plastic castle, it's like they're seeing it for the first time" (Denberg interview). In that song, "Little Plastic Castle," DiFranco adds that "it's hard to say if they're happy, but they don't seem much to mind." Seeing the familiar afresh would seem to be another weapon in Sisyphus's arsenal.

Death, Suicide, and Fighting to Survive

All of this brings us back around to the impetus for Camus's investigation: suicide. Certainly, Warren Zevon's songs deal with death. A lot. Counting work with the Hindu Love Gods, Zevon recorded over two dozen songs whose lyrics include a variation on the words "death" or "kill." Add variations on "shoot" or mentions of firearms, and the total surpasses forty. These numbers don't even include the crucifixion imagery of "Desperados Under the Eaves" or songs like "Werewolves of London" or "Keep Me in Your Heart," which certainly include some of his most obvious insinuations of death. He might have claimed that his songs were less violent than the plays of Aeschylus or Shakespeare, but the body of work tells a some-what different story (Denberg interview).

For all this, there are remarkably few references to suicide, and those that do occur come early in Zevon's career. (Kushins's description of Buddy's "apparent suicide"—p. 320—at the end of "Hit Somebody!" is absurd in a different sense of that term.) "Poor Poor Pitiful Me" opens with such imagery: "I lay my head on the railroad track / I'm waiting for the double E." But there are significant reasons not to take this apparent self-pity too seriously. First, these lyrics are the product of a self-con-sciously edgy twenty-something songwriter. Moreover, the nar-rator seems to tease us rather than beg for sympathy in relating his sexual escapades. Also, the opening line is almost instantly subverted: "The railroad don't run no more." The lis-tener immediately begins to suspect that this is all a joke; par-odic takes on serious subjects were, of course, a Zevon specialty. Finally, like "Excitable Boy," this song features an upbeat, toe-tapping tune that certainly doesn't suggest sober reflection on a very serious subject.

The other song that may refer to suicide is on that same 1976 self-titled album. "I'll Sleep When I'm Dead" features this lyric: "There's a .38 special up on the shelf / I'll sleep when I'm dead / If I start acting stupid I'll shoot myself." There are two points to make here. First, it's unclear, presumably intention-ally so, whether the shooting would be intentional, a volitional response to presumed stupidity, or whether it would be the accidental result of that stupidity. Moreover, by the time of the release of the *Stand in the Fire* live album in late 1980, the lyrics had changed. The handgun was now a .44 Magnum. More significantly, the rest of the sequence now goes, "and I don't intend to use it on myself," as Zevon offers wry self-referential commentary while simultaneously eliminating any ambiguity.

Yet again, however, it may be Zevon's life more than his lyrics that place him in company with Camus. His well-chroni-cled substance abuse certainly qualifies as reckless, and could indeed have killed him, but even in times of despair, depression, and destitution, there is little evidence of *intentional* self-harm. He was often violent towards others, but, somewhat unexpectedly in a hard-core alcoholic, not really towards himself. It's pretty unlikely that we ought to take seriously his claim that he'd have to kill himself if the producers of the TV show *Action* didn't like the theme song they asked him to write (*I'll Sleep When I'm Dead*, p. 367).

Still, there were incidents. David Landau dismisses one moment as "not . . . a serious attempt to hurt himself," but the fact remains he did slash his wrists with broken glass (p. 152). He also shot "himself," that is, his image on the cover of *Excitable Boy*, later declaring the episode "funny" (p. 161). Unsurprisingly, others failed to see the humor, which led to an intervention at a rehab center, where then-wife Crystal and virtually all of his closest friends confronted him with the impact on them of his addiction. Ultimately, he declared he "no longer had the right to pronounce and act out a death sentence" on himself (p. 163). The key words here may be "no longer." True, the death sentence in question was not specifically intentional, but it is no less real for all that. But if Camus's rejection of suicide comes only after considering it, so does Zevon's. He lived for over twenty years after these events.

Yes, there was some concern near the end of his life that he was "trying to outrace the cancer by drinking himself to death" (p. xvii). The point is that he didn't, although he had the means, in both the financial and pragmatic senses of that term, to end his life through overdose at any point during what had to have been a draining and painful last few months. He remarked that "with my vast knowledge of pharmacopeia, I can carve out a nice little comfort zone for myself" (*I'll Sleep when I'm Dead*, p. xvii). He did this, but that it was the cancer that ultimately killed him is surely as unequivocal a rejection of suicide as anything Camus ever wrote. After all, as he told Springsteen, "It's a sin not to try to stay alive" (p. 411).

Coda

What, then, is "the absurd"? At one level, it's a world in which Jesus and John Wayne are staying at the same hotel, a world populated by desperado gorillas, piña colada-loving werewolves with perfect hair, and vengeful ghosts of now-headless Thompson-gunners. In more philosophical terms—those applied by Camus, for example—it describes a universe in which cheating death is regarded by the gods as deserving of eternal punishment, in which amorality is a given, and in which the mundane, the banal, and the repetitious are the weapons used against mere mortals. We all inhabit this philosophical space, but few overcome it. Those who do, the existential heroes, are those with the perspicacity to fully comprehend the forces working against them, the mental and emotional flexibility to seize upon the brief moments of respite, and the honest self-awareness both to act according to their own will and to take responsibility for their actions. Above all, they endure.

No one would suggest that Warren Zevon was an exemplary human being. But in the end, both he and a host of the perhaps not-so-fictional characters he created checked many more of those boxes than they left blank.

Warren Zevon stands atop the hill, watching as the boulder rolls downward away from him. He contemplates eternity beneath the vast indifference of heaven, smiles sardonically, reminds us to enjoy every sandwich, and begins his descent.

We must imagine the Excitable Boy happy.

15

There's Always Room for a Goon in the Life of the Absurd

THOMAS E. MALEWITZ

The author and playwright P.G. Wodehouse, known above all for the fictional characters of farce, Bertie Wooster and his valet Jeeves, once stated that there are two ways of writing a novel. The one involves "making a sort of musical comedy without music and ignoring real life altogether," while the other involves "going right deep into life and not caring a damn" (p. 3). While we associate Wodehouse's style of playful satire with musical comedy and the ignoring of real life, the latter, more brutish perspective on storytelling aptly describes the obscure narrative genius of Warren Zevon.

The lyrical grittiness found in Zevon's ballads and song-stories can only be described as novelistic. It is widely acknowledged that he was a bibliophile. Mitch Albom, the celebrated author and journalist, and friend of Zevon, once recalled, "I had never been to his place before because he would always come down and meet me. I was amazed at how many books and books and books and books . . . everywhere" (*I'll Sleep When I'm Dead*, p. 393). Zevon's vast reading influenced the engaging song-stories he composed. His writing depicts captivating dramatic characters, while directly confronting standards of civility by acknowledging all that is menacing in the world. Zevon's portrayal of characters living on the edge, along with his frequent use of macabre imagery, is reminiscent of Gothic authors like Mary Shelley and Edgar Allen Poe, or their Southern counterpart, William Faulkner.

By elaborating scenes of the absurd and obscene, Zevon's lyrics examine human emotion through depicting a reality that, in its rawness, can be uncomfortable for those satisfied with a sanitized view of human experience. Rather than incorporating such imagery for mere shock value, these fantastical and off-kilter songs are woven from the fabric of his life, then amplified, even exaggerated, so that they evolve into a challenging examination of the meaning, or perhaps lack of meaning, of human existence.

Zevon raises questions that fall comfortably in line with the philosophical movement of existentialism, specifically absurdism. His work follows that of a previous generation of authors, including Franz Kafka and Albert Camus, who argued that traditional definitions of meaning, in a sanitized, post-industrial world, have come to be interpreted as absurd. In the wake of the cultural changes America experienced in the 1960s and 1970s, Zevon's songs focus on themes that likewise expose life's absurdity, through alienation, isolation, rejection, crises of identity, and ultimately death.

In Zevon's work, volatile lyrics accompany upbeat rhythms to create a beautiful, often haunting musical experience. Meanwhile, unnerving characters contend with uncomfortable realities, leaving listeners with an unbalanced view of existence that demands an exploration beyond more superficial accounts of reality, including those associated with civic life. Zevon's lyrical imagery at once reminds listeners that we all have deep desires that at any time could be condemned. His songs challenge listeners to consider that there is a moment of choice that lies between our unhinged desires and the achievement of civility, suggesting that there is always room for each of us to be a "goon."

Exposing the Absurdity of Civil Society

The song-stories of Warren Zevon trudge deeply and honestly into the dregs of life, without caring a damn about what they reveal. There is no patience here for romanticism, only a window into the raw brutality of human experience. Recalling the philosopher Thomas Hobbes's claim that life at its most elemental is "solitary, poor, nasty, brutish, and short," Zevon's lyrics confirm that life proceeds under the persistent threat of impending death. Zevon examines instances of rejection, addiction, revenge, murder, PTSD, rape, and self-destruction. If experience is the best teacher, then his own helped him understand thoroughly the absurdity of the world from the perspective of a reviled outcast. Battling through bouts of alcoholism, as well as acute struggles with obsessive-compulsive disorder, Zevon's well-documented exploits suggest a Jekyll-and-Hyde personality.

Through the refinement of language, Zevon's lyrics provide snapshots of events and situations, highlighting their absurdity. As a student of history, he explores topics that affirm its reverberations in and through the present age. In "Ourselves to Know," he reflects on elements of religious ideology in the context of a pilgrimage during the First Crusade of 1099. His lyrics indicate that human behavior has not changed all that much over the past millennium. Through a twist of irony, he cleverly exploits the very definition of a sacred pilgrimage—a spiritual journey to achieve more deeply one's authentic self—as a metaphor for the wayward habits of the so-called faithful. Instead of growing in their spirituality, the pilgrims in this tale live in a way distinctly at odds with the ideals they profess, everyone managing to get famous and rich, but not without going off the rails and ending in the ditch. Here, Zevon illustrates the tragic decline of a spiritual ideal, embodied in the vision of a peaceful pilgrimage on the cusp of a three hundred year-long series of religious wars. By means of a few powerful words and images, he crafts a visual story that highlights life's antic excesses.

Another example from the Zevon canon that explores the absurd in lurid detail can be found in his song "Mr. Bad Example." Relying on a first-person narrative reminiscent of a pirate ballad, complete with an upbeat, hard-drinking polka, the eponymous narrator recounts his dedicated enactment of the seven deadly sins. The list of nefarious acts recounted in the song includes stealing from both a charity and a family business, fornicating with customers, working as a lawyer and persuading clients to lie in court, selling fake hair treatments to balding men, gambling a fortune on cards in an exotic resort, hiring a prostitute and then stealing her identity to escape the next morning, and tricking Indigenous workers in Australia to slave away in an opal mine.

Ultimately, the narrator of the song decides to retire in contentment, unburdened by any consequences for his transgressions. This furnishes a classic example of life's absurdity, especially in a culture that claims to have achieved a certain level of justice and civility. It thereby constitutes a kind of political parable, which reminds us how the sins of the privileged are often excused or ignored. As James Campion rightly notes, the challenge of Zevon's lyrics is that they pose "a sneering rebuke to those who would stand apart from the fray and dare interject gratuitous opining, despite failing to understand those engaged" (p. 149). Zevon's lyrics challenge listeners to be more than passive bystanders, but to dig deeply into the lived and complex experience of those on the fringes. Together, these two songs introduce us to the complexity of Zevon's perspective, prompting questions about the received narrative concerning who are to count as the real heroes, victims, and villains.

Parallels with Existentialism

Existentialism is a philosophical movement that explores the problem of human existence, especially its meaning, purpose, and value. Evolving from the societal norms and standards of the Industrial Revolution, the philosophical school of Rationalism had long prevailed, but philosophers came to challenge its assumptions. In the nineteenth and twentieth centuries, existential questions were raised outside of a purely academic environment, being incorporated into art, and becoming especially prominent in literature. Much like the existentialists, Zevon introduced existential questions into a new format, that of popular music, challenging traditional perspectives by holding a mirror up to the harsh, often absurd, realities of life.

Born over half a century before Zevon, Franz Kafka similarly questioned the nature of what was presumed to be the civilized political order of his time. In his novel *The Trial* (1925), Kafka challenges the supposed sanity of civilized society by exposing its absurdity. *The Trial* involves a series of events surrounding the central character, Josef K., who is arrested without explanation, either to Josef or the reader. Throughout the events leading up to his trial, Josef meets several nameless individuals who mechanically fulfill their duty in the civic process, never questioning the purpose of their actions.

Traditional authorities, from lawyers to priests, seem to have a thorough knowledge of Josef's case, but are unable or unwilling to clarify the relevant issues for him. This situation enforces an inscrutable divide, for Josef, between the meaning of life, on the one hand, and the complex network of interactions that constitute civil society, on the other. Facing death for an action the significance of which is never explained to him, Josef's predicament symbolizes the absurdity of a system devoid of genuine humanity.

Kafka's novel hints at a deep truth just out of both Josef's and the reader's reach. What is clear, however, is the absurdity of Josef's looming trial and death. In many of his story-songs, Zevon acquaints us with colorful fringe characters whose predicaments and exploits often serve as parables of the absurd that illustrate for the listener that, from society's perspective, anyone can be recognized as a "goon." The following sections will provide a framework for examining the challenge Zevon poses to passive and superficial accounts of reality by exploring themes prominent in the philosophical tradition of absurdism, in particular those concerning identity, alienation, and death.

The Crisis of Identity

For the psychologist Carl Jung, since understanding the very nature of human identity is a continual struggle, man remains "an enigma to himself" (p. 45). Although human beings desire to be known authentically, they are often appreciated only in light of the value that others place upon them. Zevon explores this dissonance, along with the deep longing on the part of those who remain isolated and misunderstood to be appreciated for who they are.

In "Hit Somebody! (The Hockey Song)," which he co-wrote with Albom, Zevon crafts a fatalistic ballad about the life and career of a hockey player that invites renewed contemplation of life's absurdity. In the song, a Canadian farm boy named Buddy dreams of becoming a goal-scoring phenom, like Maurice "Rocket" Richard. Unfortunately, his coach concludes, Buddy's sorely limited talent is better suited to the role of enforcer, a grunt, like the characters portrayed by the Hanson brothers in the *Slap Shot* series, or "The Thug" from the *Goon* movie series, who is responsible for fighting the other teams' players in order to protect his own team's stars.

Zevon's ballad suggests a stark divide between our dreams for ourselves and the limitations imposed on us by others, encouraging listeners to reflect on what it means to seek to live authentically when external forces conspire to thwart our individuality. Zevon concludes the song ambiguously, with Buddy, in the final game of his final season, possibly scoring his one and only career goal, but no less possibly lying dead on the ice, having been cold-cocked on his follow-through by a head-hunting Finn.

"Lawyers, Guns, and Money," one of Zevon's most admired songs, reminds us of the litany of sins recited in "Mr. Bad Example," centering on the exploits of the unnamed narrator, which include cavorting with a waitress who is actually a Russian spy, losing a significant amount of money while gambling in Havana, and hiding out in desperation in Honduras. Like Mr. Bad Example himself, the narrator fails to take responsibility for the consequences of his actions, and, when in a bind, pleads with his father to resolve his problems for him. The refrain of the song urgently implores the father to send lawyers, guns, and money, implying that the narrator can only escape his predicament by undermining the law, including threatening violence and offering bribes. In this way, Zevon presents us with a character who expects his parents to step in and save him, thereby posing the question of what type of family in what type of society is prepared and inclined to do this.

Although we regard such stories as absurd, existential philosophers like Albert Camus remind us that human existence is characterized by a tension between insisting, on the one hand, that our lives are meaningful and suspecting, on the other, that they are entirely devoid of meaning. Camus's masterpiece, *The Myth of Sisyphus*, illustrates this tension by means of a dramatic allegory. In the story, Sisyphus, a Greek hero, is condemned by the gods to roll a boulder up a hill for all eternity. When the boulder eventually rolls down the hill, he must repeat the action of pushing it up the hill, only to watch it roll down, over and over again. The task never ends. Camus's parable challenges readers by confronting us with the fact that we often live day-to-day in a similar position to Sisyphus, pursuing a consistently meaningless routine, without often realizing it.

Zevon indicates that, although most people are restless, lost, and tired of being sold the same lie over and over again, they are condemned, like Sisyphus, to lives of numbing routine from which they can never escape. In "Mohammed's Radio," Zevon confronts us with this bleak predicament, specifically concerning our inability to change the course of our lives in the face of desperation. For Zevon, the absurdity of Sisyphus's situation is reflected in the exhausting struggle of ordinary people to survive, a consuming preoccupation that demonstrates the effort to find meaning in the midst of apparent absurdity.

Monstrosities Created Through Absurdity and Alienation

Over the past thirty years, there have occurred roughly five hundred school shootings in the United States of America. From Columbine and Sandy Hook to the more recent shootings in Parkland and Uvalde, such heinous acts unfortunately seem to be on the rise. This disturbing violence is often committed by perpetrators who have felt rejected by, or at least alienated from, society. When it's revealed that many of the perpetrators had already been diagnosed with severe behavioral problems, questions are routinely asked about why the relevant authorities hadn't intervened. Why aren't there civil protocols in place to prevent such problems from festering and such criminal behavior from escalating?

In "Excitable Boy," Zevon again relies on dissonance between an upbeat melody, reminiscent of Jimmy Buffet's classic "Margaritaville," and macabre lyrics to frame a horrific story. The lyrics recall the bizarre and unnerving actions of a teenage boy, which include him rubbing a pot roast all over his chest, biting an usherette's leg in the dark, raping and killing his date for the junior prom, spending ten long years in a psychiatric home, then digging up the bones of his victim to build a cage with them.

As with the characters in so many other Zevon songs, there are no substantial consequences for the boy's transgressions. The chorus of the song expresses the blithe detachment with which his bizarre behavior is excused: "Excitable boy, they all said / Well, he's just an excitable boy." The tendency to excuse, or simply remain indifferent to, such abominable behavior confirms how little power we have to control and contain a budding monstrosity.

In his classic ballad "Roland the Headless Thompson Gunner," Zevon offers another parable of an alienated figure, this time a headless mercenary who eternally roams the countryside, and whom the world blindly accepts. After being betrayed and decapitated by a comrade in the CIA, Roland, the now-headless tommy gunner, lives on, seeking retribution for the injustice perpetrated against him. This spectral mercenary, who was wronged by a supposedly honorable institution, now inspires others to commit themselves to, or at least see the value in, retribution.

Roland's immortal perspective suggests that actions, whether noble or not, can have bizarre and unintended consequences, well beyond the control of any individual or institution. Zevon dramatically concludes his song by linking the case of his fictional tommy gunner to the 1974 kidnapping of heiress Patty Hearst by the Symbionese Liberation Army and her eventual conversion to their insurgent cause. This final line offers an uncomfortable reminder that anyone, even members of the American elite, can, when alienated from norms they have come to regard as false and hollow, succumb to absurd outrages.

In "Werewolves of London," Zevon once more exploits the dissonance between jaunty melody and macabre lyrics. The lyrics offer an absurd image of a werewolf mutilating an old lady and threatening to rip out someone's lungs, while at the same time attending to the most ordinary functions, like eating a bowl of chow mein and tending to his perfect hair. Perhaps due to his own turbulent experience of excess, Zevon turns a sympathetic eye to those condemned as goons or outcasts by the reigning social narrative.

In his classic novella *The Metamorphosis*, Kafka explores the nature of alienation through the unexplained transformation of the focal character, Gregor, into a monstrous insect. After his transformation, Gregor can no longer support or clearly communicate with his family, so he must rely on them to take care of him. As time passes, however, the monstrous Gregor is so chronically prone to injury that he becomes too much of a burden to his family. Ultimately, he is objectified by and alienated from his family, to the point of death. The story concludes with the family feeling considerable relief at Gregor's death, so much so that they're looking forward to a new life of less financial strain and fewer hardships. In his lyrics, Zevon often slyly acknowledges that, behind the façade of social propriety, we are all one step from becoming a monster in others' eyes.

Death, The Final Act in a Life of Absurdity

Literary philosophers like Kafka and Camus challenge traditional perspectives on the nature of human existence, especially concerning the idea of freedom. Since they claim that human reality can only be understood by acknowledging its absurdity, they resort to surreal imagery in an effort to explore the depths of human consciousness. Camus defines the absurd as the "confrontation between human need and the unreasonable silence of the world" (*Myth of Sisyphus*, p. 37). By acknowledging the inescapability of this condition, he refuses to submit to despair, accepting absurdity as part of the very fabric of life.

Like Camus, Zevon never succumbed to despair, even when facing his cancer diagnosis and impending death. Zevon's frankness and humor even took comedian and late-night host David Letterman completely off guard during his final interview with Zevon on October 30, 2002. Joking about his diagnosis, Zevon stated, "Let me say that I might have made a tactical error in not going to a physician for twenty years . . . It was one of those phobias that didn't really pay off." Letterman later recalled a conversation with a *Late Show* sound assistant about having received news of Zevon's illness. "It was the most bizarre thing," said Letterman, reflecting on "the stunning revelation" of Zevon's diagnosis. "But Warren was making jokes just like that. Now how is that possible?"

Ironically, well before his own terminal diagnosis, death had already emerged as a common theme in Zevon's work. It can even be said to count as the focus of his final three albums: *Life'll Kill Ya* (2000), *My Ride's Here* (2001), and, understandably, *The Wind* (2002). The last of these albums was released two weeks before his death and served as a pseudo-requiem for his perspective on the absurd. While the album as a whole is somber and reflective, Zevon leaves the listener with a final testament concerning both life's eternal absurdity and ultimate reward, particularly through the tracks that bookend the album. The lead track, "Dirty Life and Times," reflects on his isolation from the world at large, exploring his persona as a musician and scrutinizing the life of extremes he had led. On the final track, "Keep Me in Your Heart," Zevon offers a heartfelt plea of remembrance to those who knew him most intimately, beyond the on-stage persona.

In his short story, "Borges and I," Jorge Luis Borges, a representative figure in the "magical realism" movement, addresses the absurd struggle to separate the identity of the artist from that of the actual individual. There is evidence of a similar search in Zevon's work. How do we distinguish between Zevon the over-the-top artist-musician and the introspective man off-stage, between what producer John Rhys calls the "werewolf" and the "classical" side of Zevon? Which one was fixated on death? Which Zevon longed for intimacy?

"Thus," Borges concludes his short story, "my life is a flight and I lose everything, and everything belongs to oblivion, or to the other" (p. 247). This theme of being abandoned to oblivion or to the estimation of others is a common theme in Zevon. It is apparent, for instance, in his portrayal of Elvis in "Porcelain Monkey," in the hypnotic hum of the air conditioner and the slow fade of the view of Gower Avenue in "Desperadoes Under the Eaves," and the persistent questions and unresolved hopes in "Fistful of Rain." But one of the most vivid examples of the inescapability of absurdity, alienation, and death is found in the image of the dysfunctional family celebrating to the music of "that dead band's song" in "Play It All Night Long." Here, Zevon captures the abiding sense of death, looming like a shadow just outside the frame.

In lyrics that memorialize how inescapable our encounters with the unexpected and absurd are, Zevon repeatedly challenges falsely simplified accounts of existence. People, he insists, are infinitely more complex, even contradictory, than socially approved views allow. None of us is immune to the possibility of being labeled a goon and condemned accordingly.

By introducing a gallery of colorful characters, into whose histories he often weaves elements of his own addictive behavior, Zevon offers a stark counter-narrative to prevailing views of social propriety. In his story-songs, he thereby manages, in a way unsurpassed in pop and rock, to continue the legacy of absurdism, since they manage, as Wodehouse puts it, to go "right deep into life" without "caring a damn" about what they reveal.

VII

Life'll Kill Ya

16
In the Face of Death

JAMES CARTLIDGE

It's hard to listen to or think about Warren Zevon without thinking about death, and not just because of how he died. The shadow of death looms large over his entire musical catalogue. Many of his songs are either directly about death and dying or told stories of people who either died, flirted with death, killed people, or all the above. His characters form quite the colorful ensemble: Thompson-toting mercenary ghosts, excitable boys, gangsters, gamblers, cowboys, even boxers, who all play their part in an often gleefully violent theater of murder and death.

But Zevon often took a more personal approach. On his 1995 album *Mutineer*, we find him "contemplating eternity beneath the vast indifference of heaven." *Life'll Kill Ya*, released in 2000, takes mortality as an explicit theme, containing several tracks about aging, sickness, and dying that are poignant and darkly funny in equal measure. The press kit for 2002's *My Ride's Here* described it as "a meditation on death." As his friend Billy Bob Thornton said of Zevon's songs, "the Grim Reaper made a cameo in most of them" (Read interview). Warren Zevon was one of the great songwriters of death, and all this *before* he found out he was dying of cancer.

Zevon has become known not only for his music, but for the remarkable way he approached his suddenly very real mortality, the attitude he took up in the face of death, one displayed in his actions, on his final album, and in his public remarks in interviews and TV appearances. Like Zevon's music, philosophy has also always been concerned with death. Questions about how we should understand, approach, and come to terms with death have plagued humans ever since there were humans, and philosophers ever since Plato (through the voice of Socrates) characterized philosophy as "training for dying" (*Phaedo*, 67e).

Throughout history, philosophers of all stripes have tried to make sense not just of the fact of death and what it means, but the existential angst it produces in us, a defining characteristic of the human condition and one that directly shapes our lives. But what impact does death have on how we live? And what can the case of Warren Zevon tell us about this?

Warren Zevon's Diagnosis

A journal entry from Zevon, dated August 28th 2002, reads:

> Rough day. I went to the doctors. They tell me I have lung cancer. They say I only have three months left to live. In the time I have left, I want to record as many songs as fast as I can. Right now, it's the best way I can think of to say goodbye to my friends and kids. (Read interview)

To accomplish this, Zevon made a couple of what we might call "controversial decisions," one being the refusal of a medical treatment that could, possibly, have prolonged his life. However, the treatment was potentially very debilitating, and he wanted to put whatever energy he had left into making another record. The second decision was going totally public about his illness, hoping to use his predicament to his benefit.

In Crystal Zevon's biography, *I'll Sleep When I'm Dead*, Zevon's manager, Brigette Barr, remembers what he said to her after getting the news: "We have to go into showbiz mode. I'm giving you permission to use my illness in any way that you see fit to further my career right now." Some people would prefer to keep such news private, or only tell close friends and family. Very few people, for example, knew David Bowie was ill before the announcement of his death two days after the release of his final album. Warren went the opposite route. He told everyone, did interviews, got some significant recording money, appeared on David Letterman one last time, and was even the subject of a documentary that chronicled the making of what would be his final album.

The resulting record, *The Wind*, was in many ways the perfect farewell, classic Zevon, the one we'd always known. Songs of dark, country-tinged rock, blistering guitar solos, all mixed with an intelligent, black-as-coal gallows humor. The filthy blues grind of "Rub Me Raw" and the raucous "Disorder in the

House" exemplify this aspect of the album well: hard rocking, dryly funny, utterly defiant. But *The Wind* was also a farewell to family, friends and fans, a deeply personal reflection on his life and impending death. It's an album that balances beautifully between these two aspects, beginning with the words "sometimes I feel like my shadow's casting me" and ending with "keep me in your heart for a while." *The Wind* ranks among Zevon's best, belonging in the same category as albums like David Bowie's *Blackstar* and Leonard Cohen's *You Want It Darker*, works of great artists who knew the end was coming and made that knowledge musical.

Obviously, we shouldn't define Zevon's career entirely by how it ended, because he produced consistently brilliant music since his breakthrough 1976 album, *Warren Zevon*. But his career has become particularly notable for its ending, which had a great impact on his public reputation and how his previous work is perceived. Songs like "My Shit's Fucked Up" and "Don't Let Us Get Sick" sound positively eerie when you know they were written by a man who would soon find out he was dying, as though he somehow, on some level, knew it was coming.

Zevon was asked about this profound "irony" on his famous final appearance on the David Letterman show. He said he didn't know why he was writing those songs at the time but supposed that "artists have some instincts or feelings about things that can't be put into words" that might have alerted him to his situation on an unconscious level before he actually knew about it. These instincts, coupled with an intimate familiarity with drugs and alcohol, meant he probably wasn't entirely surprised at his newfound situation.

> Well, I can't really complain. . . . I think I chose a certain path and lived like Jim Morrison and got to live thirty more years, who knows why? You have to make choices and live with the consequences, and there's always consequences. (*The Late Show with David Letterman*, October 30th 2002)

Except during the late Seventies, around the time of the release of *Excitable Boy*, Zevon was never as famous as he would perhaps have liked to have been. But with his diagnosis, how public he went with it, and his final album, he became more famous than he had been since that previous career highpoint. Due to the open, highly documented nature of his final months, we know a fair amount about how he thought and spoke about dying, how his mortality influenced him, the decisions he made, and his attitude towards his existence.

Despite the tragic nature of his final year and the sadness involved in watching these late interviews and public appearances, there is something remarkable about how he conducted himself in the face of his death—and perhaps we can learn something from it. His often-quoted injunction to "enjoy every sandwich," from his last Letterman appearance, is a simple, direct statement on the importance of appreciating even the smallest moments of our lives, because even they are marvelous, and they won't keep coming forever.

Although he says in the same interview that he'd always felt like he'd enjoyed himself and treasured these moments, his illness made him aware of just how much you're supposed to do this. I would suggest that, from a philosophical or existential point of view, what's interesting about Zevon is the fact that he refused medical treatment to pursue making a final artistic statement. What should we make of someone who does this? Is it right or wrong? Can it *be* right or wrong, or does it vary from person to person? What can it tell us about the human confrontation with mortality?

Zevon did say how he thought his actions should *not* be interpreted. To his disappointment, many of his fans had voiced this interpretation on-line.

> They're all saying it's like, heroic, that I won't get treatment, and I think there's something so incredibly morbid about that. You know I stalled the discussion of having treatment so I could finish the record 'cause I didn't want any drastic alterations to my health other than dying, and boy I was really kinda shocked and disappointed in people when I read that. "That's why he's our hero, because he won't get treatment" . . . I think it's a sin not to want to live. (Read interview)

This perception of his actions clearly displeased him, but why? Two things stand out here: he seemed not to think that refusing the treatment was "heroic," and he didn't refuse treatment because he didn't want to live. He did want to live, but in a particular way and on his own terms. He wanted as little impact on his health as possible, apart from actually dying, so he could live relatively as he wanted to (but for a shorter time) and make a final album. He also directly authorized his manager to use his illness to further his career, be properly in the public eye once more, and ultimately have a say in how he will be remembered. He even commissioned his ex-wife and lifetime friend Crystal to write his biography, which he insisted tell the unflinching truth about him, warts and all.

When faced with his imminent death, Zevon took ownership of his life and legacy to have a say about how he would go and how he would be remembered when he did. Without necessarily saying this is "heroic," there is something existentially significant about it. There might be many reasons for refusing treatment in this situation, but Zevon's was about seizing hold of the time he had left, living it on his own terms and delivering a final artistic flourish.

Martin Heidegger's *Being and Time*

In thinking about all this, it's natural and fascinating to link Zevon with the philosophy of Martin Heidegger, specifically the idea of "authentic being-towards-death" from his 1927 masterpiece, *Being and Time*. Zevon was actually familiar with this book, since a 1995 diary entry reveals he once gave it as a birthday present to fellow songwriter J.D. Souther (*I'll Sleep When I'm Dead*, p. 322). Heidegger's philosophy was driven by the word "being" from start to finish. Specifically, he wanted to answer *the question of what "being" means*. Heidegger thought no one had ever been able to answer this question, which is a concern, because he also thought that all other questions lead back to it. We can't expect to know what a molecule *is*, what knowledge *is*, or what evil *is* until we know what the "is" means. Heidegger accused the history of philosophy of "forgetting" the question of being and failing to investigate it properly. Almost all his philosophy is dedicated to trying to correct this mistake, and his most famous attempt at doing so, the work for which he is remembered more than any other, is *Being and Time*.

In this landmark text, Heidegger undertakes a painstaking analysis of human existence, attempting to figure out how it is structured, what its important and defining elements are. The guiding idea is this: to find out what being means, we should find out what it means for a particular type of entity to be, and human beings are special because only we can raise the question of being. Heidegger chose to analyze the existence of the entity which can raise the question he wanted to answer. He actually called the entity he wanted to analyse "Dasein" (an everyday German word for existence) rather than "human being."

Humans are a type of Dasein (we must be, because we can raise the question of Being), but Heidegger argued that Dasein might not be limited to humans, so his use of "Dasein" meant that, really, he was doing something different to analysing human existence. This is a controversial claim in Heidegger scholarship, but since what Heidegger wrote about Dasein clearly also applies to human beings, I will speak here only of humans.

One of the driving insights of *Being and Time* is that if we want to ask, understand, or answer a question, we must know what it is about our existence that allows us to ask, understand or answer questions. What is it about us that gives us our incredible capacity for philosophical wonder, the capacity to contemplate justice, God, time, the nature of existence, or the meaning of being? Heidegger's rationale was to start here, hoping this would provide a solid foundation for dealing with the question of being adequately. Whether or not Heidegger ever answered this question is debatable, but his attempt to do so is one of the most fascinating philosophical projects of the past century, although a very challenging one. Heidegger's writing is notoriously abstract and full of jargon words that he made up because he wanted to avoid overused traditional philosophical language, but his work concerns the most fundamental issues about what it means to be human.

One of the things Heidegger tries to do in *Being and Time* is to identify what he calls "existential structures," things that feature in *every* case of human existence, without which we wouldn't really be human. Intuitively, death seems to be one of these structures—every human being dies. But even though death is clearly part of the human condition, Heidegger points out that death is not actually part of our existence. We never experience being dead. Death is the end of our existence, so it cannot be a part of it. Heidegger says that death is always a "possibility," never an "actuality." We never *actually* experience death and are only aware of it as a constant *possibility* hanging over us. So, how can death be an existential structure if it is not actually part of our existence?

For Heidegger, it is not so much about our actual death, but the way the possibility of death determines how we live. What we do, think, consider important or meaningful, what motivates us, how we act around other people, the way we organise our worlds, our entire existence is shaped, structured by the fact that our lives are finite. Things wouldn't mean what they mean to us if we could keep experiencing them forever. This doesn't necessarily mean that we're always thinking about death, but even when we're not thinking about it, death plays an integral role in the fabric of our being. We are always, as Heidegger puts it, in a state of "being-towards-death," and this is an existential structure. From the moment we begin to exist, we are hurtling towards our death, and this fact plays a part in everything we do.

Authentic and Inauthentic Being-Towards-Death

But does this mean everyone is being-towards-death in the same way, or that everyone takes up the same attitude towards death? Heidegger claims that there are two different ways we can be, "authentic" and "inauthentic." We can be-towards-death "authentically" or "inauthentically." (The word for "authenticity" in Heidegger's German is *Eigentlichkeit*, which contains the word "eigen," meaning "own," so the original German has connotations of "owning" that the English translation does not, which is important for Heidegger's use of the term.) Heidegger argues that, by default, we are inauthentic, and we spend most of our time this way. Nobody is authentic all the time. Instead, we only achieve it in certain situations, with the right attitude.

Authenticity is connected with Heidegger's analysis of other people. Being among others, being part of a social community, plays an obviously important role in our lives. It teaches us how to be a person, how to act around people, what social norms are, how to live within them, and generally what is important about being human. Other people play a crucial role in the formation of our identity. In fact, Heidegger claims that we owe our identity to other people. He argues that what makes us who we are as individuals are not those unique features that distinguish us from everybody else, but the fact that *we do not distinguish ourselves* from other people. We know who we are by knowing that we belong to a social community, that we are human, like everybody else. This commonality with others, rather than distinguishing us from them, is the basis for our individual identities.

But this is not the whole story. Because other people play this important role in shaping our identities, it's easy to go along unthinkingly with what everyone else does and thinks. Rather than shouldering the heavy burden of deciding for ourselves who we want to be, we can unknowingly become dominated by the mood, opinions, and norms of our culture. Not only does this highlight the difference between authenticity and inauthenticity, it's also where Heidegger's idea of the "they" comes in.

When we are inauthentic, we just go along with what "they," other people in general, do. Not this person or that one, this group or another, but the neutral, indeterminate mass—*they*—that exerts this profound influence on your life because you are a social creature. Being inauthentic means succumbing to the inconspicuous power, the herd mentality of the "they," without properly taking responsibility for your existence, your thoughts, opinions, actions, and choices.

One of Heidegger's most famous passages says that when we are inauthentic "we take pleasure and enjoy ourselves as *they* take pleasure; we read, see and judge about literature and art as *they* see and judge," and "we find shocking what *they* find shocking" (*Being and Time*, p. 164). While it's impossible to escape fully from *their* influence, being authentic involves not letting your life be completely determined by them, forging your own path within the social space and taking responsibility for your identity, your choices, your being. To be authentic is to *own* your life, while to be inauthentic is to have your life owned by *them*.

Heidegger suggests that being truly authentic is difficult, and therefore not something we can do all the time. If you were totally rebellious against the "they" concerning every little thing, you would surely go insane. But authenticity is a state of being you can achieve with the right attitude in the right situations. So, being authentic requires confronting your mortality. You must understand life for what it is and live accordingly, with no illusions about the fact that your life is finite. Otherwise, you would not understand life on its own terms. While we all at some point realize that we will die, coming to terms with this fact is a different thing altogether. Not everyone manages this, which shows that it is one of the most difficult things about being human.

To fail to appreciate, to think about or accept your mortality fully, would be "inauthentic being-towards-death," in Heidegger's terms. You would still be being-towards-death, but without confronting this fact adequately, simply going along with life without really considering the significance of your finitude. One troublesome aspect of Heidegger's thoughts on this subject is that he *insists* that being inauthentic is not "worse" than being authentic. His intention is simply to describe the structure of our existence and the possibilities that lie within it. But we do not have to follow him on this. Would it not be better to be authentic, at least some of the time, when it matters?

Learning to accept your mortality is a difficult task, but one everyone must face up to. It comes to us all eventually: "life'll kill ya," indeed. For Heidegger, authentic being-towards-death involves consciously taking ownership of your life, its direction, and meaning, which cannot be achieved without a serious reckoning with your mortality, which is also your own.

No one can die for you. It's not that you must develop a morbid obsession with death, to the extent that you're always thinking about it, but once you come to terms with your death, it affects everything about how you live your life. To think about death is to think about your existence, as a whole. An encounter with your death, unpleasant as it may be, is the only way to make complete sense of your life, and you cannot live authentically without it. What can we learn about Warren Zevon's case from all of this? What questions can we use Heidegger's philosophy to ask about it?

Warren Zevon's Authentic Being-Towards-Death

Whatever you think the right thing to do in his situation would have been, you cannot accuse Zevon of failing to take responsibility for his life during the time he had left. He knew what he wanted to do, had a vision about how he wanted to do it, and used everything at his disposal to get it done on his own terms. His final album was probably as close to a perfect final Zevon album as was possible, one that contained something of every musical side of him that we'd seen throughout his career and represented a powerful attempt to make sense artistically of his life and death. His actions in the run-up to his death show a man who was (in his own way) putting his affairs in order, forcefully having a say in how he would be perceived and remembered. This is a direct manifestation of what Heidegger called "authentic being-towards-death," because Zevon properly took hold of his life and choices in light of his impending death in order to live his remaining life on his own terms. Zevon's case was quite a drastic one, given how little time he was given to live after his diagnosis. Not every case of authentic being-towards-death has to be this drastic, but it is plausible that it can arise from the right contexts, especially those which starkly confront a person with his mortality.

An important question you might raise here is, was Zevon right to do what he did? Perhaps the "right" thing to do in this situation would not be the same for everyone, because what is authentic or inauthentic also would vary from person to person. People have very different lives, emerge from very different social contexts, have different political views, different senses of what is good, bad, right, or wrong, so "authentic" cannot mean the same thing for everyone. What counts as authentic is something you must figure out for yourself, on your own, for your own reasons.

We are not all under-rated artists who want to make a final statement. Some people, in Zevon's situation, would probably

snatch with both hands the treatment he rejected, eager to pro-
long their lives as much as possible, to secure every possible
extra day on this Earth to spend with loved ones, doing the
things they love. If this comes at the cost of being debilitated
and living at a reduced capacity, so be it. They would want to
live for as long as possible, whatever that meant.

For a certain sort of person, with a certain worldview and
type of life, could this not be just as authentic as what Zevon
did? For such a person, this could be an authentic vision of owning the time that remained to him. It could be, and no doubt has
been, for many people. How you face up authentically to your
death is a solitary matter that requires you to make your own
decisions about. But precisely because it is so solitary and
because people are so different, authenticity is clearly not going
to manifest itself in the same way for everyone.

But if what Zevon did was authentic, for him, why was he so
adamant that it wasn't heroic? Presumably, he thought it was
the right, perhaps the authentic, thing to do, so why wouldn't
we view his manner of confronting death as somewhat heroic?
Truly, this is a hard question to answer, and I haven't been able
to find any other reflections of Zevon's on this point. If it has
anything to do with authenticity, perhaps that's because it's not
necessarily heroic to be authentic, but part and parcel of the
task of being human.

It's your job to be a functioning person and to figure out for
yourself the direction in which you want to take your life, and
who you want to be. It's your job to own your life and your
choices, and not have them be determined by others. No one
gets a medal for that. Zevon said, "it's a sin not to want to live,"
so presumably it would be unheroic to give up and refuse treatment for that reason. His reason for refusing treatment was
different, because he wanted to live on his own terms. But it's
not heroic to want to live either; you're supposed to want to.

Warren Zevon was one of the great songwriters of death, from
the beginning to the very end, and his conduct in the face of
death presents an interesting case for philosophers to contemplate from an existential point of view. I hope to have shown this
by referring to Heidegger's idea of "authentic being-towards-
death," which I have argued, Zevon, when confronted with his
mortality, personified in his behaviour and conveyed in his art.
His music consistently took death as a theme, but *The Wind* is
one of the great musical attempts to make sense of the fact of
impending death, while offering a final artistic statement. It is
also, in many ways, a classic Warren Zevon album, containing
everything we've come to know and love about his music.

There are probably many ways that authentic being-towards-death can be manifested from person to person, but, faced with his own death, Zevon immediately went public with his illness, assumed responsibility for his public perception and legacy, and recorded one last album. If this can't be described in terms of heroism, perhaps it can be described in terms in Heidegger's sense of authenticity.

17

Winded: Warren Zevon's Last Act

THOMAS H. KANE

> The nature of his wound was the clock-cicada winding down.
> He wound down.
>
> —LUCY BROCK-BROIDO, "Father, in Drawer"

In August 2002, Warren Zevon was diagnosed with terminal lung cancer. As his own capacity to breathe was diminishing, he composed songs for the ironically titled album, *The Wind*. The mordant title is in perfect keeping with Zevon's career, which included writing many acerbic lyrics and songs. It also importantly and humbly suggests the ephemeral in nature, that Zevon's life, like a mandala, can be swept away. Paradoxically, perhaps, the album itself still stands. But much of the content of the album verges on sentimentality, as Zevon reflects on his impending death and attempts to make amends with loved ones and listeners alike. The songs ring with his mortality.

The album exemplifies a genre I call "auto*morto*graphy," or self-representation in the face of death. I contrast it with auto*bio*graphy, where figures reflect on the *life* they've lived, whereas auto*morto*graphy shows the self anticipating and contending with its own mortality. By attending closely to the lyrics and music of songs like "Keep Me in Your Heart," we can appreciate Zevon facing his mortal predicament and attend to his witness. Zevon's automortography, *The Wind*, holds a special place in his catalogue, allowing for a greater appreciation of his humanity, as his signature irony is turned inward, where he settles accounts with an existential humility.

Flipping the Hourglass

From the start, Warren Zevon sought fame. He wrote clever, pithy songs that played like biting ironic folk tales and a critique of power *after* the idealism of the 1960s. He was a folksinger for the Me Generation. Having been trained in classical piano in his youth, he wrote melodic songs usually initiated with the piano. On top of his riffs, he laid witty lyrics, often about the dark comedy of human folly. His biggest hit came in 1977 with "Werewolves of London," a piano stomp with a literal howl for a chorus.

Zevon never attained the kind of fame he sought. With his icy lyricism and his "genius" for musical composition, he was always well-respected by fellow musicians. But pop music stardom eluded him. In the early Eighties, Zevon's fame came more from his own bad behavior, due to drug and alcohol use, than from his music. But he eventually attained sobriety and continued to write and tour. By the mid-1990s, the venues had shrunk to breweries, which could make him sullen. Still, David Letterman remained a steadfast promoter of all-things-Zevon, having him stand in for Paul Shaffer for two weeks in 2000, and devoting a full show to him after his cancer diagnosis was disclosed, in October 2002.

Zevon first started feeling short of breath when he performed at an outdoor festival in Calgary, Alberta, in the summer of 2002. He maintained a deep skepticism and maybe even existential laziness about medicine, but was pushed by a cousin to see a doctor, who told him he had three months to live. Zevon responded to the diagnosis with urgency. It is not uncommon for those who feel or know the end is nigh to turn on a productivity switch, flipping over the hourglass. Indeed, a whole genre, *automortography*, is the result.

There can be a wide range of motivations behind such work. For Charles Bukowski, it was liberating, as he dedicated his final novel, *Pulp*, "to bad writing." Raymond Carver turned to poetry. David Bowie recorded the songs and videos for *Blackstar*, including the song, "Lazarus." The writer Kathy Acker recorded an album with The Mekons. David Wojnarowicz left photographs of himself in Chaco Canyon with explicit instructions not to expose them for twelve months after his death. Many wish to leave *something*, while some wish to use that something to play with the boundaries between life and death.

Warren Zevon knew that at the end he would benefit from a period of genuine attention and good feeling, and he was determined to make the most of it. He was transparent about this paradox—as he could be about many things. He used his dead-pan irony to describe it: "If you're lucky, people will like something you do early and something you do just before you drop dead. That's as many pats on the back as you should expect."

This knowledge (of his death) and attention (from the media) does not diminish the authenticity of Zevon's automortography, although it does elevate some of the self-consciousness. But then, Zevon was always self-conscious. Indeed, it suggests that part of Zevon's motivation stemmed from an appreciation for the special status of last acts. The songs that were recorded as *The Wind* have a different status than other of Zevon's songs; we can *hear* them differently because we listen in the context of his mortality, because we listen *for* his mortality.

Zevon knew that publicizing his diagnosis would attract considerable attention. And it did. He then had to deal with economizing that attention, along with husbanding his limited time. For years, he'd wanted VH1, the video channel, to do a "Behind the Music" episode on him. For years, they'd declined. He did not want to be included in a One-Hit Wonder series when it was pitched to him in the late-1990s. He cared deeply about his fame. Now, with the diagnosis public, VH1 came with their cameras and Zevon wasn't too proud to turn them away. He collaborated in the making of "(Inside) Out: Warren Zevon, Keep Me in Your Heart," an hour-long documentary directed by Nick Read on the recording of *The Wind*. Zevon's manipulation of the media concerning his diagnosis shows that he understood and anticipated the implications of this unique status. And, with the footage, he left an intimate and compelling portrait of himself at the end, surrounded by friends, working toward the completion of that one final album.

Life'll Kill Ya

At the age of fifty-three, Zevon released what would be his third-to-last album, *Life'll Kill Ya* (2000). Collapsing his celebrity and self, Zevon's promotion for the album included comments in interviews that were particularly morbid, like, "my career is as promising as a Civil War leg wound," and, "I'd say the hearse is at the curb at this point, both professionally and personally." There are two essentially automortographic elements of *Life'll Kill Ya* that I want to concentrate on, as they set up Zevon's choices to record his final album. The songs show, first, the genre's uncanny sense of time and, second, how one approaches limited time.

The closing song is "Don't Let Us Get Sick." It's an acoustic waltz that leads with the lines, "Don't let us get sick, don't let us get old, don't let us get stupid, alright?" The lines *play differently* upon Zevon's eventual diagnosis; his wish not to be "sick" echoes with prophecy and denial. It opens up speculation about his intuition or bodily knowledge: did he *feel* it on some level? And, it serves as an uncanny portal to review and revive numerous allusions to death and the body in earlier songs. Most famously, perhaps, "he'll rip your lungs out Jim," from "Werewolves of London," fixates the listener on that part of Zevon's body, his lungs, that would fail him, would be the site of his sickness. This is not to suggest that *he knew* in the 1970s what his fate would be, but it does suggest that his fate forces a recontextualizing, a fresh and fated new way of hearing these and numerous other lines. So, when we now hear lines from "Don't Let Us Get Sick," they ring differently. For instance, "Just make us be brave" sounds now like Zevon rehearsing the stoic response.

After his diagnosis, he sent his doctor copies of *Life'll Kill Ya* and *My Ride's Here*, with a note explaining how his reserved response to hearing his diagnosis may have been due to his (unconscious) preparation evident in these songs. Now, when we hear the line, "I thought of my friends and the trouble they've had, to keep me from thinking of mine," we can appreciate Zevon's choice to record in his final months. He is deflecting, while at the same time existentially *acting*. The automortographic songs pre-occupy him, granting him agency at the end; he can both defer mortal reflection and produce songs that stand as a testament. After the end, Zevon and others who produce automortographies appear to have anticipated their memory, creating works that occupy a future anterior tense, "what will have been."

Issues of temporality arise frequently in automortography, with motifs of clocks, sunsets, or the ephemeral proving quite common. Zevon's choice to record songs, given his three-month prognosis, was held up in chat rooms as taking a stand against conventional therapies. He was appalled that internet chats called him a hero for not seeking treatment, saying, "I think it's a sin not to want to live." It is clear that had he been given a different horizon of time—six years, two years—instead of three months, he likely would have approached the situation differently. Laura Carstensen calls this "socio-emotional selectivity theory"—deciding how to spend time depending on an existential horizon or finitude. People who have limited time, a diagnosis of a few months, commonly give up seeking worldly accolades and, instead, opt to spend time with loved ones. To a degree, Zevon's choice to record an album defies Carstensen's research: he goes to work. But recording gives him a legitimate excuse to reconnect with beloved musicians and to write songs for, and in a sense to, those he loved. Given how little time he thought he had, he insisted on concentrating on writing and producing as many songs as possible.

The Wind

Zevon's diagnosis, and its public disclosure, invites a distinct posthumous listening, just as it invited a pre-posthumous recording. That is, the fact of Zevon's mortality served as a siren call for numerous famous and skilled musicians to help him record these last songs. This unique time also, then, served as an opportunity for Zevon to reconcile with specific musicians whom he'd fallen out of favor with (some for decades, after his debauchery of the late-Seventies and early-Eighties), while providing them with a sense of fulfillment in lending a hand at his end.

The list of contributors to *The Wind* reads like a super-group on a Rock'n'Roll Hall of Fame induction night: Don Henley, Jackson Browne, Gil Bernal, Bruce Springsteen, Ry Cooder, Joe Walsh, Tom Petty, Mike Campbell, John Waite, and Emmylou Harris, among many others. The songs reflect Zevon's typical range, what he called "grunge classical," but the concentration of star-power elevates them in comparison to much of Zevon's previous work.

Now, for a closer look at these final songs, I *listen for* Zevon's mortality. While I might be accused of overreading, the context of automortography *invites* that. The songs now stand between Zevon's dying intent and my living listening. It is in this space that the unique status of automortography literally *plays* out. Zevon is seen and heard leaning toward his mortality. And I hear these songs *through* the fact of his death. The songs, then, have what Paul Ricoeur, in *Time and Narrative,* calls, "double intentionality." I hear back through the fact of Zevon's death, and, at the same time, hear Zevon *anticipating* my listening. By the time anyone hears the album, the fact of his death is (literally) immutable.

The Wind, in keeping with Zevon's previous work, includes a range of song styles: upbeat piano-based compositions, raucous blues, slide-guitar numbers, melancholic ballads, and acoustic pieces. While one could organize the songs in terms of Kübler-Ross's famous "stages of grief," I find the theory too linear, and the album more nuanced. I am going to consider them not in the order they appear on the album, but by style, because the genres and aesthetics reflect different aspects of Zevon's mortal predicament and his response to it. For instance, a ballad may be more reflective, and a raucous number may sound more resistant, existentially, when considered as automortography. I will close with the more meditative songs, which sound more direct, and, as a result, benefit from a distinctly automortographic sentiment.

Were this a rock'n'roll tour, Bruce Springsteen would clearly get top billing. Zevon and Springsteen had co-written "Jeannie Needs a Shooter" in the late-1970s. During sessions for *The Wind*, Springsteen recorded for a day, producing a boisterous blues number, "Disorder in the House," that would go on to be chosen as the first single from the album. While the title might be misread to allude to Zevon getting his own "house" in order, it is an early-'oughts political song that today sounds as if it might have been written in the aftermath of the January 6th 2021 insurrection.

The closing lyrics are: "It's home of the brave / and land of the free / where the less you know / the better off you'll be." Springsteen's vocals are a gutbucket shout, with emotion summoned from the energy and tenor more than the intelligibility of the lyric. After the third verse, he also rips a raw and unpredictable guitar solo. "Disorder" is a raucous number, though Zevon sounds as if he is laboring. He's nearly lost in the musical haze, his voice incapable of keeping pace with Springsteen's shrill shout. It's as if Springsteen's raw vigor is trying to *enliven* Zevon, and refuse his mortality. Bruce lends his stardom to Zevon here at the end, creating a single that helps Zevon and his heirs financially, and propelling *The Wind* up the music charts, enough for it to land at number twelve on the Billboard charts, the highest for Zevon since his bestselling 1978 album, *Excitable Boy*. And the single "Disorder in the House" did climb, winning a Grammy for Best Rock Vocal Performance (Group or Duo). *The Wind* itself ended up as Zevon's *only* Grammy-winning album, for Best Contemporary Folk Album. People *heard* the album differently.

Zevon was not afraid of including autobiographical material in his songs. Indeed, the critic Robert Christgau ironically praised Zevon's collaboratively written 2002 album, *My Ride's Here*, because it spared listeners from hearing songs about Zevon's love life. That said, some of Zevon's songs depend on absurdist conceits, some of which suggest alienation or dissociation. If they are autobiographical, they are dreamlike, as if they happened to someone else. In part, this may be due to Zevon's history of drug use. In response to an inquiry from the comedian Kathy Griffin about a contributor to one of his albums, he quipped, "I'm not even sure *I* played on that record."

His darker periods are essential to understanding Zevon at the end, not as someone who is redeemed, but by offering him a register of his self that is alien or dissociated—there but not there. On "Numb as a Statue" and "Dirty Life and Times," Zevon invites an alienated autobiographical listening, with each song serving as an object that is both his and ours. His non-feeling (numbness) is both a metaphor for this state, and a literal description of his desire for feeling at the end (perhaps due to his use of pain-killers). And the statue serves as an icon of immortality. "I'm numb as a statue, I may have to beg borrow or steal some feelings from you, so that I can have some feelings too." Riding a guitar that sounds like Zevon's compadres from the 1970s, it's a song in search of sentiment. A song about the effects of medical treatment, it refuses to be saccharine, standing instead as a fine example of Zevon's mordant wit. In a moment of sincerity, he sings, "I'm pale as a ghost but you know what I love about you, that's what I need the most." And then, over the bridge, he hollers, "Can I get a witness?" Indeed, the entire album is an act of witness—both his and ours. He is testifying to his mortality, and listeners are bearing witness to it.

Zevon never tried to deny his ugly past. Instead, the bad-boy mythology fueled him, giving him the credibility of a rock star and the narrative of redemption, a narrative he was not wholly comfortable with. As much as he appreciated the effects of the intervention in the 1980s that eventually led to sobriety, he was deeply skeptical of any addict's congratulatory impulse. Still, he plays with self-mythologizing (a more direct, but still alienated, register of autobiography), in the first song on the album, "Dirty Life and Times."

With a slide guitar, and the rhythm of a southern shanty, the song is staged as a confession. It begins: "Some days I feel like my shadow's casting me / Some days the sun don't shine / Some days I wonder what tomorrow's gonna bring / When I think about my dirty life and times." This sounds like Zevon dealing with his present predicament and reflecting on his bad-boy past. Importantly, there is no hint of self-pity here. Still, he does not disclose any actual dirt, convinced that there are plenty who would "hunt me down and hang me for my crimes / If I tell about my dirty life and times." So, the piece verges on a confession, and is rife with witty lines ("I'm looking for a woman with low self-esteem"), but it is *about* confession, while not being one. The piece resolves itself with the line entertaining the possibility that he might be able to ease his worried mind, "while winding down my dirty life and times." It is clear-eyed, but, while we hear about his "worried mind," we are not given any glimpse of it. His worries remain his own. As a death-bed tell-all, it is a failure, but as a pop song, its self-deprecating wit typifies Warren Zevon. In his recent book *The Philosophy of Modern Song,* Dylan describes it as "a daredevil of a song" and "undaunted and unafraid" (p. 192).

Two songs, "The Rest of the Night" and "Rub Me Raw," might sound like filler on another album, each peppered with clichéd couplets that a Zevon fan who values his intricate lyricism can only chalk up to existential haste. But these two songs reflect a common tactic of automortography, taking up the issues of time and pain. What's more, the clichés resonate less as lazy than as a gesture to the universal: I am dying and there are only so many ways to say it. "The Rest of the Night" is a *carpe diem* anthem punctuated with the chorus, "We may never get this chance again / Let's party for the rest of the night." Zevon is joined by Mike Campbell and Tom Petty, whose voice hovers above Zevon's for most of the lines. Many of the lyrics are counting the hours on the clock as the night winds down. Zevon may be his most full-throated in this song, suggesting it was recorded earlier in the process. He still had time to *sound* like himself even if the lyrics are fairly clichéd. "Rub Me Raw" is a traditional electric blues piece, with Joe Walsh playing a Muddy Waters-style guitar that evolves into a wailing slide over the chorus later in the song: "Oh no, these blues are gonna rub me raw." Zevon is up to the task, but *he* is the one who is getting rubbed raw, with that word "raw," sounding like his own bodily pain. The plaintive wail of the "oh, no" sounds like a cry, but one that still has vigor—the "rubbing raw" is in the future, a promissory pain.

Songs of Humility

The Wind alternates between more upbeat rock and blues numbers and more meditative ballads. In the ballads, Zevon's biography and mortality are inescapable, and framed by a male sentimentality, or gendered melancholy. For all his claims of needing to feel on "Numb as a Statue," Zevon's ballads show a man both indulging in and provoking feeling. Two of these songs were written by Zevon alone (while all of the other songs on the album were co-written with Jorge Calderón, Zevon's long-time song-writing partner), namely, "She's Too Good for

Me" and "Please Stay." And, taken together, they reveal an un-guarded vulnerability in Zevon at the end.

"She's Too Good for Me" is an acoustic piece, punctuated by maracas and bongos. The song addresses a love who has left. There is self-pity, but also a maturity, in wanting the best for an ex. It sounds like Zevon wishing that a lover will find love after his death. The vocals sound weak and tentative.

"Please Stay" is a plodding piano number. Zevon begins with a wobbling voice that climbs, "Please stay. Two words I thought I'd never hear you say. Don't go, don't go, please stay." Zevon tries out a falsetto, then "I need you near, to me." Emmylou Harris seems to relieve him of the falsetto, providing backing vocals, and Gil Bernal plays a melancholic sax that serves as counter-point. But the point of view is complicated here. As opposed to the maturity of letting go in "Too Good," the speaker here is plainly begging not to be left alone. But in keeping with the slip-pery self of automortography, the point of view in the song is unstable. That is, Zevon sets it up so that *he* is the one hearing someone else beg him to "please stay." This then fits into a nar-rative of redemption for Zevon: he never thought he'd hear her say, "please stay." He is now beloved. The tribulations in the past meant that he was the one always sent packing. But, because the lines are sung by Zevon himself, they become his words, the plea in his actual voice rings as *his* in a death bed, grasping. He is the one begging, "please stay." He is direct, vulnerable and needy, even as he's given his self the space of plausible deniability.

Winding Down

There are two songs that I'd like to focus on in thinking about questions of authenticity and self-representation at the end, "Knocking on Heaven's Door" and "Keep Me in Your Heart." When Bob Dylan learned of Zevon's diagnosis in September 2002, he began to cover his song "Mutineer" in concert. Zevon was touched by this and was determined to return the favor by covering a Dylan song on his final album. Zevon's signature irony, most often seen in his lyrics, is very apparent in the choice of Dylan song, "Knocking on Heaven's Door," a song cov-ered by many, but none so obviously and literally facing "heaven's door." This is the most self-conscious version of the song, with everyone involved already knowing Zevon's diagno-sis. Ry Cooder's slide guitar makes the song sound like it has sprung from Lynyrd Skynyrd's vault. But the music carefully complements while refusing to eclipse Zevon's subdued and understated vocals.

Zevon's performance is utterly authentic. Whereas other singers have to affect a break in their voice or some desperation, Zevon simply speak-sings the song straight, knowing that the listener will not be able to unhear the death that mediates and silently saturates the whole thing. Even the tenor of his cracking voice plays as existential. Zevon's one real addition to Dylan's song is an incantation of a phrase in counterpoint. Late in the song, as the backup singers are repeating, "Knock, knock, knocking on heaven's door," Zevon can be heard repeating the phrase, "Open up! Open up!" and in the closing seconds, "Open up for me!" It works musically because the counterpoint adds syncopation. But it also reverses the logic of Dylan's original, where a cowboy is slowly dying, resigning himself in his final moments. Instead, we have Zevon imploring that heaven be open to him. This might reflect a wish that he will receive an affirmative divine judgment, or it may be a recognition that he's on the outside, wanting in. Either way, the insistent repetition of "open up" tells the listener that Zevon has agency, is ready and embracing his own end.

The final song on the album, "Keep Me in Your Heart," was nominated for two Grammys, Song of the Year and Best Vocal Performance. While it did not win either, the piece is *the* signature song of the album. (It lost Song of the Year to another automortographic song, Luther Vandross's "Dance with My Father.") It is Zevon's second most popular song, when it comes to streaming statistics, and is a quintessential example of automortography.

The song begins almost matter-of-factly: "Shadows are falling and I'm running out of breath, keep me in your heart for a while." Zevon's voice is strong and clear at the start, betraying none of the sense of an ending, despite the lyric. In the second verse, one can hear some shortness of breath, including during the bridge (on the word "view"). He uses the metaphor of a train and an engine driver. "These wheels keep on turning but they're running out of steam / Keep me in your heart for a while." *The Wind* is winding down.

"Keep Me in Your Heart" is a song of humility, as the speaker is not seeking immortality, but instead asking to be "kept" for "awhile," an indeterminate amount of time that sounds nothing like eternity. It is addressed to an intimate, who is being asked to remember. It has strong echoes of one of Raymond Carver's final poems, "Late Fragment," which begins as a question, a bit of internal dialogue, "And did you get what / you wanted from this life, even so?" Here, the "even so" refers to Carver's acknowledgement of his terminal cancer diagnosis at fifty, much like Zevon's. The poem continues with the response: "I did. / And what did you want? / To call myself beloved, / to feel myself beloved on the earth." There is a directness and acceptance here, a sense of fulfillment that sounds like satisfaction, fulfillment and humility. But the last line of the poem also reveals that it is all about *how he feels*. "Keep Me in Your Heart" reflects the same logic, one that reveals the male ego acknowledging mortality and provoking the feeling of others to recognize and remember.

Because Carver has been "beloved," he implies and imagines the feeling of future loss for those who have made him feel beloved. Zevon's song is similarly phantasmatic. In the bridge, he sings in falsetto, asking to be held in the other's thoughts, kept in her dreams, touched as he falls into view, and to be near one another when the winter fires are lit. Relying on the future anterior tense, he is imagining what will have been. On the bridge, Zevon's voice becomes thin, the breathiness belying the urgency that the speaker feels, as its tone shifts from wishing to imploring. Here, on this particular day, recording in his living room, he's imagining and, indeed, *willing* someone to, one day, in the distant winter (the vocal was recorded in April), think back and feel for him. A *man* facing his death is not only allowed such a sentiment, but is applauded for it. It is one of the common gender markers in some works of automortography: men feeling for themselves as they imagine others in the future feeling for their absence.

Even the likes of Howard Stern have expressed how moving he found the song, as he asked Eddie Vedder to cover it. As a side note, in listening to Eddie Vedder's over-stylized vocals in his cover, one can gain an appreciation for the straightforward candor of Zevon's original. There were reasons for Zevon's style; it was the last set of vocals he recorded. It may be the most direct song Zevon ever performed or recorded. It refuses his signature irony. In this aesthetic reversal, the song seems akin to what Edward Said calls "late style," when artists assert a kind of artistic autonomy by refusing the expectations of their audience at the end. Regardless, Zevon has left us with this spare, direct, plaintive self-elegy.

In the VH1 special, the recording of "Keep Me in Your Heart" is the concluding footage, far too powerful to place anywhere but at the end. The film shows the mic being set up near the couch, Zevon singing while his son and daughter look on, and then fades to a posthumous montage of moments in Zevon's life, encapsulating and containing the energy, chaos, and sadness of a complex life in three melancholic minutes of video, as Zevon's lyrics humbly ask not to be forgotten.

Encore

Zevon had more time than he thought he'd have. In August 2002, he thought he had three months to live. The album was released the last week of August 2003, and Zevon died on September 7th 2003. He managed to see its release and enjoy its initial success.

The Wind proved Zevon right: his work at the beginning and end of his career is most noteworthy and popular—two "pats on the back." But these songs at the end are recorded and heard in a space that is distinct from the earlier songs, emerging from the shadows of Zevon's mortality and ringing with existential angst. Part of our pleasure comes from the authenticity that is staged as the pieces stand as testament to Zevon *facing* death.[1]

---

[1] For Papa. I'll keep you in my heart.

EPILOGUE

Finishing Touches

JOHN E. MACKINNON

> There are three types of person. Those on top, those on the bottom, and those who fall.

> —TRIMIGASI, *The Platform* (directed by Gaztelu-Urrutia, 2019)

> . . . good writers come back. Always.

> —HEMINGWAY to Fitzgerald

Beyond a love for his music, there are two principal reasons why Warren Zevon attracts the interest and devotion reflected in the chapters of this book. The first is the appeal of his intelligence and wit.

Robert Craft, who joined him during his sessions with Stravinsky, described the teenaged Zevon as "self-possessed and articulate far beyond his years," able to support his musical judgments "with acute arguments" (*I'll Sleep When I'm Dead*, p. 13). Jackson Browne notes the rare "literary quality" of Zevon's compositions, observing that, while plenty of songwriters have literary pretensions, Zevon clearly had "literary muscle" (p. 428). Christened "the Dorothy Parker of rock'n'roll," he was, according to Danny Goldberg, "the most literary of rockers" (p. 119; *Bumping into Geniuses*, p. 247). The critic Mark Deming insists that, though Zevon's music is "full of blood, bile, and mean-spirited irony," it nonetheless possesses "a steely intelligence, a winning wit, and an unusually sophisticated melodic sense," while Carl Hiaasen describes his lyrics as "cunning, cutting . . ., yet often elegant," arguing that he "left behind a wildly intelligent and captivating body of music."

But Zevon's life and work are compelling, too, because of the trajectory of his career: his brilliant early achievement, followed by years of dissipation and a succession of self-inflicted disappointments, then by attempts at recovery, both personal and professional, by near-misses and occasional flashes of the old brilliance, and, eventually, a reputation reclaimed in illness, and, finally, in death. As Zevon declares in "Disorder in the House," the standard against which all forms of despair are measured is no less than fame itself. Two of his finest songs, "Jesus Mentioned" (1982) and "Porcelain Monkey" (2000), are meditations on the fate of Elvis Presley and, as such, the ravages of fame.

According to the great Australian critic Clive James, fame may be radiant, but "its radiance burns." It must, therefore, be "handled with care." The real story of fame in the contemporary world, he says, is "how to live with it" (*Fame,* pp. 48, 45). At the height of his success, however, Zevon was clearly ill-equipped to cope. A veteran of the *Excitable Boy* tour, guitarist David Landau recalls that "Warren was a hit. He was getting raves in *Rolling Stone.*" And yet, in the middle of what ought to have been the celebration of a brilliant "career-making album," Zevon was drunk during sets, disappeared between shows, messed up songs and petulantly blamed his band, and, at a show in Chicago, fell off the stage (*I'll Sleep When I'm Dead,* pp. 146–149). "The memories I have of Warren," says Mark Hammerman, who briefly managed Zevon and accompanied him on an earlier tour, "are mainly of trying to get him from one place to another without him falling down" (p. 131). On the *Excitable Boy* tour, Landau reports, Zevon was "out of his mind" (pp. 147, 149).

The *Ur*-text of Zevon Studies is Crystal Zevon's *I'll Sleep When I'm Dead: The Dirty Life and Times of Warren Zevon,* a compulsively readable oral history, comprising the personal recollections of friends, lovers, and musical collaborators, along with a representative sample of entries from Zevon's journals, all knitted together by Crystal's own interjections and commentaries. About a week before he died, Zevon phoned Crystal and announced to her, "You are my witness. The story is yours. But you gotta promise you'll tell 'em the whole truth, even the awful, ugly parts" (pp. 395, 430). Although "he wanted it all told after he was gone," writes Hiassen, the resulting memoir is, in many ways, "ugly and unflattering" (p. xii). Like Mister Johnson in "Lord Byron's Luggage," Zevon was clearly "hard on his friends and family," and, along the way, Crystal laments, "there were casualties" (p. 276). To read her unstinting account is, as Fred Schruers wrote in the *Los Angeles Times*, "to swing between admiring and abominating the man."

Zevon's sometime-producer-and-collaborator Waddy Wachtel discerns in the "orchestral dynamics" of "Mohammed's Radio" what he calls "strong punches in between delicate lines," just as James Campion describes Zevon's music, more generally, as offering a "plaintive mixture of balladry and raunch" (pp. xi, 97). As friends and colleagues amply attest, however, this same "anomalous combination of traits" was evident in the man himself (*I'll Sleep When I'm Dead*, p. 176). "Warren had two distinctive personalities," observes producer John Rhys, one "the classical side," the other the untamed werewolf (p. 72). "He could change direction like a cutting horse," adds Howard Burke, who briefly managed Zevon in the late Seventies. "It was astounding" (p. 157). And David Landau recalls how, having rendezvoused with Zevon at a Mexican restaurant, he watched him "transform over lunch," until, after three martinis, he became "unreachable" (p. 159).

Though given to adolescent bravado when drunk, and though his live shows were said to be "like watching an exorcism," he was, when sober, and in his personal life, quiet, shy, and introspective (pp. 72, 205, 231; *Nothing's Bad Luck*, p. 288). "He was interesting," Bruce Springsteen reminisces, "because he was very sweet of heart on one hand, and then he had this very tough nature, tough part of his personality, on the other" (p. 232). In his personal and professional lives, Hiassen concludes, Zevon "could be a saint or a son-of-a-bitch. . . . There were times when he treated people who adored him pretty severely. He could be so charming and wonderful, but then he could vanish, too. He could break people's hearts" (pp. xv, 313).

"One is fruitful," Nietzsche declares in *Twilight of the Idols*, "only at the price of being rich in opposites," of being full of conflict and ambiguity. In *The Birth of Tragedy*, he affirms that even the clearest figures of drama retain "a comet's tail" that seems "to point to the uncertain, to darkness beyond illumination" (*Twilight*, p. 22; *Birth*, p. 67). Just as, according to Marilynne Robinson, "the reflex of disparagement" so prominent in our culture treats ambiguity "as a synonym for corruption," so, according to Milan Kundera, the urge of naive idealists everywhere is to "banish all contradictions" (*Death of Adam*, p. 26; *Unbearable Lightness of Being*, p. 54). But human beings can hardly be reduced to the artificial tidiness of a psychological vignette. "Pop psychology instructs us that men are from Mars, women from Venus," writes Stewart Justman. "The

Wife of Bath is from both" (p. 190). Likewise, Theodore Dalrymple observes that, in *Henry IV*, Sir John Falstaff "is a man who is lazy, a coward, a boaster, a fornicator, a would-be thief, a sponger on others, a glutton and a drunk." Not only is there not much virtue in him, but he manages to cast doubt on the very possibility of virtue. "And yet," writes Dalrymple, "far from hating or despising him, we feel the deepest affection for him. When he says 'Banish plump Jack, and banish all the world,' we not only know exactly what he means, but agree with him" (p. 149). Although we are unlikely to indulge anyone who pleads "ambiguity" to excuse his misbehaviour, we're at least inclined to respect him if he struggles to temper the internal conflicts that threaten to consume him. And there's ample evidence that Zevon was no stranger to this struggle.

Works by Jerks

I live and work in a city where it has lately become a holiday ritual for pious radio hosts to interview even more pious Women and Gender Studies professors about the outrage of allowing the Christmas classic "Baby It's Cold Outside" to be played on the airwaves. What generations of listeners have mistaken for a cooing, lightly lusty winter tune, we are now advised is a barely disguised apology for date rape. In many a local home, idling car, or coffee shop, well-meaning citizens uncertainly nod their agreement, not necessarily because it's what they think, but because they know it's what they're *supposed* to think.

In this, our utopia of scolds, what possible chance does Warren Zevon have? In his song "Dirty Life and Times," he himself is well aware of how eager some would be to hunt him down and hang him for his crimes. It's not just the content of the songs that, in certain quarters, would cause concern—the scenes of violence, drug-fueled revelry, and sex: rough, kinky, or otherwise—but for what we now know about the life he led, what sometimes seemed to have been his appetite for, not just excess, but ruin.

In the field of philosophical aesthetics, the relation between art and morality is a perennial concern. It's no secret, as Bernard Wills and Jason Holt contend, "that many first-rate artists are also first-rate jerks." Is it wrong, they ask, to enjoy the work of a jerk, even if work and jerk are first-rate? Often, this question is raised concerning artists who hold repugnant political views, but for a generation assured that "the personal is political," even the most private of peccadilloes can immediately assume a political character. While it may be pernicious to dismiss or deny the importance of an artist's morally suspect behaviour simply because we happen to like his work, it's nonetheless worth asking whether it's wrong to enjoy that work because of the unpalatable opinions, and, especially, wayward conduct, of the artist who produced it ("Art by Jerks").

To pursue this issue, Wills and Holt identify five types of artist, ranging from the thoroughly admirable to the criminal and beastly. At either extreme, our question can be answered rather easily, though of course differently. Of far greater interest are the intermediate cases, ranging from what they call the morally "flawed" and the morally "ambivalent" to the morally "reprehensible." If we were constrained by a "moral hygiene" so exacting that we were permitted only to endorse those works produced by artists who are "morally exemplary people" with "sound views about the world," we would be free to enjoy very little. At the same time, though an "inhuman monster" may be unable to make great art, perhaps a human, all-too-human sinner can. We may conclude, for instance, that a particular artist, as a person, is "callous, lecherous, vain, spiteful," or worse, and yet recognize aspects of these traits in ourselves, perhaps not as "outright evils," but as "ordinary imperfections." Why limit ourselves, in any case, to only certain forms of fault or infraction? Why not detail a list of all that offends us and silence artists accordingly?

Wills and Holt argue that, since "works and their creators are normally distinct entities," a "moral flaw in one need not confirm a corresponding flaw in the other." In most cases, therefore, we have sound reasons for distinguishing between ethical and aesthetic judgments. Not only is the moral character of the artist distinct from that of the work, but the moral status of the work's subject matter is distinct from that of the work overall. Murder and mayhem, depravity and defilement are by themselves, no doubt, morally objectionable, but can nevertheless be represented artfully and humanely. The moral imagination, Wills and Holt insist, "has its own necessity and integrity, its own freedom." When sufficiently vital, it ensures that the works in which it finds expression are sources of moral insight of the sort that, as ethical beings, "we should not deprive ourselves." But while the moral imagination "is essential to the development of morality," it is hardly sufficient, since imaginative capacity is one thing, the will to act morally quite another. It is on these rather curious and troubling grounds that not just admirable, but often morally valuable, works of art can be produced by morally compromised artists.

Art in the Valley of Its Making

In his book *Authority and Freedom*, Jed Perl discusses the case of the poet William Butler Yeats, whose fascist sympathies in the 1930s have alienated many readers (p. 140). In his poem "A Prayer for My Daughter," Yeats commends to his daughter Nietzsche's Overman, that paragon of individual vitality and amoral aristocratic virtue. According to David Bromwich, the mood of Yeats's later writing combines "elegiac regret" with "an unembarrassed affinity" for "a power sufficiently muscular to remake the world," what Bromwich later describes as Yeats's "wish for destruction" (pp. 64–66). In light of these assessments, how could anyone be drawn to such poetry?

W.H. Auden confronts this difficult question in one of his most famous poems, "In Memory of W.B. Yeats," as well as a handful of essays. Even though Auden concedes that Yeats "carried on alarmingly" and was guilty in many of his public pronouncements of "silliness," he suggests that the various charges against Yeats "bear an extraordinary resemblance to the belief of an earlier age that a great artist must be chaste," since, if we "take away the frills," the argument of his critics amounts to a demand that a poet provide prescribed answers to select questions and be blamed indiscriminately should he fail to do so. On this view, poetry amounts to little more than "the filling up of a social quiz," but this, says Auden, is "nonsense" (*Prose*, pp. 4, 5, 173).

According to Perl, when Yeats threw his support behind Mussolini and the Irish fascists, he was *doing* something: defending a position, advocating a point of view, committing himself to a cause. When he turned to his poetry, however, he was *making* something. "However false or undemocratic" Yeats's ideas, writes Auden, "his diction shows a continuous evolution towards what one might call the true democratic style." It is the diction, Auden affirms, of "a just man" (*Prose*, p. 7). The world of action, in other words, is distinct from that of language, the poet's vocation, where "words can survive even a person's follies" (*Authority and Freedom*, pp. 141–42).

Auden provocatively claims that "art is a product of history, not a cause," that poetry, presumably along with the others arts, "makes nothing happen." Instead, it survives, he says, "in the valley of its making" ("In Memory of W.B. Yeats," *Prose*, p. 7); whereas *doing* involves acting in the world, *making* amounts to what Bromwich calls "symbolic action," which itself is the working out of the very moral imagination that proves so vital to Wills and Holt (Bromwich, p. 79). "Nothing matters to the artist," according to Perl, "except the perfect object," the finished work, in the service of which he must subject himself to the authority of his art, remaining "true to both the order and the disorder," as well as the "linguistic virtues of strength and clarity," all the while seeking patterns, through the arrangement of "words on a page, the sound of instruments and voices in the air, and the shaping of stone, paint, or thread" (*Authority and Freedom*, pp. 142, 143; Auden, *Prose*, p. 7).

Bromwich's observation that, although Yeats failed ever to "set anything like a good example," his work was nevertheless "exemplary," calls to mind no one more than Mr. Bad Example himself (p. 80). Auden, too, recalls Jon Landau's judgment that Zevon, unlike many of his contemporaries, continued to grow as an artist, when he claims that a major poet likes Yeats "continues to develop. He learns how to write new poems. He goes on to attempt something new, new subjects, new ways of treatment or both," attempts at which "he may quite possibly fail" (*Prose*, p. 288). Poets, Auden adds, "stop writing good poetry when they stop reacting to the world they live in. The nature of that reaction . . . matters very little." What is essential is that their reaction be genuine and unabated (*Prose*, p. 6).

Noël Coward famously quipped that "the secret of success is the capacity to survive failure." Elaborating this remark, Clive James says that, "unlike heartbreak, which really is a dead loss, failure has a function. It asks you whether you really want to go on making things" (*North Face*, p. 264). Zevon's response to this was emphatic. The same man who gave us "Roland the Headless Thompson Gunner," "Lawyers, Guns, and Money," and "Poor, Poor Pitiful Me," gave us, decades later, "Suzie Lightning," "Renegade," "Worrier King," "Genius," and the entirety of *Life'll Kill Ya*.

A Strange Constellation

"Achievement without fame can be a good life," reflects James. "Fame without achievement is no life at all. Somewhere between those two principles," he suggests, "there's a line of argument" (*Fame*, p. 12). In his absorbing book, *Always Crashing in the Same Car*, it's a line of argument that Matthew Specktor strenuously pursues, while at once attempting to lend it substance. Written with intelligence, wit, a keen critical eye, and a sort of consoling beauty, it is, like Crystal Zevon's *I'll Sleep When I'm Dead*, almost impossible to put down. Part memoir, part literary and film history, it's also a meditation on the personal and cultural significance of Los Angeles, Specktor's hometown, confirming the common suspicion that the place we come from and the stories we tell are inseparable. Above all, though, Specktor's book is a study of the ideas of success and failure that, by turns, animate and haunt our imagination.

In *Always Crashing*, Specktor devotes chapters to screenwriters Eleanor Perry and Carole Eastman, to the novelist Thomas McGuane, the actress Tuesday Weld, directors Hal Ashby and Michael Cimino, the critic Renata Adler, and to Warren Zevon. Together with a supporting cast that includes writer and visual artist Eve Babitz, actor Bruce Dern, and director Charles Burnett, as well as Specktor's own mother and his dear friend "D," these figures constitute what he calls "a strange and decidedly limited constellation."

Traditionally, philosophers have assumed that membership in a constellation, or, as they would prefer, inclusion under a concept or in a category, must be due to all members, or particular instances, sharing an essence, fulfilling some defining criterion. In his *Philosophical Investigations*, however, Ludwig Wittgenstein challenges this view. What unites members of a class, he says, is "a complicated network of similarities overlapping and criss-crossing: sometimes overall similarities, sometimes similarities of detail" (section 66). To belong to a given category, then, to count as a particular *type* of thing, is not a matter of containing some mysterious essence, but of what Wittgenstein calls "family resemblances" (section 67).

How, then, are the members of Specktor's strange and limited constellation related? What family resemblances can we identify among them? Specktor attributes to Perry and Eastman an impulse to self-erasure or self-negation, which Campion implies we can attribute to Zevon as well (*Accidentally Like a Martyr*, p. 27). He identifies in Weld and Cimino an appetite for "selective mythmaking," just as he does in Zevon. That Eastman was "afraid to fly, afraid to have her photograph taken, agoraphobic, picky about food, reluctant to enter any restaurant she'd never eaten at before" recalls Zevon's own obsessive-compulsive struggles. Just as Specktor describes *Five Easy Pieces*, for which Eastman wrote the screenplay, as a movie "about failure," and McGuane's *Panama* a novel "about failure . . ., a chronicle of anomie, of excess and collapse," so he praises Weld's later performances, which suggest Weld herself as "a poet of failure." The anti-heroes of *Five Easy Pieces* and *Panama*, Bobby Dupea ("a flaming asshole, and also a musical prodigy") and Chester Pomeroy (emerging from a "blizzard of self-inflicted misery" an "existentially tired, morally frayed, but unbroken, creator"), respectively, recall Zevon in their different ways. The evolution of McGuane's writing, from "the antic, reckless, machine-gun craziness," the "bucking, deranged vitality," of his early work, to the calm, patience, and elegance of his later work recalls few things more strikingly than the evolution of Zevon's music from the Asylum to the Artemis years. That Weld was cast in films "that were the victim of poor distribution, negative reviews, or just plain terrible timing" reminds us of Zevon's often fraught dealings with the music industry, the series of labels who signed and dropped him, the often very good albums that fell flat. While Eastman was "given to solitary and voracious reading," McGuane inherited a love of language and of books from his parents. Specktor refers to how Perry "ate, lived, and breathed literature" and how, though born Jewish, she, like Zevon, "contemplated a conversion to Catholicism." Just as Specktor remarks on the "relentlessness" of Adler's intelligence, her "keen eye for the specific," he characterizes Eastman's intelligence variously as "prickly" and "magnetic," as "weird, fierce, and original," her cool wit and odd ear as "delicious," qualities that remind him of another "incandescent young intellect," Babitz, and the rest of us of Zevon. Eastman "did not suffer fools," preferring, like Ashby, like Zevon, "to be left alone. She liked . . . silence," Specktor says, "splendid isolation."

The lodestar of Specktor's strange constellation is the novelist F. Scott Fitzgerald, who, after a series of brilliant early successes, arrived in Los Angeles to write for the movies, came up short, washed out, and, at the age of forty-four, died "the sorry ruin of Hollywood." Fitzgerald was a flawed man, Specktor acknowledges, his alcoholism having "generated suffering in those who stood close to him," inflicting pain and humiliation. But he was "a kind man, a generous man." The sharpness of his intellect is confirmed by his having mastered what one of his favorite poets, John Keats, called "negative capability," meaning, the condition where someone is "capable of being in uncertainties, mysteries, doubts, without any irritable reaching after fact or reason." It refers, that is, to the capacity to confront and struggle with, rather than be defeated by, ambiguity. In his memorable essay "The Crack-Up," Fitzgerald lends the notion of negative capability his own formulation, declaring that "the test of a first-rate intelligence is the ability to hold two opposed ideas in the mind at the same time, and still retain the ability to function" (p. 69). And what two ideas could be more opposed, Specktor asks, than, on the one hand, the impulse to save yourself and, on the other, "the one that makes you want to grind yourself to dust, to drown yourself in gin and set your house on fire?" The spirit of choice needn't be gin, of course. It might be vodka. And you might not just set your house on fire, but find yourself huddled in the hallway when the house burns down.

Specktor describes the subjects in his book as "preternatural talents" who "soared and then collapsed," or who barely even soared, but "were dropped to the ground almost before they left the runway," artists "who found a way to take their brilliant careers and end them prematurely," whose "modestly masterful bodies of work, or whose rare freak successes, crested the surface every now and again only to disappear." His interest is in those "half-realized talents," whose careers "carry an aura of what might, also, have been. Those who failed, those who faltered, those whose triumphs are punctuated by flops or by periods, often lasting years, of obscurity."

Where does it begin, he wonders: the disintegration? What makes a writer, a musician, fall silent? How does "the earlier, confident promise" curdle into "something darker"? Ultimately, he replies, the difficulty, which is often enough a collapse, can be traced to the "moral arc of a personality that never lets itself off the hook, but never lets well enough alone, either." These are people who don't want to destroy themselves, but "don't quite *not* want to, either." What they seek is "the risk, the threat, the muddle, the crisis," whatever manages to shake them from their torpor. But while "their flaws are obvious," he says, "their rewards are substantial." However incomplete and truncated their legacies, however "aborted or abridged" their careers, all deserve a more sustained appreciation than they have so far received, since their work frequently has "as much claim to greatness as that of those better known." Each "might illuminate, in different ways, what it means to be a person," writes Specktor: "how to square one's desires, one's dreams and disappointments, with the act of being a citizen of the world." Even if not exactly a model citizen.

Specktor says that what he loves most about life are "the things that fail, that crash and burn without any particular fanfare." But this can't be what he means. It's not failure, as such, that he loves, but the things that *tend* to fail, that *tend* to crash and burn, since so often they are distinctive, demanding, masterful, and, as in the work of Eleanor Perry and Carole Eastman, Tuesday Weld, Warren Zevon, and others, chronically underappreciated. An unreceptive public is among those disappointments that, together with the hopes, are inescapable in creative lives. What Specktor misses in his own life, he says, "are not the things that never came to pass but rather the illusion, the bright hope for the future that you know…is false, that even if you should somehow fulfill it, you will be left, in part, with a fistful of sand."

Or rain.

Making Amends

In his assessment of Zevon, Specktor is unsparing. Having acquainted himself with Crystal Zevon's recollections in *I'll Sleep When I'm Dead*, he knows Zevon to have been "a drunk, a violent and abusive alcoholic, . . . a serial philanderer, negligent toward his children when they were young," and occasionally "unkind and ungenerous to cowriters." His life story, Specktor says, is "miserable" and "sordid," noting the "groupies, sexual exploitation, alcoholic blackouts, ruinous behavior onstage and off . . ., the callousness." Zevon himself, Specktor alleges, was "a real prick," a "rock'n'roll asshole," perhaps even "something of a monster," the very sort of guy, you'd think, who should be, "y'know, cancelled." As Specktor asks about Cimino, so he might just as easily ask about Zevon, "why waste even a speck of empathy upon this man?"

As it happens, the criss-crossings and overlappings apparent in the lives of his various subjects extend to Specktor himself—the passions, obsessions, disappointments and failures. Sometimes, however, these family resemblances have a more circumstantial aspect. During the period of personal struggle and reflection that Specktor recounts, he lived in an apartment building across the street from the very one in which Fitzgerald died. Upstairs, meanwhile, Specktor's kind, fiercely intelligent neighbour turned out to be a former girlfriend of Zevon's. Given the parade of women identified, and often quoted, in *I'll Sleep When I'm Dead*, it's easy enough to name this woman—Zevon's very own "angel dressed in black"—but since Specktor doesn't, neither will I.

On three separate occasions, he tries to coax from her incriminating, and clinching, evidence against Zevon. In every case, however, she disappoints him. "What was it like," he asks, "when you were with him?" "He was so smart," she replies. "He made me feel smart." "Was he kind to you?" Specktor persists. "He wasn't very kind to himself," she snorts. Later, when he reflects on how monstrous Zevon could be, it's clear that she wouldn't describe him "as anything of the kind." He was just a crummy boyfriend. "I've had better and I've had worse," she says. "Did you ever forgive him?" he finally asks. "Who?", she wonders, before replying, "I never thought of it that way." It's the wrong question. "He was just a person," she adds, meaning that he was simply the person that he was, with all the quirks of personality and contours of character that made him a whole man.

It's tempting to characterize *Always Crashing in the Same Car* as a book about gifted failures, except that every member of Specktor's strange constellation knew success, often considerable, while others who foundered, flopped or flamed out eventually recovered, reclaiming themselves, their careers and reputations. Others, too, "passed out of their prime, like *that*, overnight."

Apart from the ideas of success and failure, there is perhaps none other more central to Specktor's reflections than that of forgiveness. This bears on several people in his own life, particularly his parents, especially his mother, but also on many of his subjects, though none more so than Zevon. He recalls borrowing his neighbor's collection of Zevon records, settling down with them, and slowly growing to love them, and Zevon, "without apology." Although he insists that it's "no real answer to seek refuge in the work," he ultimately concedes that real answers can be found if appreciating the work enables us to appreciate more deeply, more fairly, the artist himself.

"Creative spirits . . . aren't consensus builders," writes Perl. Their many parts may account for what Nietzsche considers their fruitfulness, but they also divide opinion, prompting all manner of responses, from adulation to contempt. The novelist Howard Jacobson cheerlessly predicts that, soon, "all that literature understands by drama, subtlety, and equivocation will be gone, and bald statements"—the thumbs-up or the thumbs-down—"will be all we have left" (*The Dog's Last Walk*, p. 2). Among such bald statements he counts the notes on gallery walls, which present everything concerning the artist and his art as "so neat and understood. Every mystery solved. Every inconsistency ironed over. The age, the man . . ., rendering precise that which was once tumultuous" (*Whatever It Is*, p. 26). Obsession with false simplicity is the hobgoblin of little, and literal, minds. A work of art, like a human life, is subject to shifting forces, grainy and knotted with detail, the sources of turmoil threatening to erupt at any moment, imposing themselves on our consciousness, calling for judgment, but always, too, a fair mind and even hand.

"Morality," writes Peter Marin, "is an activity, not a sentiment." Just as private struggles occur in "the debauched moral landscape," so, in guilt, "one is moved by reason and conscience to rethink and remake the nature of one's moral life." For his part, Zevon was determined, not only to achieve and maintain his sobriety, but also to make amends—to Crystal, his children, friends and former lovers, even businesses whose property he had trashed in blind rages years before. In the latter half of *I'll Sleep When I'm Dead*, the imperative to make amends emerges as something close to a theme. It's possible that when Zevon urged Crystal to reveal all in her biography, he hoped to scandalize us all from beyond the grave. But I have a strong suspicion that he expected to be called to account, and that being called to account was part of his determination to make amends.

Problems of the Penumbra

According to Specktor, the movies that Hal Ashby directed in the Seventies, taken together, are "as satisfying a run as I can think of, a straight flush." There "isn't a clunker in the bunch." And yet, Ashby's decline from the dizzying heights of Hollywood prestige was "steep and sudden." Still, Specktor asks, "isn't every artist entitled to the occasional dud?" Identifying the duds in Dylan's discography, Dickstein insists that even they reflect a "distinctive direction and purpose." This calls to mind Bromwich's reference to the "obscure momentum" that runs through all the forms and phases of Auden's poetry (p. 80). However distinct the varied "shades of feeling," however successful, or not, each new attempt, Auden's work, like Dylan's, is sustained by whatever imperatives of art propelled him forward.

Even when an artist produces consistently exemplary work, retaining the public's favour is another matter. As Nick Wernicki nicely expresses it in his chapter, good song-writing puts listeners in conversation with the artist. If listeners are distracted or indifferent, however, how far should the songwriter go to appeal to, or appease, them? To seek complete acceptance, writes Greil Marcus, is to seek complete assimilation, which entails adopting "an aesthetic where no lines are drawn and no choices are made." In such cases, the principle, and quality, of what Marcus calls "selection," which is precisely what's at stake when an artist attempts to present his version of anything, is missing. And when an artist is no longer able to create anything new, when he is no longer interested in testing his own worth or that of his audience, there is nothing he can tell or do for them (p. 123).

Although Springsteen famously describes Zevon as "a moralist in cynic's clothing," many would resist, even resent, any attempt to portray him as a moralist of any kind. So, what kind of moralist, exactly, does Springsteen have in mind? According to Saul Bellow a writer is moral to the degree that, when responding to the question, "In what form shall life be justified?", his imagination suggests to us "how we may answer naturally, without strained arguments, with a spontaneous, mysterious proof that has no need to argue with despair" (p. 165). It's in his efforts to address this most inescapable of questions that the moral artist exhibits a commitment to the demands of his art, and how that art in turn exhibits an obscure momentum, a direction and purpose.

Peter Gallagher describes the cover photo of Zevon's self-titled Asylum debut as "a slightly blurred night-time shot of a bespectacled Warren wearing a suit" (p. 25). Jimmy Wachtel, art director, photographer, and Waddy's brother, recalls the circumstances in which the photo was taken, during the Grammys, while the awards were being handed out inside, with Zevon standing outside the Palladium on the deserted red carpet, "uninvited" (*I'll Sleep When I'm Dead*, p. 116). Somehow, this image, and the story behind it, neatly captures Zevon's oddly indeterminate status in the music world. Specktor refers to the members of his strange constellation as "faintly marginal." In Zevon's case, however, this won't do. We should regard him, instead, as penumbral. Whereas artists are moved, or move themselves, to the margins, the penumbral figure remains where he's always been. It's the light that changes. There, he confronts what the great philosopher of law H.L.A. Hart calls "problems of the penumbra," those where uncertainty and doubt prevail, where it's tough to know how to proceed or how to make the right call (p. 607). But if the light has shifted once, it can shift again, catching him once more in its brilliance.

Adapting Marcus's discussion of Herman Melville to our concerns, we might say that only the artist who resists assimilation to any official, or otherwise fashionable, aesthetic is a free man (p. 123). According to Mark Slouka, Melville's novel *Pierre*, subtitled, of all things, *The Ambiguities*, calls attention more than any other work in American literature "to its own silences, its fragility." There, Melville offers us a hero whom he "propels . . . toward death" with what Thomas Mann famously calls "the voluptuousness of doom." Reading the novel, says Slouka, is akin to witnessing an artist "painstakingly put the finishing touches on his own epitaph" (p. 45).

Listening to his radiant valediction, *The Wind*, it's hard not to conclude the same about Warren Zevon.

Book Soup

Allaby, M. 2010. *Animals: From Mythology to Zoology*. Infobase.

Applebaum, Anne. 2021. The New Puritans. *The Atlantic* (August 31st).

Aristotle. 1995. *Politics*. Oxford University Press.

———. 2019. *Nicomachean Ethics*. Hackett.

Auden, W.H. 1976. In Memory of W.B. Yeats. In Edward Mendelson, ed. *Collected Poems*. Random House.

———. 1996. *Prose*. Volume II (1939–1948). Princeton University Press.

Avery, Keith. 2011. *Everything Is an Afterthought: The Life and Writings of Paul Nelson*. Fantagraphics Books.

Barry, Sam, and Lou, Jennifer, eds. 2013. *Hard Listening: The Greatest Rock Band Ever (of Authors) Tells All*. Sam Barry.

Bell, Macalester. 2014. Grizzly Man, Sentimentality, and Our Relationships with Other Animals. In Susan Wolf and Christopher Grau, eds. *Understanding Love: Philosophy, Film, and Fiction*. Oxford University Press.

Bellow, Saul. 2015. *There Is Simply Too Much to Think About: Collected Nonfiction*. Penguin.

Bloom, Harold. 1973. *The Anxiety of Influence*. Oxford University Press.

Boorse, C. 1975. On the Distinction Between Disease and Illness. *Philosophy and Public Affairs* 5.

———. 1977. Health as a Theoretical Concept. *Philosophy of Science* 44.

———. 1997. A Rebuttal on Health. In J.M. Humber and R.F. Almeder, eds. *What Is Disease?* Humana.

Borges, Jorge Luis. 2015. *Labyrinths: Selected Stories and Other Writings*. Virgin.

Borges, Ron. 2007. Twenty-Five Years Is a Long Time to Carry a Memory. ESPN (November 13th) <www.espn.com/sports/boxing/news/story?id=3107079>.

Boyiopoulos, Kostas, and Michael Shallcross. 2020. Like a Burr: Aphoristic Writing and Modernity. In Boyiopoulos and Shallcross, eds. *Aphoristic Modernity: 1880 to the Present*. Brill.

Bromwich, David. 2019. *How Words Make Things Happen*. Oxford University Press.

Brownstein, Ronald. 2021. *Rock Me on the Water: 1974, The Year Los Angeles Transformed Movies, Music, Television, and Politics*. HarperCollins.

Butcher, S.H. 1951. *Aristotle's Theory of Poetry and Fine Art, with a Critical Text and Translation of The Poetics*. Dover.

Butler, Judith. 1999. *Gender Trouble: Feminism and the Subversion of Identity*. Routledge.

Campion, James. 2018. *Accidentally Like a Martyr: The Tortured Art of Warren Zevon*. Back Beat.

Camus, Albert. 1955. *The Myth of Sisyphus and Other Essays*. Vintage.

———. 1958. Le Malentendu. In *Caligula, suivi de Le Malentendu*. Gallimard.

Carstensen, Laura. 2013. Social and Emotional Aging. In *Annual Review of Psychology* 61.

Carter, Ian. 2022. Positive and Negative Liberty. *The Stanford Encyclopedia of Philosophy* <https://plato.stanford.edu/archives/spr2022/entries/liberty-positive-negative>.

Cartlidge, James. 2020. Heidegger's Philosophical Anthropology of Moods. *Hungarian Philosophical Review* [Special Issue: "Self, Narrativity, Emotions"] 15.

Chesterton, G.K. 1990. *What's Wrong with the World*. Sherwood Sugden.

Culler, Jonathan. 1981. *The Pursuit of Signs: Semiotics, Literature, Deconstruction*. Routledge.

Dalrymple, Theodore. 2011. *Anything Goes*. New English Review Press.

Deming, Marc. 1976. Review of *Warren Zevon* <www.allmusic.com/album/warren-zevon-mw0000312155>.

Denberg, Jody. 2000. Interview with Warren Zevon on Radio KGSR in Austin, Texas, originally conducted and aired on January 22nd, 2000, and then included in the Warren Zevon album, *Preludes: Rare and Unreleased Recordings* (New West, 2008) <www.youtube.com/watch?v=jseKHl8lOa8>.

DeVito, S. 2000. On the Value-neutrality of the Concepts of Health and Disease: Unto the Breach Again. *Journal of Medicine and Philosophy* 25:5.

Devon, Ivie. 2023. The Best and Funniest of Warren Zevon, According to David Letterman. *Vulture* (April 26th).

Dickstein, Morris. 2015. *Gates of Eden: American Culture in the Sixties*. Liveright.

Doctorow, E.L. 1991. Standards: How Great Songs Name Us. *Harper's* (November).

Doino, William, Jr. 2013. Warren Zevon's Secret. *First Things* (September 16th).

Domínguez Barajas, Elías. 2010. *The Function of Proverbs in Discourse: The Case of a Mexican Transnational Social Network*. de Gruyter.

Dostoyevsky, Fyodor. 1994. *Notes from the Underground*. Vintage.

Duncan, Stewart. 2022. Thomas Hobbes. *The Stanford Encyclopedia of Philosophy* <https://plato.stanford.edu/archives/sum2022/entries/hobbes>.

Dylan, Bob. 2022. *The Philosophy of Modern Song*. Simon and Schuster.

Elgat, Guy. 2018. Aphorisms and Fragments. In B. Stocker and M. Mack, ed. *The Palgrave Handbook of Philosophy and Literature*. Palgrave Macmillan.

Epstein, Mark. 2013. *Thought Without a Thinker: Psychotherapy from a Buddhist Perspective*. Basic Books.

Esslin, Martin. 1973. *The Theatre of the Absurd*. Revised edition. Overlook.

Feinberg, Joel. 1970. *Doing and Deserving*. Princeton University Press.

Fitzgerald, F. Scott. 2009 [1945]. *The Crack-Up*. New Directions.

Frankfurt, Harry. 1982. Freedom of the Will and the Concept of a Person. In Gary Watson, ed. 1982. *Free Will*. Oxford University Press.

Freeman, Hadley. 2013. Warren Zevon: The Man Behind the Demons. *The Guardian* (August 1st).

Freud, Sigmund. 2003. *The Joke and Its Relation to the Unconscious*. Penguin.

Fricke, David. 2002. Warren Zevon and the Art of Dying. *Rolling Stone* (November 28th) <www.rollingstone.com/music/music-news/warren-zevon-and-the-art-of-dying-38326>.

Fürstenberg, Henrike. 2013. Aphorisms. In Steven M. Emmanuel et al., eds. *Kierkegaard's Concepts*. Volume I. Ashgate.

Fusilli, Jim. 2003. Warren Zevon, "Song Noir" Storyteller of Wit and Irony. *Wall Street Journal* (September 9th).

Gallagher, Peter. 2022. *Warren Zevon: Every Album, Every Song*. Sonicbond.

Gardner, John. 1991. *The Art of Fiction: Notes on Craft for Young Writers*. Vintage.

Gimbel, Steven. 2017. *Isn't That Clever: A Philosophical Account of Humor and Comedy*. Routledge.

Goldberg, Danny. 2008. *Bumping into Geniuses: My Life inside the Rock and Roll Business*. Gotham.

Gray, John. 1992. The Virtues of Toleration. *National Review* (October 5th).

Gruner, Charles R. 2017. *The Game of Humor: A Comprehensive Theory of Why We Laugh*. Routledge.

———. 1978. *Understanding Laughter: The Workings of Wit and Humor*. Nelson-Hall.

Hanh, Thich Nhat. 1987. *The Miracle of Mindfulness*. Beacon Press.

Hart, H.L.A. 1958. Positivism and the Separation of Law and Morals. *Harvard Law Review* 71.4.

Hasted, Nick. 2002. Life'll Kill Ya. *Uncut* (September) <https://zevonaticism.tripod.com/lifellkillya.htm>.

Hazlitt, William. 1819. On Wit and Humor. In *Lectures on the English Comic Writers*. Taylor and Hessey.

Heidegger, Martin. 1962. *Being and Time*. Blackwell.

Helsel, Philip Browning. 2007. Warren Zevon's *The Wind* and *Ecclesiastes*: Searching for Meaning at the Threshold of Death. *Journal of Religion and Health* 46.2 (June 2nd).

Heylin, Clinton. 2011. *Bob Dylan: Behind the Shades*. Faber and Faber.

Higgins, Aidan. 1989. *Ronda Gorge and Other Precipices*. Secker and Warburg.

Hobbes, Thomas. 1968. *Leviathan*. Penguin.

Hubbard, Alan. 2011. Barry McGuigan: "Every Fighter Has a Story That Could Break Your Heart." *The Independent* (June 5th) <www.independent.co.uk/news/people/profiles/barry-mcguigan-every-fighter-has-a-story-that-could-break-your-heart-2293134.html>.

Hugo, Victor. 2002. *L'Homme qui Rit*. Gallimard.

Hutcheson, Francis. 1750. *Reflections upon Laughter and Remarks upon "The Fable of the Bees."* University of Glasgow.

Hyden, Steven. 2018. His Sh*t's F***ed Up: The Complicated Legacy of Warren Zevon. *The Ringer*. <www.theringer.com/music/2018/9/7/17830460/warren-zevon-career-music-albums>.

Iglesias, Gabino. 2019. Review of C.M. Kushin's *Nothing's Bad Luck: The Lives of Warren Zevon*. Broadcast on npr.org (May 14th).

Isserow, Jessica. 2020. Moral Hypocrisy. In Edward Craig, ed. *The Routledge Encyclopedia of Philosophy*.

Jacobson, Howard. 2011. *Whatever It Is, I Don't Like It*. Bloomsbury.

———. 2018. *The Dog's Last Walk*. Bloomsbury.

James, Clive. 1993. *Fame in the 20th Century*. Random House.

———. 2006. *North Face of Soho*. Picador.

James, William. 1900. On a Certain Blindness in Human Beings. In James, *On Some of Life's Ideals*. Holt.

Jaspers, Karl. 2000. *Basic Philosophical Writings*. Humanity Books, 2000).

Jung, Carl G. 2006. *The Undiscovered Self*. Signet.

Justman, Stewart. 2005. *Fool's Paradise: The Unreal World of Pop Psychology*. Ivan R. Dee.

Kafka, Franz. 1995. *The Metamorphosis and Other Stories*. Schocken.

———. 1998. *The Trial*. Schocken.

Kant, Immanuel. 2007. *Critique of Judgement*. Oxford University Press.

Katz, Michael. 1982. Referee Defends His Decision. *The New York Times* (December 12th) <www.nytimes.com/1982/12/12/sports/referee-deefnds-his-decision.html>.

Keats, John. 2014. *Selected Letters*. Penguin.

Kierkegaard, Søren. 1944. *The Concept of Dread*. Princeton University Press.

———. 1980. *The Concept of Anxiety*. Princeton University Press.

———. 1987. *Either / Or*. Princeton University Press.

———. 1992. *Concluding Unscientific Postscript to Philosophical Fragments*, Volume 1. Princeton University Press.

Kinsey, Tara Christie. 2013. "Rave on, John Donne": Paul Muldoon and Warren Zevon. *The Yellow Nib* 8 (Spring).

Kozintsev, Alexander. 2012. *The Mirror of Laughter*. Transaction.

Kriegel, Mark. 2012. *The Good Son: The Life of Ray "Boom Boom" Mancini*. Free Press.

Kübler-Ross, Elisabeth. 1964. *On Death and Dying*. Scribner's.

Kundera, Milan. 1984. *The Unbearable Lightness of Being*. Harper Perennial.

Kushins, C.M. 2019. *Nothing's Bad Luck: The Lives of Warren Zevon*. Da Capo.

Labash, Matt. 2022. Enjoy Every Sandwich. *Slack Tide* (November 23rd).

Latta, Robert L. 1999. *The Basic Humor Process: A Cognitive-Shift Theory and the Case Against Incongruity*. Mouton de Gruyter.

Layton, Irving. 1969. *The Whole Bloody Bird: Obs, Aphs, and Pomes*. McClelland and Stewart.

Lazar, Seth. 2020. War. *The Stanford Encyclopedia of Philosophy* <https://plato.stanford.edu/archives/spr2020/entries/war>.

Leopold, David. 2018. Alienation. *The Stanford Encyclopedia of Philosophy* <https://plato.stanford.edu/archives/fall2018/entries/alienation>.

Levitas, Ruth. 2011. *The Concept of Utopia*. Peter Lang.

Marcus, Greil. 1991. *Mystery Train: Images of America in Rock'n'Roll Music*. Fourth edition. Penguin.

Marin, Peter. 1995. *Freedom and Its Discontents: Reflections on Four Decades of American Moral Experience*. Steerforth.

Mill, John Stuart. 1978. *On Liberty*. Hackett.

Miller, Arthur. 2012. *Timebends: A Life*. Bloomsbury.

Miller, Jesse James, director. 2013. *The Good Son: The Life of Ray "Boom Boom" Mancini*. Sophia Entertainment <www.youtube.com/watch?v=Gfgt5WlkwJk>.

Morreall, John, ed. 1987. *The Philosophy of Laughter and Humor*. SUNY Press.

Muldoon, Paul 2006. *Horse Latitudes*. Faber and Faber.

Murdoch, Iris. 1959. The Sublime and the Good. *Chicago Reader* 13:3.

Murphy, D. 2021. Concepts of Disease and Health. *The Stanford Encyclopedia of Philosophy* <https://plato.stanford.edu/archives/spr2021/entries/health-disease>.

Niebuhr, Reinhold. 1995. *The Nature and Destiny of Man: A Christian Interpretation*. Westminster John Knox Press.

Nietzsche, Friedrich. 1967. *The Birth of Tragedy and The Case of Wagner*. Vintage.

———. 1968. *The Will to Power*. Vintage.

———. 1974. *The Gay Science, with a Prelude in Rhymes and an Appendix of Songs*. Vintage.

———. 1990. *Beyond Good and Evil*. Penguin.

———. 1997. *Twilight of the Idols*. Hackett.

Nordmann, Alfred. 2005. *Wittgenstein's 'Tractatus': An Introduction*. Cambridge University Press.

Pence, Gregory. 2020. *Medical Ethics: Accounts of Ground-Breaking Cases*. Ninth edition. McGraw-Hill.

Perl, Jed. 2021. *Authority and Freedom: A Defense of the Arts*. Knopf.

Plasketes, George. 2016. *Warren Zevon: Desperado of Los Angeles*. Rowman and Littlefield.

Plato. 1981. *Five Dialogues: Euthyphro, Apology, Crito, Meno, Phaedo*. Hackett.

———. 1993. *Philebus*. Hackett.

———. 1994. *Republic*. Oxford University Press.

Potter, Jordan. 2022. Warren Zevon: The Man Bob Dylan Called the "Musician's Musician." *Far Out Magazine* (January 24th).

Radford, Colin. 1988. Utilitarianism and the Noble Art. *Philosophy* 63:243.

Raskin, Jonah. 2019. Review of C. M.Kushin's *Nothing's Bad Luck: The Lives of Warren Zevon*. *New York Journal of Books* (May 7th).

Read, Nick, director. 2004. VH1 Documentary (Inside) Out. *Warren Zevon: Keep Me in Your Heart* (February 10th).

Reid, Graham. 1992. Warren Zevon Interviewed: Tales from the Dark Side. *New Zealand Herald* (September).

Ricoeur, Paul. 1988. *Time and Narrative*. University of Chicago Press.

Robinson, Marilynne. 2005. *The Death of Adam: Essays on Modern*

Thought. Picador.

Roche, Mark W. 2002–2003. Hegel's Theory of Comedy in the Context of Hegelian and Modern Reflections on Comedy. *Revue internationale de philosophie* 221.

Roeser, Steve. 1995. Warren Zevon: Left Jabs and Roundhouse Rights. *Goldmine* (August 18th).

Rossinow, Doug. 2015. *The Reagan Era: A History of the 1980s*. Columbia University Press.

Said, Edward. 2007. *On Late Style: Music and Literature Against the Grain*. Vintage.

Sandy, Mark. 2020. "A Ruin Amidst Ruins": Modernity, Literary Aphorisms, and Romantic Fragments. In Boyiopoulos and Shallcross, eds. *Aphoristic Modernity: 1880 to the Present*. Brill.

Santayana, George. 1955. *The Sense of Beauty*. Dover.

Sargent, Lyman Tower. 2010. *Utopianism: A Very Short Introduction*. Oxford University Press.

Sartre, Jean-Paul. 1965. *Existentialism Is a Humanism*. Methuen.

———. 1966. *Being and Nothingness: A Phenomenological Essay on Ontology*. Washington Square Press.

———. 1969. *Nausea*. New Directions.

Satel, Sally. 2001. The Indoctrinologists Are Coming. *Atlantic Monthly* (April).

Savile, Anthony. 1982. *The Test of Time: An Essay in Philosophical Aesthetics*. Clarendon Press.

Schaler, Jeffrey A. 2002. Moral Hygiene. *Society* (May–June).

Schjeldahl, Peter. 2020. *Hot, Cold, Heavy, Light: 100 Art Writings, 1988–2018*. Abrams.

Schoenberg, Arnold. 1975. *Style and Idea: Selected Writings of Arnold Schoenberg*. St. Martin's Press.

Schruers, Fred. 2007. Crystal Zevon's Crusade: Warren from A to Z. *Los Angeles Times* (May 4th).

Schulman, Bruce J. 2001. *The Seventies: The Great Shift in American Culture, Society, and Politics*. Da Capo.

Sennett, Richard. 1970. *The Uses of Disorder: Personal Identity and City Life*. Norton.

Siegel, Alan. 2022. "Thank You, and Goodbye": The Night Warren Zevon Left the *Late Show* Building. *The Ringer* (October 28th).

Silverman, Stephen M. 2003. Zevon to Be Honored at Private Service. People.com (September 10th).

Slouka, Mark. 2010. *Essays in the Nick of Time*. Graywolf Press.

Sokol, D.K. 2004. The Not-So-Sweet Science: The Role of the Medical Profession in Boxing. *Journal of Medical Ethics* 30.5.

Sounes, Howard. 2011. *Down the Highway: The Life of Bob Dylan*. Grove.

Specktor, Matthew. 2021. *Always Crashing in the Same Car: On Art,*

Crisis, and Los Angeles, California. Tin House.

Spencer, Herbert. 1864. The Physiology of Laughter. In Spencer, *Illustrations of Universal Progress: A Series of Discussions*. D. Appleton.

Stebbing, L. Susan. 1939. *Thinking to Some Purpose*. Penguin.

Stratton, Allan. 2022. Dave Chappelle vs. the New Puritans. *Quillette* (August 3rd).

Sutton, John William, ed. 2006. *The Dicts and Sayings of the Philosophers*. Medieval Institute Publications.

Suzuki, Daisetz T. 1955. The Awakening of a New Consciousness in Zen. In *Eranos Jahrbuch* XXIII. Rhein-Verlag.

Sykes, Christopher, director. 1987. *Getting to Dylan*. Documentary for *Omnibus*. BBC.

Szwed, John F. 1988. *Space Is the Place: The Lives and Times of Sun Ra*. Da Capo.

Taylor, Barry. 1992. Medieval Proverb Collections: The West European Traditions. *Journal of the Warburg and Courtauld Institutes* 55.

Tillich, Paul. 2000. *The Courage to Be*. Yale University Press.

Torn, Luke, 2003. The Life and Times (and Music) of Warren Zevon. *Wall Street Journal* (March 25th).

Tremain, Shelley. 2020. Interview with Quayshawn Spencer. *Biopolitical Philosophy* (May 20th) <https://biopoliticalphiloso-phy.com/2020/05/20/dialogues-on-disability-shelley-tremain-inter-views-quayshawn-spencer-redux>.

Vaughn, Lewis. 2021. *Doing Ethics: Moral Reasoning, Theory, and Contemporary Issues*. Sixth edition. Norton.

Viljetić, G. 2017. "An Overview of the Findings of the Research Accompanying the Exhibition of Animals and Humans: A Dog, a Woman, a Cat, a Man—In Search of the Lost Past. *Etnološka istraživanja* 22.

Visković, Nikola. 1996. *Životinja i ovjek: prilog kulturnoj zoologiji*. Književni Krug.

Wakefield, J.C. 1992a. The Concept of Mental Disorder: On the Boundary between Biological Facts and Social Values. *American Psychologist* 47.

———. 1992b. Disorder as Harmful Dysfunction: A Conceptual Critique of DSMIII-R's Definition of Mental Disorder. *Psychological Review* 99.

———. 1995. Dysfunction as a Value-free Concept: A Reply to Sadler and Agich. *Philosophy, Psychiatry, and Psychology* 2.

Warren, Ron. 2016. Intruder in the Dirt. *Glide Magazine* (August 16th).

Watkins, Sean. 2019. Interview with Jackson Browne (November 13th) <https://anchor.fm/this-is-who-we-are/episodes/Suzie-Lightning-with-Jackson-Browne-e8vjra>.

Wegierski, Mark. 1996. Canadian Conservatism and the Managerial

State. *Telos* no. 108 (Summer).

Weil, Simone. 1945. *The Iliad*, or the Poem of Force. *Politics* (November).

Williams, Tennessee. 1948. The Catastrophe of Success. *New York Times* (November 30th).

Wilde, Oscar. 1979. *Letters*. Harcourt Brace.

Wills, Bernard, and Jason Holt. 2017. Art by Jerks. *Contemporary Aesthetics* 15.

Wittgenstein, Ludwig. 1974. *Philosophical Investigations*. Blackwell.

Wittusen, Carl. 2010. Philosophical Method as a Technique of Art. *Literature and Aesthetics* 20.

Wodehouse, P.G. 1963. *The Indiscretions of Archie*. Penguin.

Wolff, Jonathan, and David Leopold. 2021. Karl Marx. *The Stanford Encyclopedia of Philosophy* (Spring) <https://plato.stanford.edu/archives/spr2021/entries/marx>.

Wood, Mikael. 2023. "The Soul of L.A.": Twenty Years after His Death, the Stars are Aligning for Warren Zevon. *Los Angeles Times* (January 31st).

Zevon, Crystal. 2007. *I'll Sleep When I'm Dead: The Dirty Life and Times of Warren Zevon*. HarperCollins.

Zoglin, Richard. 2009. *Comedy at the Edge: How Stand-Up in the 1970s Changed America*. Bloomsbury.

Zola, Irving Kenneth. 1972. Medicine as an Institution of Social Control. *Sociological Review* 20:4 (November).

Discography

Studio and Live Recordings

Wanted Dead or Alive (Imperial, 1970)
Warren Zevon (Asylum, 1976)
Excitable Boy (Asylum, 1978)
Bad Luck Streak in Dancing School (Asylum, 1980)
Stand in the Fire (Asylum, 1980)
The Envoy (Asylum, 1982)
Sentimental Hygiene (Virgin, 1987)
Transverse City (Virgin, 1989)
Hindu Love Gods (Giant, 1990)
Mr. Bad Example (Giant, 1991)
Learning to Flinch (Giant, 1993)
Mutineer (Giant, 1995)
Life'll Kill Ya (Artemis, 2000)
My Ride's Here (Artemis, 2002)
The Wind (Artemis, 2003)

Compilations

A Quiet, Normal Life: The Best of Warren Zevon (Asylum, 1986)
I'll Sleep When I'm Dead (Rhino, 1996)
Genius: The Best of Warren Zevon (Rhino, 2002)
Warren Zevon: The First Sessions (Varese Sarabande Records, 2003)
Reconsider Me: The Love Songs (Artemis, 2006)
Preludes: Rare and Unreleased Recordings (New West Records, 2007)
Warren Zevon's Greatest Hits . . . According to Judd Apatow
(Rhino, 2020)

Zevonistas

JAMES CARTLIDGE is a post-doctoral researcher in Philosophy with a PhD from the Central European University, Vienna. His background is in continental philosophy, especially phenomenology, existentialism, and post-structuralism. His doctoral thesis was on Heidegger's philosophy of anxiety and boredom, and his recent research projects have concerned the philosophy of sport, deep disagreement, and video games. He recently held a fellowship at Vienna's Institute for Human Sciences, working on the philosophy of Jan Patočka, and has previously held teaching positions at Eötvös Loránd University, Budapest, and the Central European University. James first heard "Disorder in the House" on a CD given away with a music magazine in 2003 and has been an ardent fan of Warren Zevon ever since.

CONALL CASH completed his PhD in the Romance Studies department at Cornell University in 2022, and is currently Melbourne Early Career Academic Fellow in French Studies at the University of Melbourne. His published work includes articles on Flaubert's modernism, the politics of phenomenology, and the philosophy of film. His chapter "Self-Hatred and Identity" is included in *Better Call Saul and Philosophy* (2022). As background music while writing, he listens to the air conditioner hum at the Hollywood Hawaiian Hotel.

BRUNO ĆURKO is an Assistant Professor in the Faculty of Humanities and Social Sciences, University of Split. He teaches logic, philosophy of education, critical thinking, and philosophy for children. He received his PhD at the University of Zagreb in 2012. He is a leader of the Croatian delegation to the International Philosophical Olympiad (2007–today), founder and secretary of the Association for the Promotion and Advancement of Philosophy for Children ("Petit Philosophy"), and has organized and led about 1300 workshops associated with various projects of the Association (www.petit-philosophy.com). He has been a researcher in more than ten different

EU educational projects. His research interests include bioethics, cultural zoology, philosophy of education, philosophy for children, Mediterranean culture, and philosophy of popular culture, especially rock, hard rock, and heavy metal. Too many interests, perhaps, but, like Zevon, he's just looking for the next best thing.

HEINRIK HELLWIG is Visiting Assistant Professor of Philosophy at Seton Hall University. One of his teaching and research interests is philosophy of law, an area that deals with issues relevant to lawyers, and some topics that deal more directly with guns and money. He contributed a chapter to *The Ultimate Supernatural and Philosophy: Saving People, Killing Things, the Family Business* (2022) and purposely listened to "Werewolves of London" while writing it.

RICHARD JONES is Professor Emeritus of Theatre at Stephen F. Austin State University. Over a career that has stretched from the 1970s to the 2020s, he has taught courses in theatre history, dramatic literature, and dramatic theory. He has directed dozens of theatre productions, many of them "absurdist," and has used Zevon songs in pre-show, entr'acte, or curtain-call music in five shows he's directed. Rick has been a fan of Warren Zevon since first hearing cuts from the *Excitable Boy* album on a radio station in Birmingham, England, early in 1978. The title track was darkly intriguing, but the deal was sealed when Roland the Thompson Gunner became "headless."

THOMAS KANE has published articles on the automortographies of figures such as MLK, Tupac, Raymond Carver, Kathy Acker, Donald Barthelme, and Charles Bukowski—and now, Warren Zevon. As more people die, he publishes more articles. He teaches at Phillips Academy in Andover, Massachusetts, offering courses on mass incarceration, last acts, and Roland Barthes's notion of mythologies. He tries to enjoy every sandwich.

ERIC V.D. LUFT earned his BA *magna cum laude* in Philosophy and Religion at Bowdoin College in 1974, his PhD in Philosophy at Bryn Mawr College in 1985, and his MLS at Syracuse University in 1993. From 1987 to 2006, he was Curator of Historical Collections at SUNY Upstate Medical University. He has taught at Villanova University, Syracuse University, SUNY Upstate, and the College of Saint Rose. He is the author, editor, or translator of over 670 publications in philosophy, religion, librarianship, history, history of medicine, politics, humor, popular culture, and nineteenth-century studies. He owns and runs Gegensatz Press and is listed in *Who's Who in America*. He'll sleep when he's dead.

JOHN E. MACKINNON was born in Halifax, Nova Scotia, and raised in the Atlantic Provinces of Canada and the New England States. He has degrees in Philosophy from McGill University, the University of Toronto, the University of Exeter, and Cambridge University, where he earned his PhD in the field of Aesthetics. For the past twenty-five years, he has taught in the Department of Philosophy at Saint Mary's University in Halifax, where he lives with his wife, two sons, and their handsome black lab, Abner. His articles have appeared in the *British Journal of Aesthetics*, *Journal of Aesthetics and Art Criticism*, *Law and Literature*, *Philosophy and Literature*, and elsewhere. Once, his hair was perfect.

THOMAS MALEWITZ serves as Assistant Professor and Director of the Ed.D. Leadership Program in the College of Education at Spalding University in Louisville, Kentucky. He holds a PhD in Education and Social Change. Tom has taught courses in Mathematics, Philosophy, and Theology at the secondary level for over a decade, during which he wove popular culture, film, and music between the mystics and statistics. He is a Catholic Media Association book award-winning author and has presented national workshops on adolescent spirituality, ethical leadership, and the philosophy of education. He's a hobby musician and occasionally sings sad songs, sweetly and slightly out of key.

MARINA MILIVOJEVIĆ PINTO is a psychologist at the Community Service Center in Zadar, Croatia, which is part of the social welfare system. She is also a psychotherapist, working with children who have behavioral problems and mental health issues, as well as with their parents. It is a very demanding, but also useful and humane, job, which is made much easier when listening to hard rock and heavy metal, but also Zevon and his poetry. She's also a big fan of good books and philosophy.

CHRISTOPHE POROT sometimes becomes a were-puppy, but has never been a werewolf. When not undergoing this metamorphosis, he writes, podcasts, and conducts research, especially in ethics, political philosophy, and philosophy of religion. He has been a Dean's Fellow recipient at Harvard University and a Managing Editor, along with Charles Taliaferro, of a series on Philosophy of Religion in the journal *Religious Studies Review*. His publications include contributions to *Pokémon and Philosophy* (forthcoming) and to academic journals, including the *European Journal for Philosophy of Religion*.

ROSS CHANNING REED is a philosopher, writer, musician and part-time woodsman. He lives on a rock farm in the Missouri Ozarks. As a child, he was an avid stamp collector, but that fell by the wayside as soon as he learned about girls. He had intended to write a book titled *Everything You Ever Wanted to Know about Life You Can Learn from Running a Five-Hour Marathon in Under Three Hours*, but instead wrote a number of other books on unrelated topics. A trombonist, he holds an MM in Jazz and Studio Music from the University of Memphis, a BA in Philosophy from Millersville University, an MA in Philosophy from Baylor University, and a PhD in Philosophy from Loyola University Chicago.

HANNAH RUBIN is an Associate Professor in the Department of Philosophy at University of Missouri. She is an evolutionary game theorist, researching how social structures come to be, from communication and cooperation between our cells in our body, to vervet monkeys yelling at each other about nearby predators, to the complexities of human societies. She has recently won an NSF grant to study under-representation in scientific communities. As a game theorist, she knows when not to take a risk gambling in Havana.

ZACH RUBIN is an Assistant Professor of Sociology at Lander University, where he teaches classes on social problems, deviant behaviors, and the concept of utopia, among many others. He also does research on intentional communities, which are attempts at implementing a utopian ideal through small group living. This has earned him the distinction of being a two-time winner of the Communal Studies Association's "Outstanding Article" award. Introduced to Zevon at a young age, he is a lifelong fan and is always asking for lawyers, guns, and money from his father (who did the introducing) to help get him out of this.

LUCIE TARDY often howls at the moon, but was never invited to the werewolves' club. She is finishing her PhD at the Sorbonne (Paris I) on Islamic philosophy and has participated in many public conferences on subjects ranging from mysticism and physics (especially atomism) to the representation of God in the Islamic tradition.

JARKKO S. TUUSVUORI is a Finnish philosopher and independent researcher with a doctoral dissertation on Nietzsche (University of Helsinki, 2000) and a bulk of books and articles (written and translated) on various philosophical, social, and historical subjects. His particular expertise is nineteenth-century thought and twentieth-century popular culture. Recently, he participated in the anthology *Graphic Novels as Philosophy* (2017), and his contribution to Will Eisner's *A Contract with God* stood out, in a review of the book, as an "admirably researched piece." Tuusvuori works as a publisher of ntamo books in Helsinki and leads a never-ending library tour that concentrates on Bob Dylan and the allure of folk and rock songs.

SHALON VAN TINE is a cultural historian who specializes in twentieth-century American and world history. As a PhD candidate at Ohio University, she is currently writing her dissertation on the history of Generation X. She also teaches History and Humanities courses for University of Maryland Global Campus and Virginia Peninsula Community College. She's very well acquainted with the seven deadly sins, and she keeps a busy schedule trying to fit them in.

NICHOLAS J. WERNICKI is the Director of Continuing Education at Santa Fe Community College in New Mexico. Prior to his move to SFCC, he served as an Associate Professor of Philosophy at colleges in

Pennsylvania, where he taught courses in Popular Culture and Philosophy, Philosophy of Self, and Continental Philosophy. He has a PhD in Theological and Philosophical Studies from Drew University, and his scholarly interests include existentialism and religious naturalism. He plays guitar with his keyboardist wife, Abby, and her guitarist dad, Joe. The band is yet unnamed and audiences include close friends and Nick's dog Laika, named after the first dog in space. The band covers Warren Zevon's "Carmelita" and "Mutineer." They have tried to play "Keep Me in Your Heart," but it's just too sad. Laika remains ambivalent about the future of the band.

FERNANDO ZAPATA is the Ted DeLaney Postdoctoral Fellow in Philosophy at Washington and Lee University. He has taught philosophy courses at Hunter College, John Jay College of Criminal Justice, and LaGuardia Community College, all within the City University of New York. His research and teaching interests are in the history of philosophy, especially the American philosophical tradition, social and political philosophy, and ethics. A native New Yorker, he aspires to live on the Upper East Side and never go down in the street.

Index

Liner Notes

Jungle Pilots: George A. Reisch and David Ramsay Steele, Chicago, Illinois

The Gentleman Boys: Larry Rubin in St. Louis, Missouri, Rich Rubin in Guerneville, California, and Calum T. MacKinnon and Sethuram B. A. MacKinnon in Halifax, Nova Scotia

Hindu Love God: Paroo Parmar MacKinnon, Halifax

Shadowboxing: Jason Holt, Acadia University, Wolfville, Nova Scotia; David Collins, Oxford University

Aides-de-camp: Fatema Ali, Department of Philosophy and Religious Studies, Saint Mary's University
Matthew Salah, Software and Applications Support, Saint Mary's University

Dr. Babyhead: Abner R. MacKinnon

Flugelhorn: Wendell Eisner, Italy Cross, Nova Scotia

Pennywhistle: Trinity Gadway, North Bay, Ontario

Junk Culture Emissaries: Calum and Seth MacKinnon

Whoops, Hollers, and Handclaps: David Heckerl in Halifax, Nova Scotia; Andrew Mylne in Edinburgh, Scotland; and Daniel F. Rosen in Baltimore, Maryland

Harmonies: Daniel Trainor-McKinnon, Halifax, N.S.; Dylan Mackenzie, Fortune, P.E.I.; Alex Baker, Dartmouth, N.S.

Turd Handlers, Mud Jugglers, Hammerheads, and Bedwetters: Too many to mention.

Il miglior fabbro—Bernie MacKinnon in Memphis, Tennessee

Thanks always to Jackson!

QUEEN
and Philosophy
GUARANTEED TO
BLOW YOUR MIND

EDITED BY JARED KEMLING AND RANDALL E. AUXIER

ALSO FROM OPEN UNIVERSE

Queen and Philosophy

Guaranteed to Blow Your Mind

VOLUME 5 IN THE OPEN UNIVERSE SERIES,
POP CULTURE AND PHILOSOPHY®

Edited by
Jared Kemling and Randall E Auxier

"This is your brain on Queen! A book filled with intoxicating and dangerous delights for thoughtful disciples of the most momentous London quartet of all time."

—RAY SCOTT PERCIVAL, author of *The Myth of the Closed Mind: Explaining Why and How People Are Rational* (2012) and editor of *Steven Pinker: Critical Responses* (2024).

"This book gives us thought-provoking ideas and theories, seeking to unravel some of the mystery of where Queen's amazing songs may have come from, and what we could learn from them. The result is a captivating book that is likely to inspire contemplation and debate amongst Queen fans, and beyond."

—TONY RIGG, University of Central Lancashire, co-editor of *The Future of Live Music* (2020) and *Popular Music in the Post-Digital Age* (2018).

"With excellent musicianship and a singer with a unique and powerful voice (and from a Zoroastrian background, no less!), Queen is one of the most important bands of the post-classic era. The excellent essays in this volume do a superb job of helping us understand the brilliance of Queen!"

—BILL MARTIN, author of *Avant Rock* (2002) and *Music of Yes* (1996)

JARED KEMLING, a longtime aficionado of both Queen and philosophy, is Philosophy Instructor at Rend Lake College. He edited *The Cultural Power of Personal Objects* (2021).

RANDALL E. AUXIER is Professor of Philosophy and Communication Studies at Southern Illinois University, Carbondale. He is the author of a whole lot of books, including *As Deep as It Gets: Movies and Metaphysics* (2022) and *Metaphysical Graffiti: Deep Cuts in the Philosophy of Rock* (2017).

ISBN 978-1-63770-032-7 (paperback)
ISBN 978-1-63770-033-4 (ebook)

AVAILABLE FROM ALL BOOKSTORES AND ONLINE BOOKSELLERS

For more information on Open Universe books, visit us at

www.carusbooks.com